Life, Death, and Other Inconvenient Truths

Life, Death, and Other Inconvenient Truths

A Realist's View of the Human Condition

SHIMON EDELMAN

The MIT Press
Cambridge, Massachusetts
London, England

This book was set in ITC Stone Serif Std and ITC Stone Sans Std by New Best-set Typesetters Ltd. Printed and bound in the United States of America.

Library of Congress Cataloging-in-Publication Data

Names: Edelman, Shimon, author.
Title: Life, death, and other inconvenient truths : a realist's view of the human
  condition / Shimon Edelman.
Description: Cambridge : The MIT Press, 2020. | Includes bibliographical references
  and index.
Identifiers: LCCN 2020002123 | ISBN 9780262044356 (hardcover)
Subjects: LCSH: Life.
Classification: LCC BD431 .E2155 2020 | DDC 128—dc23
LC record available at https://lccn.loc.gov/2020002123

10 9 8 7 6 5 4 3 2 1

To my readers—
pedo mellon a minno—speak friend and enter

Contents

Preface

tat tvam asi

(thou art that [too])

—Uddalaka (to his son Śvetaketu), *Chandogya Upanishad*

Thou thyself art the subject of my discourse.
   Whate'er men do, vows, fears, in ire, in sport
   Joys, wand'rings are the sum of my report
—Robert Burton, *The Anatomy of Melancholy*

. . . for those who want to learn one of the ways to make a soul. To them, to the children I say: Listen! Avoid magic! Be aware!
—Ursula K. Le Guin, "Solitude"

Long ago, in a galaxy far, far away, I had written a book that bore the title *The Happiness of Pursuit*. To this, the publisher added the subtitle *What neuroscience can teach us about the good life.*[1] It was implied that appealing to neuroscience would help my opus stand out from the spate of self-help books on happiness—fair enough, although my take had more to do with how and what brains compute than with the "neuro" angle, which is about what they're made of.

It was the "good life" bit, though, that came to haunt me, as I might have expected but did not. For one thing, during live interviews, I would get call-ins from people who described their life as a mess and wanted to be told how to be happy. As is often the case with those who have both privilege and luck, I was slow to realize that people who have little of either are kept too busy by their daily struggle and do not care much for the science of happiness—unless perhaps it offers a simple, surefire prescription for being happy. And although my book did include a seven-word "recipe" for happiness that echoed its title, I could no longer pretend that it was a match for the "slings and arrows of outrageous fortune."

This realization pushed me to try and redress what I eventually perceived as a serious mistake that I had committed in putting that book together: my glossing over the vast darker tracts of human nature and human affairs. Because focusing on the negative would amount to committing another mistake, in this book I tried to step back from both happiness and unhappiness as such and to examine instead some of the general parameters that shape our existence. To be sure, HAPPINESS does have a short chapter all of its own, but so do thirty-seven other categories of human experience: in alphabetical order, from ACTION and AMBITION, via LANGUAGE and LOVE, to WAR and YOUTH (throughout the text, I use small capitals to highlight chapter names).

This book, then, is a kind of reference volume, a partial one for sure, for making sense of the human world and of the hard work of human soul-making, or simply life. The entries are cross-referenced and contain quite a few notes and pointers to primary sources, all collected at the end of the book.[2] Each chapter ends with a list of films, music, stories, and places—any product of human endeavor or feature of natural environment that may help illuminate its theme.

No synthesis is offered for the list of inconvenient TRUTHS collected here, for the simple reason that there isn't—nor can there be—a single underlying cause that makes life what it is. If this book has a central thesis, it's one that is neither a revelation, nor a secret: the human condition has much room for improvement. Working out possible ways of improving it is left as an exercise for the reader.

Human nature being what it is, the truths described here are not iron-clad: you'll likely be able to hone or perhaps overturn them, if you have a mind for it and are willing to learn and live an examined life. You may hope that the more inconvenient an item seems, the less truth there is to it, but I am afraid that such hope would be unfounded. The mirror is dark, but it is not warped; and breaking it will not make the dim land it reflects disappear.

—"Do you advise me to look?" you may ask, as Frodo asked of Galadriel, when she brought him to her Mirror.

—"No," she said. "I do not counsel you one way or the other. I am not a counsellor. You may learn something, and whether what you see be fair or evil, that may be profitable, and yet it may not. Seeing is both good and perilous. . . . Do as you will."

Executive Summary: A Rhyming Lore of the Human Condition

Learn now the Lore of Living Creatures!
—J. R. R. Tolkien, *The Lord of the Rings: The Two Towers*

ACTION is good except when it's not.
AMBITION unchecked is a kind of mind rot.
ANXIETY is our constant companion.
BEAUTY awaits in a desert canyon.
CHILDREN are a joy that can give us a pause.
COMPLEXITY has the mind grasping at straws.
CONSCIOUSNESS is a fancy illusion.
DEATH is the ultimate end to confusion.
EMPATHY is an angel that gave up its wings.
EMPTINESS is the nature of things.
EVOLUTION and culture pull on our strings.
EXISTENCE is a gift that hides many stings.
FEAR is POWER's tool of oppression.
FREE WILL may not be worth a digression.
HAPPINESS, misery—each has its turn.
HOME is where you can never return.
LANGUAGE is how we influence others.
LOVE only makes sense to the lovers.
MATHEMATICS is strangely effective in SCIENCE.
MEMORY and hindsight are a wicked alliance.
MORALITY is shaped by those in POWER.
OLD AGE brings insights that make us dour.
PARENTS are the ones whom we leave behind.
PERCEPTION is a world made up by the mind.
POLITICS is corrupted by POWER and money.
POWER is that which is sweeter than honey.

POVERTY means that the rich don't care.
REGRET is a door that can lead to despair.
RELIGION is opium for the masses.
SCIENCE reports to the ruling classes.
STUPIDITY will be our species' perdition.
SUFFERING is a mark of the human condition.
TECHNOLOGY is often a mixed blessing.
THINKING should not be so depressing.
TIME is a teacher that kills its students.
TRUTH preservation calls for prudence.
WAR is fought at POWER's behest.
YOUTH is a treasure that contains all the rest.

1 Action

The native hue of resolution. The pale cast of thought. And lose the name of action.

Mir hilft der Geist! Auf einmal seh ich Rat
Und schreibe getrost: Im Anfang war die Tat!

(The spirit aids! from anxious scruples freed,
I write: In the beginning was the Deed!)
—Johann Wolfgang von Goethe, *Faust*

It is my job to create universes. . . . And I have to build them in such a way that they do not fall apart two days later.
—Philip K. Dick, "How to Build a Universe That Doesn't Fall Apart Two Days Later"

Praise then darkness and Creation unfinished.
—Ursula K. Le Guin, *The Left Hand of Darkness*[1]

The native hue of resolution

In the beginning was a motive. The motive must have been urgent: not a whole lot of deliberation seems to have preceded the action that it had provoked. Any hasty action is risky, but for a particularly momentous undertaking, such as creating a universe, the risk is compounded by the difficulty of telling ahead of time how things will turn out. In such a project, it makes sense at least to take it easy, let the dust settle, and look around before proceeding to the next stage: "And God said, Let there be light: and there was light. And God saw the light, that it was good."

Self-supervision is, however, rarely an effective approach to quality control. As the gnostics might argue, the biblical act of Creation could have benefited from a full-scale prelaunch review, seeing that its product is so sweepingly defective (witness the pervasive and unavoidable SUFFERING in the world).[2] Assuming that the intentions on the part of the responsible party had been good, this nevertheless imperfect outcome should give a pause to any aspiring world-maker—"Between the idea / And the reality / Between the motion / And the act / Falls the Shadow."[3]

Mere finite beings such as ourselves may not be in the business of creating entire universes (yet),[4] but we do routinely try to remake what we can of our little world to our advantage through our actions. In that, we run into occasional failures, and the consequences of these may be no less momentous to us and to others than a faulty universe would have been for its Maker (had the latter not excused itself from responsibility to its denizens by remaining outside of it). And a bad run of attempts at action that miscarry can shell-shock a person into passivity for the rest of their life.

Principled inaction has its advocates. Laozi, in line with the rest of his teachings, even proffered it as military philosophy (which, if adopted universally, might end WAR): "A great warrior has said, 'I dare not be the host, I would rather be the guest; I dare not advance an inch, I would rather retire a foot.'"[5] Now, inaction is not inherently safer than, or MORALLY preferable over, action. It is not so in war (precisely because one can never be certain that everyone else will refrain from hostile action). And for those who are witnessing POWER being exercised that causes the SUFFERING of others, doing nothing *is* taking a moral stance. Still, it seems advisable to learn to mistrust one's motives, wishes, and beliefs,[6] and for those that are deemed worthy, to try to anticipate the consequences of action and inaction before committing to a decision. And there, as Hamlet puts it, is the rub.

The pale cast of thought

Hamlet's famous indecision is so very human, and yet it is rooted in mind traits that we share with many other species:

> If you watch an aging cat consider a doubtful leap onto the dryer, you will suspect that what [William] James said is true, "Where indecision is great, as before a dangerous leap, consciousness is agonizingly intense."[7]

The reasons behind the agony of wavering and indecision have no less to do with the nature of the world we inhabit than with human (or feline) nature.

The prime reason is the inordinate COMPLEXITY of the web of cause and effect:[8] the possible repercussions of any weighty act, or inaction, especially in human affairs, ramify exponentially as one tries to see farther into the future. Even if all the relevant parameters of the situation at hand were known, and even if our THINKING from those perfect premises were faultless, no amount of it can match this complexity—corners must be cut and approximations made, and even then at some point the die must be cast before all the desired insights are in.

The complexity of forethought is exacerbated by the difficulty of emotional forecasting.[9] At each stage in the expanding avalanche of possible events triggered by the act under consideration, we are liable to experience various emotions. What these might be depends in complex ways both on the history and on the context of the imperfectly imagined future situation. As the unrelenting TIME drags us into that future, action sets us up for possible REGRET.

And lose the name of action

From the beginning to the end, then, action is beset and at times marred by trouble: from irresponsible wishes, via incomplete information and imperfect reasoning, to irreparable consequences and regret. Dwelling to no end on potential pitfalls will not, however, make them disappear or make one happy:

> Thus conscience does make cowards of us all;
> And thus the native hue of resolution
> Is sicklied o'er with the pale cast of thought,
> And enterprises of great pith and moment
> With this regard their currents turn awry,
> And lose the name of action.[10]

After so much deliberation, one might just as well act, consequences be damned. In the end, that was Hamlet's choice, which he did not live to regret. Most of our daily enterprises are not as momentous as his was, and most of them don't spell death. Life is what we are stuck with, and it is the unexpected that makes life possible.[11]

Of related interest

To watch:

Claude Lelouch, *Les Uns et les Autres* (1981)

Tarsem Singh, *The Fall* (2006)

To listen:

Maurice Ravel, *Boléro* (1928)

To read:

John Brunner, *The Compleat Traveller in Black* (originally *The Traveler in Black*, [1971] 1982)

Stanisław Lem, "Non Serviam" in *A Perfect Vacuum* ([1971] 1999)

To go:

Away from Elsinore.

2 Ambition

Pelf and place. A small goat.

Place . . . is the end of half the labours of human life; and is the cause of all the tumult and bustle, all the rapine and injustice, which avarice and ambition have introduced into this world.

—Adam Smith, *The Theory of Moral Sentiments*

Ambition; a passion, which when it keeps within the bounds of prudence and justice, is always admired in the world.

—Adam Smith, *The Theory of Moral Sentiments*[1]

Pelf and place

It is fair to say that ambition is to the body politic what table salt is to the human body: impossible to live without, but seriously life shortening if overused. This suggests that ambition should be subject to the Goldilocks Principle, but it isn't: none of the "modern" societies has *everyone's* ambition in the sweet spot between too much and too little.

My guess is that the social dynamics of ambition is to blame.[2] Many people do have what would count as just about the right amount of ambition, but some are ambitious beyond the "bounds of prudence and justice," to use Adam Smith's phrase. Merely observing those strivers and climbers in action is likely to kick the members of the modest majority right out of the sweet spot. Some contract learned helplessness (as when coming within an upstart's POWER) and end up depressed. Many others have their own ambition stoked and get drawn into the rat race, only to experience continual disappointment with their achievements, as these fail to keep up with their aspirations.[3]

Ambition being a fundamentally interpersonal phenomenon, the social comparison that it implies is a force with which all societies must contend.[4] With very few exceptions,[5] our economies and our POLITICS are driven by ambition for "pelf and place."[6] Adam Smith, a figurehead of the Age of Enlightenment[7] who is often referred to as capitalism's "founding father," remarked that pelf and place—economics and POLITICS—are inseparable:

> The objects of avarice and ambition differ only in their greatness. A miser is as furious about a halfpenny, as a man of ambition about the conquest of a kingdom.

As might be expected from a man of money and privilege, Smith in this passage from *The Theory of Moral Sentiments* glosses over the possibility of a person being furious about a halfpenny for the simple reason of being poor, yet having the ambition to be fed and sheltered; as well as over the possibility of a "conquest of a kingdom" at the hands of the king's own subjects whose ambition is not to be ruled by an autocrat.[8]

The famous (or infamous) idea behind Smith's other book, *The Wealth of Nations*, is that each person's economic ambition will have the side effect of benefiting the society at large. It has been put forward as an account for the enormous economic growth that the world has seen in the past two centuries; an alternative explanation credits growth to the exploitation of the many by an overly ambitious few.

Be that as it may, growth is a problematic phenomenon. On the one hand, it makes personal economic betterment possible, and it is hard to blame people for wanting to be as well off as their neighbors (or, thanks to the media TECHNOLOGY, as someone halfway around the globe). On the other hand, an incessant global "arms race" over standards of living (which is spurred along by the pursuit of profit by those who profit from others' consumption) demands constant growth. This, when compounded, turns exponential, which, as MATHEMATICS tells us, is unsustainable when the resources it depends on are finite.[9]

With just one planet to exploit, the looming resource shortage increasingly forces the economic game to be zero-sum: one person's gain must be another person's, or many other people's, loss. Thus, the nature of growth makes ambition, whether "merely" for self-advancement or for the domination of others, problematic too, in a purely empirical-economic sense. As I already noted, it is also problematic because it causes unnecessary ANXIETY and stress.[10] And it is not even guaranteed to be conducive to professional success.[11] Why can't we all just chill instead?

A small goat

An insight into why a state of general moderation in matters of ambition (which is what Adam Smith was advocating) is unstable over time can be found in the dynamics of POWER. As Hannah Arendt observed, "Power, like action, is boundless; it has no physical limitation in human nature, in the bodily existence of man, like strength. Its only limitation is the existence of other people, but this limitation is not accidental, because human power corresponds to the condition of plurality to begin with."[12] The nature of power would thus seem to ensure that for as long as there is a society, ambition will be prone to getting out of control.

In elementary school, I once scandalized a teacher by claiming not to want to become a cosmonaut, presumably because there was "enough to do on earth" (this was during the first few years of the space race, when the Soviets were still winning the prestige war). Little did she know that I was being groomed by my PARENTS for a much more illustrious—in their eyes, and soon in mine—career as a scholar. My father, who was in charge of this aspect of my upbringing, never told me in this many words that he expected me to become a famous scientist; it was merely explained to me that as a Jew I must always be "better than the *goyim*" to get anywhere at all in life (true enough for the USSR). At the same time, edifying stories about Nobel laureates somehow kept creeping into conversation.

Adam Smith, who grew up fatherless, never married, and had no CHIL-DREN, offered this advice on ambition to his young students at Glasgow, where he taught MORAL philosophy:

> Never enter that play from whence so few have been able to return; never come within the circle of ambition; nor ever bring yourself into comparison with those masters of the earth who have already engrossed the attention of half of mankind before you.

I sometimes wish I had read Smith's *The Theory of Moral Sentiments* in my YOUTH or at least that social media were invented a bit earlier. I just might have come in time across a pearl such as this post by an anonymous Twitter user who goes by the name of "spacegirl incognito" and who may or may not have read Smith:[13]

Career Advisor: Well, there are a number of job options available in all
of your potential fields.

Me: please I just want to be a small goat on the side of a mountain.

Of related interest

To watch:

Akira Kurosawa, *Throne of Blood* (1957)

Werner Herzog, *Aguirre, der Zorn Gottes* (*Aguirre, the Wrath of God*, 1972)

Francis Ford Coppola, *Apocalypse Now* (1979)

Miloš Forman, *Amadeus* (1984)

Nicolas Roeg, *Insignificance* (1985)

To listen:

Gustav Mahler, *Symphony No. 10* (1910)

Foreigner, "Juke Box Hero" (1981)

To read:

William Shakespeare, *Macbeth* (1606)

William Butler Yeats, "What Then?" (1939)

Sandra Newman, *The Heavens* (2019)

To go:

Visit the Ozymandias ruins and the stele of Merneptah.

3   Anxiety

Possession. What you know you don't know can hurt you. What—me worry? Yes.

Complete freedom from stress is death.
—Hans Selye, "The Evolution of the Stress Concept"[1]

Possession

As Hans Selye, the originator of the concept of stress in physiology, liked to point out, there is no such thing as stress-free life. No surprise there: being stressed means being properly mobilized for taking on a not entirely friendly world—an existential need whose passing seems as remote as world peace. The problem with stress, though, is not just that being in dire straits causes it: the choice of what to stress about and of how dire is really dire is never even up to us. This is not all: in addition to stressing over a fix we actually are in right now, we are beset by anxieties about problems that we will be, or might be, facing in the future.

To see why stress and anxiety are not up to us, it helps to understand what "us" means. What I am, and what you are, is this: myriad cognitive computations, all running in parallel.[2] All of them are suffused by emotions— computations that are *felt*, whose evolutionary role in regulating behavior requires that they be impossible to switch off at will. At any given moment, any number of them can be out and about chasing each other in the brain. Certain varieties of their little games we experience as anxiety.

All sentient beings are capable of physiological stress response, but it takes special skills to also do anxiety. Even if other animal species can worry in the same sense that we do, it is safe to assume that none of them are as good at it as we are. To be capable of getting stressed, it's enough merely to be alive; worrying takes a certain cognitive sophistication. The human mind rises to the occasion, bringing to the table MEMORY, THINKING and imagination, and LANGUAGE. These in turn allow CONSCIOUSNESS to take aim at itself and ponder its condition. And our environment—natural (what is left of that) or constructed, physical, or social—serves as a reliable supply of grist for its mill.

In computer software engineering, a process that runs in the background of the main task and takes care of system monitoring or maintenance is called a daemon. Monitoring and maintenance are clearly important for the system's health, which is why permanently shutting these processes down would not be a good idea, whether in a computer or in an embodied mind. Sometimes, however, a mind process that tracks present and future stress becomes hyperactive to the point of disrupting[3] the usual order of things. What happens in such cases is literally daemonic possession.

What you know you don't know can hurt you

The very idea of a "generalized anxiety disorder"—an official diagnostic category, which comes across as a kind of allergy to the conscious experience of life—might suggest that there is no rhyme or reason to when and where the daemons of worry can strike. There is, however, a pattern to what triggers anxiety in general. The common denominator appears to be uncertainty about the future, coupled with a FEAR of the unknown.[4]

There is little that one can do about the uncertainty part of this equation. It is predicated by the fundamental asymmetry of the arrow of TIME and the computational COMPLEXITY of trying to predict the future (including the consequences of our own ACTIONS). It is unclear, however, that the opposite of it—certainty about life outcomes—would be at all bearable, let alone better than uncertainty (see the quotation by Ursula Le Guin at the end of chapter 38).

Focusing specifically on action leads to a veritable pile-up of anxieties. The popular advice not to worry about what you cannot change is of no help, as it merely begs the question of FREE WILL. Do I or do I not have it? If I do not, what unpleasant and unavoidable surprises does life hold in store for me? And if I do, what am I missing out on by not acting in this or that way? This latter "fear of missing out" grows steadily in OLD AGE as the door on the opportunities for action is about to slam shut, provoking what the Germans call *Torschlusspanik*.

If the uncertainties of life are inescapable, existential anxiety can only be alleviated either by escaping life (as per Hamlet's advice to Ophelia, "get thee to a nunnery"), or by taking measures against the FEAR that life instills. A familiar source of thoroughly spelled out and often quite effective ideas along these lines is of course RELIGION. A clear example is the Buddhist concept of refuge,[5] as expressed in the Triratna or Three Jewels formula:

I take refuge in the Buddha.
I take refuge in the dharma [teaching].
I take refuge in the sangha [community].

In contrast, in Proverbs 3:25, the down-to-earth Old Testament tells the readers to carry on with what they're doing, while deflecting their fear with a promise of personal protection:

Be not afraid of sudden fear, neither of the desolation of the wicked, when it cometh.
For the Lord shall be thy confidence, and shall keep thy foot from being taken.

If one's fears are not thereby reduced to naught, there are still a few things to try: several cognitive behavioral therapeutic methods developed in recent decades are known to be effective in alleviating anxiety.[6] Just how effective they turn out to be in each case depends on the patient.

What—me worry? Yes

It may be that cognitive therapies work better than other therapies against anxiety because anxiety arises from THINKING and other cognitive processes to begin with. People's predisposition to anxiety seems to depend on intelligence, but not quite in the way the popular culture has it. In the general population, there is no clear association between IQ and anxiety.[7] Some studies, though, show a U-shaped dependence: both lower and exceptionally high cognitive functioning are associated with an elevated risk of anxiety.[8]

Lower than average cognitive functioning promotes generalized anxiety because it implies more difficulty in understanding how the world works. On the other side of the cognitive ability scale, understanding the world too well is not an unallayed good either. One reason for this may be the increased ability of high-IQ individuals to imagine negative outcomes, in a world where, thermodynamically speaking, there are generally many,

many ways for things to go wrong for each way in which they can come out right. Another mechanism may have to do with a generally increased awareness of the goings-on in the world, mediated by what has been called the "overexcitability" of the intellectually gifted. The original Polish word for this concept, coined by Kazimierz Dabrowski, is *nadpobudliwosc*. This word shares the Indo-European root morpheme *bud* with "Buddha," the appellation of the Awakened One, whose insights into SUFFERING seem pertinent here.

Of related interest

To watch:

Andrei Tarkovsky, *Solaris* (1972)

Tom Tykwer, Achim von Borries, and Hendrik Handloegten, *Babylon Berlin* (2017)

To listen:

The Rolling Stones, "Mother's Little Helper" (1966)

R.E.M., "Losing My Religion" (1991)

To read:

Maurice Sendak, *Where the Wild Things Are* (1963)

Arkady and Boris Strugatsky, *Град обреченный* (*The Doomed City*, 1972/ 1989/2016)

Philip K. Dick, *Flow My Tears, the Policeman Said* (1974)[9]

To go:

Peek under the bed.

4 Beauty

The imminence of a revelation. Evolutionary bait and switch. Between the world and a grain of sand. The pathos of things. The seven sad senses of beauty.

La música, los estados de felicidad, la mitología, las caras trabajadas por el tiempo, ciertos crepúsculos y ciertos lugares, quieren decirnos algo, o algo dijeron que no hubiéramos debido perder, o están por decir algo; esta inminencia de una revelación, que no se produce, es, quizá, el hecho estético.

(Music, states of happiness, mythology, faces belabored by time, certain twilights and certain places try to tell us something, or have said something we should not have missed, or are about to say something; this imminence of a revelation which does not occur is, perhaps, the aesthetic phenomenon.)
—Jorge Luis Borges, *The Wall and the Books*[1]

"If you can see a thing whole," he said, "it seems that it's always beautiful. Planets, lives. . . . But close up, a world's all dirt and rocks. And day to day, life's a hard job, you get tired, you lose the pattern. You need distance, interval. The way to see how beautiful the earth is, is to see it as the moon. The way to see how beautiful life is, is from the vantage point of death."
—Ursula K. Le Guin, *The Dispossessed*

The imminence of a revelation

More and more often as the years go by, beauty makes me feel as Moses must have felt, I imagine, when from the top of Mt. Nebo he beheld the promised land that he knew he himself was fated never to attain. Everything that ever strikes me as beautiful—a thistle poppy blooming in a desert canyon, a thunderbird petroglyph on the canyon wall, a well-turned pot, the old potter's hands, a poem, a face glimpsed in a crowd, purple shadows creeping up a mountain range at sunset—always evokes yearning, and always remains elusive: intangible, or fleeting, or utterly unattainable, a promise made to be broken, an obscure revelation.

At such times, when I should in fairness be content to just *be* in the presence of beauty, I feel driven to *do* something, anything, about it. But what can one do? What could I possibly do about a beautiful face that would stem the yearning? I once knew a girl who loved to be kissed on the eyelids while I held her face by the ears, which were of perfect size, shape, and position for that purpose. It felt great. And then what? You can't hold a person by the ears forever. And all those flowers and sunsets, why are they even in the same category here? What do you hold those by? And what's with the urge to hold on to things, anyway? Craving and attachment are bad for you—wouldn't we be better off not knowing beauty?

It seems to me that those by whom beauty goes unnoticed—whether because they were never trained to notice it, or because life beats them down and keeps them too hungry and afraid to look out, or because they, having read Laozi or the Buddha, choose peace and quiet over beauty and anguish—are worse off for it. My views in this matter have been shaped by a secondhand rendition of a Sufi parable, which I chanced across as a teenager:

> And I recall again the words of Saadi, who "used his life to embrace the Beauty of the World":
>
>> "You who stop by the poet's grave, think well of him!
>> – He gave his heart to the earth, even though he had circled the world like the wind that spread around the universe the perfume of his heart's garden.
>> – For he had ascended the Towers of Maan, Contemplation, and heard Simaa, the Music of the World, leading one into halet, joy.
>> – The entire world is full with this joy and dance—are we the only ones who are oblivious to its wine?
>> – A drunk camel makes light of his load. When hearing an Arab song, he becomes joyous. How then would we call a man who does not feel this joy?
>> – He is a donkey, a dry log."[2]

A Sufi saint may be capable of contemplating beauty without acting on it—not I. I never managed to develop a penchant for not-acting—for standing down, standing back, choosing "not-doing," *wu wei*—even as I approach the age at which ACTION grows tiresome.[3] I like to think that there is a consistency, as well as a certain rebellious quality, to my stance. Were I to forgo trying to do something about beauty, I would be surrendering it unconditionally to TIME—that which makes the face disappear in the crowd, the sun set, the flower fade. With my rational mind I *know* that there will be another sunset tomorrow, another desert bloom next year, another beautiful face lit momentarily by a streetlight, at dusk, in the rain, in a foreign city. But I still *feel* saddened by today's beauty in its passing. And even if I am still around tomorrow or next year, and am brought again into the presence of beauty, will I know any better what to do, or how to be? And how will I *feel* about it?

Evolutionary bait and switch

The distinction between rational THINKING and feelings, which I just invoked, is a classical one. Young John Keats, who went on to equate beauty with TRUTH in a poem that brought him posthumous fame, had avowedly preferred feeling over thinking: "O for a life of sensation rather than of thoughts! It is a 'Vision in the form of Youth,' a shadow of reality to come."[4] Truth to be told, though, this distinction is less clear-cut than the Romantics would have it: neither feeling without thinking nor thinking without feeling is what people normally do, or can do with any ease. EVOLUTION has seen to it that all perception and all thinking are tinged with emotion and are accompanied by valuation, which in turn brings about craving or aversion, and predisposition to ACTION. The experience of beauty, which involves both feeling and thinking, is no different.[5]

We can thank—and blame—this twofold nature of beauty for making us capable in principle of seeing it even in the most abstract realms of thought, such as SCIENCE or pure MATHEMATICS.[6] The deeper you think about the world and the stronger you feel it, the more likely you are to experience the imminent revelation of its beauty—and to feel let down when in the end it eludes you.

It is the emotional essence of the sense of beauty that keeps it from being an unadulterated blessing. This makes it unexceptional, as none of evolution's gifts are perceived by us as purely good. Like HAPPINESS, which is always shadowed by and alternates with unhappiness, our capacity to experience beauty is a complicated evolutionary legacy. The complications began as the emotions felt toward certain objects and situations started to spill over from the realm of sex and survival. The eventual emergence of the capacity for abstract thought, which yet remained enmeshed in emotions, extended our sense of beauty, until it encompassed all of human experience, in the one world we inhabit and in the manifold worlds of our minds.

Between the world and a grain of sand

When beauty is perceived in the abstract—in a mathematical formula, or a tile design—it is in a sense the farthest removed from its evolutionary origins, and so especially lucid and pure. I have found out, though, that to experience the most limitless and limpid variety of beauty, I need not seek rarefied abstractions or negate my animal nature. On the contrary, I can do so by heading to the one kind of place where my senses are overrun by the concrete and my continued existence is predicated on an animal sense of self-preservation: the arid desert.

The evolutionary roots of the sense of beauty being utility and survival, it seems perverse that the desert, as deadly a landscape as one can find on this planet, should be seen as sublimely beautiful. Richard Francis Burton, the nineteenth-century adventurer who had been brought up "in Britain's green and pleasant land" and fell in love with the great deserts of India and Arabia, reveled in this paradox:

> Desert views are eminently suggestive; they appeal to the Future, not to the Past: they arouse because they are by no means memorial. To the solitary wayfarer there is an interest in the Wilderness unknown to Cape seas and Alpine glaciers, and even to the rolling Prairie,—the effect of continued excitement on the mind, stimulating its powers to their pitch. Above, through a sky terrible in its stainless beauty, and the splendours of a pitiless blinding glare, the Samun caresses you like a lion with flaming breath. Around lie drifted sand-heaps, upon which each puff of wind leaves its trace in solid waves, flayed rocks, the very skeletons of mountains, and hard unbroken plains, over which he who rides is spurred by the idea that the bursting of a water-skin, or the pricking of a camel's hoof, would be a certain death of torture,—a haggard land infested with wild beasts, and wilder men,—a region whose very fountains murmur the warning words "Drink and away!" What can be more exciting? what more sublime?[7]

If you have not yet lived the beauty of the desert, I envy you your first hike away from the road and into the open space.[8] Between a high place, where the horizon in every direction is a hundred miles away, and a slot canyon through which one cannot squeeze without taking off one's pack, there is an infinite variety of beauty there to lose yourself in. Be forewarned, though: unless your inclination or fate, like that of Everett Ruess,[9] is to disappear into the wild, brace yourself for the moment of having to turn back, which will remind you that, while the desert is timeless, your journey through it must come to an end.

The pathos of things

Unlike the awe-instilling vista seen from a desert summit, the little things that wait for us back at home are easy to relate to, maybe because each of them can be taken in all at once, or held in hand, or is actually hand-made. Some of these project *mono no aware*: the pathos of things that are beautiful in a small and subdued way.

To my mind, the teapot that appeared in some of Yasujiro Ozu's films, such as *Tokyo Story*, is one such object. A signature move of Ozu's as a director was to make the camera linger for many seconds on a just-vacated space, with a teapot in a corner or a mirror on the far wall underscoring the room's EMPTINESS. In his last films, shot in color, the teapot was revealed to be a lively fire-engine red, which is what all black-and-white movie teapots probably are like, in teapot heaven.

Speaking of which: the luckiest teapots get to retire to a warm and sunny place—Death Valley. A variable number of teapots, a few of them red, can be found at all times hanging off the signpost at the Teakettle Junction, where Hunter Mountain Road and Racetrack Road part ways. They are surrounded by glorious emptiness, the scale of which is so vast that it makes you forget for a while the pathos of small things.[10]

In the house where I live, the role of the red teapot is played by a heavy mesquite burl, turned into a Greek-style urn by a woodworker from Jerome, Arizona. It has been sitting in the living room, on a stool placed in between two bookshelves, bearing witness to the slow accumulation of my books, which I, as all readers, acquire in exchange for TIME.

The seven sad senses of beauty

We can now count them:

- First, the dialectic: "When the world speaks of beauty as being beautiful, ugliness is at once defined."[11]
- Second, the fleetingness: beauty is prone to be changed by time, and, in the long run, not to the better; under the aspect of eternity none survives.

- Third, the futility: there is (again, in the long run) nothing that we can *do* about beauty.

- Fourth, the tension: on the one hand, the ubiquitous beauty of the world and on the other hand—the hardships of EXISTENCE.

- Fifth, the ass-backwardness: we get better at discerning beauty as we get older, by which time most of it is behind us, like the great desert of Sinai was for Moses at Mt. Nebo.

- Sixth, the inescapability: once we discover beauty and are moved by it, there is no way back to the peaceful status quo ante.

- Seventh, the letdown: the better we know beauty, the clearer it becomes that there are at least seven senses in which it is rather sad.

Of related interest

To watch:

Yasujirō Ozu, *Equinox Flower* (1958)

Julie Taymor, *Frida* (2002)

Jennifer Peedom, *Mountain* (2018; based on a book by Robert Macfarlane)

To listen:

Georges Brassens, "Ballade des dames du temps jadis" (1953; lyrics by François Villon, 1489)

Leonard Cohen, "Suzanne" (1967)

Elis Regina and Antônio Carlos Jobim, "Águas de Março" (1972)

To read:

Ryūnosuke Akutagawa, "Autumn Mountain" (1921)

W. L. Rusho, *Everett Ruess: A Vagabond for Beauty* (1983)

Shimon Edelman, *Beginnings* (2014)

To go:

Sinai; Death Valley; Dasht-e-Lut.

5 Children (The Raising of)

Be good. Plan B. Other ways to be.

וְהֵשִׁיב לֵב־אָבוֹת עַל־בָּנִים וְלֵב בָּנִים עַל־אֲבוֹתָם

(And he shall turn the heart of the fathers to the children, and the heart of the children to their fathers.)

—Malachi 3:24

Comprendió con alguna amargura que nada podía esperar de aquellos alumnos que aceptaban con pasividad su doctrina y sí de aquellos que arriesgaban, a veces, una contradicción razonable. Los primeros, aunque dignos de amor y de buen afecto, no podían ascender a individuos; los últimos preexistían un poco más.

(He comprehended with some bitterness that he could expect nothing of those students who passively accepted his doctrines, but that he could of those who, at times, would venture a reasonable contradiction. The former, though worthy of love and affection, could not rise to the state of individuals; the latter pre-existed somewhat more.)

—Jorge Luis Borges, *Las Ruinas Circulares*[1]

Be good

According to an old academic joke, God would be denied tenure at a university because he had only one publication (and even that was not peer-reviewed).[2] *One* happens also to be the number of children raised by my late father. Mine was the case he cut his parenting teeth on and, for better or for worse, it had his undivided attention.

EVOLUTION sees to it that child-rearing works—on the average. One of my kids asked me once when he was small how he would know how to raise *his* children once he had them. My reply at the time sincerely tried to reassure ("No worries, you just will"), but now I know better. Considering how much room there is for PARENTS to screw things up, his apprehension was entirely justified. It is always heartwarming to see an individual case that has not been completely botched, but low-to-moderate expectations should really be the rule here.[3]

ANXIETY about one's performance as a parent is a sign of caring about one's children. Such caring would seem to go without saying, yet it cannot be taken for granted—surprisingly, for reasons that are also evolutionary.[4] Just how much *I* must have meant to my father I eventually inferred from a remark of his: if you have children, you can be made to do anything—an inconvenient TRUTH to share with a child, but perhaps forgivable if offered by a survivor of a world WAR and a decade in the Gulag.

There was another thing he said to me once, which any child of privilege would find it easier to relate to: being a parent means always trying to anticipate where your child will stumble, so that you can rush there and spread some straw to soften the fall. This sounds almost too good to be true, until you remember that there can be too much of a good thing, including protectiveness. The trick is to decide, on a case by case basis and ahead of time, how much straw, if any, is called for, and to act accordingly. The same goes for every other thing that you may be conceivably be called to decide upon in relation to your kids. Do that, and you're good.

Plan B

You can tell you've been good if your children grow up and leave and get a life and occasionally come back HOME to visit and everyone gets a kick out of it and looks forward to the next visit. But what if your intentions have been good all along, yet the plan of ACTION turns out years later to have been faulty? The "arrow of TIME" bars the undoing of any past action, but it hurts the most if it's between you and your kids.[5] The only available options are either to make amends for past mistakes going forward, or to make your experience into an example for someone else—perhaps for your own children—of how not to behave.[6]

In either case, this can only work if at least some insight is gained into what happened. This is not easy, to say the least. Whatever intuitions we have about the dynamics between parents and children, there is also an objective reason for it being difficult: the overwhelming COMPLEXITY of social interactions. An individual's behavior is unpredictable enough; in a nuclear family, the matters are much complicated by strong emotions, the POWER differential in favor of the parents, and the countermeasures deployed by children, making the dynamics exponentially harder to fathom. Because of this, it is very hard to figure out in each particular case what exactly went wrong and when, or to devise an intervention even if the causes of the situation do become clear.

The parents' suspicion that things are not going as well as they should often intensifies as the kids grow up. Once they hit adolescence, the simmering conflict is ready to boil over. The several years that follow are not much fun either for the parents or for the kids. It may be a scant comfort to a family that feels under siege, but it pays to remember that the conflict serves a purpose: power must be redistributed and relationships redefined, to prepare the kids for leaving HOME—preferably, without burning the bridges.[7]

Other ways to be

In managing the parent-child conflict, and in identifying and making up for past mistakes, we can and should rely on any human qualities that can offset basic evolutionary urges. Dispersal (the technical term for leaving home) may be a universal biological trait (even plants do it), but only humans can negotiate the terms for it, rather than being driven exclusively by blind instinct. In doing so, we have recourse to many tools that are part of our cultural traditions.[8]

My own views on these matters are necessarily skewed by my being an only son and a father only to sons. They have also been shaped by the culture I grew up in, which values individuality and resoluteness over sociability and compromise, as well as by the culture into which I assimilated myself, which in addition also encourages seeking professional help in matters of personality and of social life. But there are as many or more ways of being human as there are cultural groups on earth, and many ways of being a parent.[9] The more we learn about those and the more we reflect about what we have learned, the better we can cope with the burden that we bear together with our children. And there is no better place for setting the burden down for a while and for reflecting together on what it all means than the desert:

Out here, there is another way to be.
There is a rising brightness in the rock,
a singing in the silence of the tree.
Something is always moving, running free,
as quick and still as quail move in a flock.[10]

Of related interest

To watch:

Yasujirō Ozu, *Late Spring* (1949)

Wim Wenders, *Paris, Texas* (1984)

To listen:

Cat Stevens, "Father and Son" (1970)

Paul Simon, "Mother and Child Reunion" (1972)

Steve Miller Band, "Fly Like an Eagle" (1976)

To read:

Jorge Luis Borges, *The Circular Ruins* (1970e)

Ursula K. Le Guin, "Solitude" in *The Birthday of the World* (2002)

To go:

Hiking in the wilderness, with the kids.

6 Complexity

The dark forest. A spotlight shines on an enigma. Back in the forest.

The view that machines cannot give rise to surprises is due, I believe, to a fallacy to which philosophers and mathematicians are particularly subject. This is the assumption that as soon as a fact is presented to a mind all consequences of that fact spring into the mind simultaneously with it. It is a very useful assumption under many circumstances, but one too easily forgets that it is false.
—Alan M. Turing, "Computing Machinery and Intelligence"[1]

The dark forest

If we still fail to appreciate computing machinery's potential for vastly complex behavior, it may be because for the entire human history, we have all been conditioned to look down on "mindless automata."[2] Before the invention of computer science in the 1930s, this blind spot had been universal, but then came the cataclysmic transformation of the logical foundations of MATHEMATICS at the hands of Gödel, Turing, and others (see chapter 19). It was driven in part by the discovery that certain seemingly simple and innocuous questions about computation are mathematically impossible to answer.

The new field of computational complexity soon followed up on these *undecidability* proofs with the development of the concept of *tractability*. The new formal tools could be used to rank abstract computing devices by power, and computational problems by their complexity. These tools revealed entire classes of problems to be provably intractable in a specific and relevant sense, despite obviously having a solution. A familiar example is the "traveling salesman" problem: how to visit each of a number of cities once, while keeping the traveled distance to a minimum. For such problems, finding the optimal solution requires a number of steps that scales exponentially with problem "size" (in this case, the number of cities that need to be visited). Problems whose complexity is exponential are considered intractable because for them finding a solution may take more time than is left until the Universe fizzles out.[3]

Computational complexity is relevant to all living creatures (and not just to computer scientists) because all brains are fundamentally computing devices, which evolve to meet computational challenges presented by the Universe—itself is a kind of computer.[4] According to Turing's insight, dealing with any computing machine, let alone a staggeringly complex one, could in principle pose undecidable or intractable challenges. Why then do all the problems that must be solved to ensure survival happen to be tractable, as our existence demonstrates them to be?

To see why this is so, remember that EVOLUTION too is a computational process, which is subject to the constraints of tractability. Evolution is an embodiment of the art of the possible. It computes feasible (but not necessarily optimal) paths through the "landscape" of potentially viable forms, each capable of a certain range of ACTIONS. As failed actors keep being discarded by selection, those creatures that temporarily manage to escape extinction do so necessarily by building and occupying niches of tractability in clearings carved out of the great dark forest of complexity.[5]

A spotlight shines on an enigma

Although computational intractability sounds like it's all about what *cannot* be done, people had been putting it to use long before the invention of programmable computers and the science of complexity. For one thing, intractability can make encryption secure: a good substitution code, for instance, is one for which the number of combinations that must be tested to break it by brute force is prohibitively large, compared to the time and computing power available to the would-be code-breakers—assuming that the latter do not happen to have a better grasp of the underlying math than the code's designers.

How large is "prohibitively large" depends on many additional factors, which in real-life usage moderate the ideal, inherently non-negotiable mathematical nature of complexity. A lesson to that effect can be found in the history of World War II. Before and during that WAR, all communication security of Nazi Germany (including its army, navy, air force, the Nazi party, the Gestapo, military intelligence, and the foreign service) was founded on the supposedly intractable combinatorial complexity of a certain coding method, a "polyalphabetic substitution cipher." This was incorporated into a family of electromechanical rotor-based encryption/decryption devices, the Enigma. Unfortunately for the German war effort, both the physical and the mathematical components of the Enigma project met with bad luck.

First, an employee of the German defense ministry's cipher division sold information about the Enigma machine's rotor construction to the Poles, who at the time were frantically preparing for the looming German aggression. This critical intelligence allowed Polish mathematicians to make significant progress in understanding how the Enigma encryption scheme worked. Then, just before Poland was overrun by the German tanks in September 1939, the Poles sent all the intelligence they had on the matter, as well as an actual Enigma machine they had captured, over to England. There, it soon landed on the desk of another mathematician, Alan Turing.[6]

Back in the forest

The Enigma story shows that computational intractability can sometimes be effectively countered by a combination of mathematical genius and computing power made possible by TECHNOLOGICAL ingenuity (not without help from other human traits such as greed and STUPIDITY).[7] We must recognize, though, that this piece of action, along with the war of which it was part, and indeed the entire history of our species to date, has been playing out in one of those metaphorical "clearings" in the surrounding dark forest of complexity.

The tractability of basic-survival tasks such as foraging for food or finding a mate, to which we owe our existence, is a sign of a deeper regularity in the make-up of the Universe. The "laws" of physics that describe the Universe are fundamentally simple, and it is this simplicity—think of the physical inertia of the body of an antelope, which prevents it from making too sharp a turn when it flees from a cheetah—that makes the Universe predictable enough to enable foresight-based survival (it is also what makes SCIENCE possible).[8]

The effects of complexity, in contrast, kick in when we try to figure out "the" cause of an actual event, or to anticipate the behavior of a given complex system such as a particular animal's brain in a specific case (as opposed to the statistical traits of a species). Complexity also besets all attempts at optimizing one's behavior instead of "satisficing" the known constraints.[9] It also disproportionately characterizes "unnatural" problems such as predicting the behavior of a herd of stock market investors (as opposed to natural ones such as predicting the behavior of a herd of wildebeest). In those unnatural situations, we find ourselves straying too far from our clearing into the thickets of complexity.

Over the course of EVOLUTION, we have developed certain safeguards that keep us from getting bogged down in intractability while taking care of the business of daily survival. One such mechanism is emotions, which are computational shortcuts designed to avoid problems that are intractable when attacked frontally.[10] It is relevant that emotions are obligatory in that we cannot consciously choose not to experience them (the ability to do so would be a serious evolutionary handicap). Another mechanism is the subjective feeling of having FREE WILL, a good objective excuse for which is the intractability (and in some cases undecidability) of questions concerning the future behavior of self and others.

Complexity also dictates the kind of MORALITY that creatures with finite computational resources might go by. The full potential consequences of any nontrivial ACTION are too complex for the human mind to compute, and so we must rely on emotions, EMPATHY, generalizations from MEMORY, and rules of thumb instead. As to the ultimate evolutionary adaptation to the complexity of the Universe, it may be, as Robert Musil has surmised,[11] nothing other than STUPIDITY:

> All of us are stupid on occasion: there are also times when we must act blindly (or at least half-blindly), otherwise the world would stand still; and if one derived from the hazards of stupidity the general rule: "refrain from all judgments and decisions which you don't sufficiently understand," we would simply be paralysed!

It looks like even people who never heard of Musil know enough about life to do just that, which explains a lot about the state the world is in.

Of related interest

To watch:

Michael Apted, *The Imitation Game* (2014; or just read the book about Turing, listed below)

To read:

Jorge Luis Borges, "The Aleph" ([1940] 1970a)

Andrew Hodges, *Alan Turing: The Enigma* (1983)

To go:

To Bletchley Park.

7   Consciousness

The Tempest in a teapot. The insubstantial pageant. We are such stuff as dreams are made on. The splendor and the misery.

Con alivio, con humillación, con terror, comprendió que él también era una apariencia, que otro estaba soñándolo.

(With relief, with humiliation, with terror, he understood that he also was an illusion, that someone else was dreaming him.)

—J. L. Borges, *Las Ruinas Circulares*

The Tempest in a teapot

When Shakespeare's Jaques, in *As You Like It*, speaks his most famous lines— "All the world's a stage, / And all the men and women merely players"— his very act of uttering these words confirms their truth: inside the Globe Theater, the stage *is* the world. There is a deeper truth here, however. It can be glimpsed in Shakespeare's last play, *The Tempest*, in the revelation made by Prospero, the weary magician and his creator's alter ego:

> . . . These our actors,
> As I foretold you, were all spirits and
> Are melted into air, into thin air:
> And, like the baseless fabric of this vision,
> The cloud-capp'd towers, the gorgeous palaces,
> The solemn temples, the great globe itself,
> Ye all which it inherit, shall dissolve
> And, like this insubstantial pageant faded,
> Leave not a rack behind. We are such stuff
> As dreams are made on, and our little life
> Is rounded with a sleep.

Let us indulge the playwright's vision here for a moment: could what Prospero says be true? Indeed it could—if the entire play were happening inside Prospero's head: a tempest in a brain pan.[1]

The insubstantial pageant

The idea of Prospero's world being imaginary—all of it, including "the great globe itself"—is perfectly in line with it having in fact been imagined, by Shakespeare. The world of *The Tempest* first came together inside Shakespeare's head, then was shared with his spectators and readers. When I read the play, I am effectively staging it for private viewing inside my head, in what must be the cheapest approach ever to producing Shakespeare. As I put the script aside, the cast takes a break, but the imaginary show goes on, with different actors and props for each new scene, for as long as I am conscious—that is, awake and aware.

The rabbit hole runs deeper than that, though. To follow it deeper down, consider how reading is like PERCEPTION: one is externally guided THINKING, and the other—guided hallucination.[2] Because all our sensory reality is virtual (see chapter 24), a play attended by a spectator is mirrored by a virtual one, consisting of brain events that unfold inside the spectator's head. That is where representations of the actors, the stage, the theater, and the rest of the perceived world are to be found.

Shakespeare's choice of words—"insubstantial pageant"—is an eerily precise description of the SCIENCE behind these brain events. The sound-and-vision show hallucinated by the viewer is *insubstantial* because it does not inhere in the substance of a particular brain: it is made up of the relations among the activities of the brain's parts. Another brain or even an electronic device that supports the same pattern of activity would be harboring the same "hallucination." And the show is a *pageant* and not a tableau because the pattern of activity is dynamic: it unfolds in TIME.[3]

The virtual reality that we inhabit *feels* real enough. Like all other major aspects of the mind, consciousness helps shape behavior and is therefore itself shaped by EVOLUTION. The task of basic consciousness—being awake and aware of one's surroundings—is to glue together bits and pieces of the virtual world as constructed by the senses, and to paint it over with emotions, so that events in the real world are easier to interpret and to act upon. A failure to take at face value our virtual reality—to *feel* it—would undermine the very reason for being awake and aware of the world, which is to be able to better deal with it.[4]

This is why merely hearing and even accepting an explanation of how perception and consciousness give rise to a virtual reality do not make the world feel less real. Explanations aside, it takes a transcendental insight for us to really see through the self-deception. When that happens, the person's state becomes exactly analogous to that of a dreamer who has attained lucidity: a conscious realization of being in a dream, which is often accompanied by the ability to exert "magical" control of the reality within it.

Lucid dreams are a lot of fun (as I have discovered), which makes me wonder what waking-world enlightenment would be like. By definition, direct insight into the nature of reality must be a first-person experience. I have never had one, but my guess is that this experience could be at the same time liberating and terrifying: liberating, because it reveals a TRUTH; terrifying, because at the core of this truth is EMPTINESS.[5]

We are such stuff as dreams are made on

The terror in the face of irreality arises out of a reasoned conclusion (and, in the case of actual enlightenment, also out of direct and deeply felt PERCEPTION) that one is surrounded by nothingness, or perhaps by empty props behind which there lurks something that is unknown and unknowable. But this discovery, whether merely reasoned or also felt, stops short of revealing the complete truth. To get to the bottom of the rabbit hole, ask this: the *I* at the center of the hurricane of experiences, the dreamer who dreams my world—*what* is it?

The conclusion to *The Circular Ruins*, whose final sentence serves as the epigraph to this chapter, merely postpones the showdown. If my world, along with my self, is dreamed by someone else, the mystery of the nature of that other self remains (as Borges had no doubt intended). There is, however, an intriguing possibility here that does not amount to running around in circles in pursuit of an explanation: if I am "such stuff as dreams are made on," perhaps *I* am a dream that dreams itself.

Everything that we know about how the mind works confirms this, the deepest, insight.[6] What all the mind's faculties and doings are made of— PERCEPTION, MEMORY, THINKING, LANGUAGE, ACTION, as well as all emotions—is the processing of information by otherwise inanimate matter, or in other words, computation. The same goes for consciousness of the world and for the eye at the center of the world. Self-consciousness emerges when a representation tasked with modeling the world, so as to better understand and predict its workings, turns back on itself, giving rise to a *self-model.*

The full account of how this could be true, and of why it most likely *is* true, can here only be pointed at in passing.[7] Particularly telling, though, are experiments that have demonstrated that all the components of the experienced self boil down to computations that can be easily subverted. It is now possible to induce controlled illusions of body ownership, out-of-body experiences, and the ownership of actions coupled with the ability to anticipate their outcomes, which we experience as a sense of agency. The outcomes of these interventions on self-consciousness are fully explained by a computational theory built around the notion of a virtual self.[8] Had Prospero been of this world, rather than dreamt by Shakespeare and his readers, there is a clear and definite sense in which he would be a dream of Prospero's.

The splendor and the misery

Basic consciousness, or being aware of the world, with all its BEAUTY, can bring much joy. Self-consciousness—being aware of that awareness, as well as of one's self—is a different matter. Given the frequency of mind-wandering and the predominance of unconscious processes in cognition, it would seem that awareness of awareness and of the self is not absolutely necessary for dealing with the world.[9] Why have it, then, if it brings more misery than splendor?

An indictment of self-consciousness runs to several counts. First, it is a well-known impediment to the pursuit of HAPPINESS, which goes astray when done consciously. Second, it is a precondition for SUFFERING: although the capacity for pain is included with basic consciousness, which always involves emotions, self-consciousness adds the *awareness* of suffering and of its subject. Third, it takes self-directed THINKING to reveal the absurdity of EXISTENCE, insofar as "the main condition of absurdity" is, as Thomas Nagel so vividly described it, "the dragooning of an unconvinced transcendent consciousness into the service of an immanent, limited enterprise like a human life." And, lastly, self-consciousness is what has brought DEATH into the human universe: all other animals, as Borges has noted, are immortal, because they have no conscious awareness of their own mortality.[10]

The standard retort to complaints about the human condition—putting it down to EVOLUTION—is scant solace for the poor self-aware self-models, but here, as in many other cases, it's all we have. Self-consciousness indeed does what it does mostly for our own good, in part because the self-model makes learning from the outcomes of ACTION more effective, by serving as a lightning rod for blame, as well as a receptacle for credit. Liberation from the self, as envisioned by some philosophers and preached by certain religions,[11] would annul those benefits.

To be complete, such liberation cannot be merely informational, as when the self attains insight into its own illusory nature, only to carry on with life as usual, subject to suffering and all. A full and true liberation, as preached by the Buddha, is supposed to involve letting go of all worldly desires and attachments. Individuals who are sheltered and provided for, such as monks or people with a trust fund, need not be concerned about this requirement, while for others it presents an economic obstacle. But the real question is whether or not there is *willingness* to do it, given the scope of the sacrifice that it requires: no less than the dissolution of the mainstay of one's identity. The stage notes for the actors who play some of the spirits in the scene in *The Tempest* with which I opened this chapter provide a fitting description for what this may feel like:

> PROSPERO *starts suddenly, and speaks; after which, to a strange, hollow, and* confused noise, they heavily vanish.

Of related interest

To watch:

Peter Greenaway, *Prospero's Books* (1991)

Richard Linklater, *Waking Life* (2001)

To listen:

Pyotr Ilyich Tchaikovsky, Буря (*The Tempest*, 1873)

To read:

William Shakespeare, *The Tempest* (1610–1611)

W. H. Auden, *The Sea and the Mirror* (1944)

Kij Johnson, *The Dream-Quest of Vellitt Boe* (2016)

To go:

See *The Tempest* at The Globe.

8 Death

The tragic sense of life. The Switch. Still The Switch. Only in silence the word.

הַאַתָּה הוּא הַקֵּץ? עוֹד צָלוּל הַמֶּרְחָב
עַרְפָלֵי הַחַיִּים עוֹד רוֹמְזִים מֵרָחוֹק
עוֹד הַשַּׁחַק תָּכֹל וְהַדֶּשֶׁא יָרֹק
טֶרֶם סָתָו

(So then, are you the end? But the air is still clear,
The mists of existence beckon still from afar,
And the sky is still blue and so bright is the star
At the end of the year.)
—Rachel, "Are you the end?" (excerpt)

Двум смертям не бывать, одной не миновать.

(There's no dying twice, no avoiding dying once.)
—Russian proverb

¿De qué otra forma se puede amenazar que no sea de muerte? Lo interesante, lo original sería que alguien lo amenace a uno con la inmortalidad.

(How else can you threaten someone other than with death? It would be interesting and original to threaten someone with immortality.)
—J. L. Borges[1]

The tragic sense of life

I inherited my copy of Miguel de Unamuno's *The Tragic Sense of Life in Men and Nations* from the man to the failure of whose suicide attempt at age nineteen I owe my EXISTENCE: my father.[2] Any book on a serious enough topic that fell into my father's hands would come out amply marked.

Unamuno's rant against death—sustained, brilliant, and passionate (it has more exclamation marks per page than any other philosophical tract that I know)—stands out in that it received only one annotation from my father, and that too in the afterword. This is the passage he singled out:

> Personal immortality offers some serious ambiguities of its own: it can be a terrifying rather than a comforting thought. So at least felt Kierkegaard, who in his *Sickness Unto Death* analyzes ultimate despair as the recoil from this possibility of having to be oneself, of not being able to escape oneself, for all eternity.

Unlike Unamuno, my father was not a man of RELIGION. This makes his lifelong ambivalence toward life and death, and his choice of the one passage to underscore in that book, easier for me to relate to. The ambivalence is endemic among nonbelievers: in the absence of faith, the contest between emotion and reason over the proper attitude to death tends to resemble World War I trench warfare. For all of us in the trenches, it is not the impending nothingness as such, but rather the impasse between our feelings about death and our THINKING about it that imparts to life a certain tragic sense.

The Switch

Reason insists that death is nothing more and nothing less than the cessation of existence. If so, opting for instantaneous (and therefore necessarily painless) death has the unique distinction of being the one ACTION that can serve as a reasonable response to both extreme HAPPINESS and extreme SUFFERING. I sometimes imagine having at my disposal a switch—The Switch—such that throwing it would immediately and painlessly terminate my EXISTENCE. Immediacy is important, lest REGRET awakens when it's already too late to change one's mind. Painlessness is important too: Hamlet's "bare bodkin" is out of the question for most people, as it is for me.[3]

Would living my life in the shadow of The Switch make me happier or more miserable? How likely would I be to use it eventually? Had my father had it at nineteen, he would definitely have used it instead of those sleeping pills. What about at eighty, with his strength and his health gone, slowly descending into dementia? I like to think that *I* would, in his place, but words are cheap and the door that The Switch opens is exit-only.[4]

Medical science may soon make The Switch easy to implement, but this would not cause pondering death to be any easier: if anything, TECHNOLOGY tends to complicate difficult personal and societal issues and to spawn new and unexpected problems, rather than delivering clean solutions. That which makes death so hard to think about clearly and dispassionately has been known for a long time. Our stance on death is a matter in which time and again feelings give reason a drubbing and cause it to retrench a few kilometers to the west, where it holds onto its positions by the skin of its teeth.

The root of the problem is that our attitude toward death is asymmetrical with respect to TIME: as Roman philosopher-poet Lucretius noted, we do not mind not having existed in the past, before we were born, yet we dread our future non-existence after death.[5] It took two thousand years' worth of science and philosophy to place the blame for this attitude where it belongs. Derek Parfit, writing in the 1980s, concludes that "we ought not to be biased toward the future. In giving us this bias, EVOLUTION denies us the best attitude to death."[6]

Still The Switch

Having identified the culprit in this, the greatest, crime ever perpetrated against humanity does not help us escape its consequences. It is unreasonable for us to fear a future state that we will by definition be unable to experience, and it is unclear that the potential loss of future happiness through death should be valued more than the suffering that it may avert, but, in Unamuno's words:

> These ratiocinations do not move me, for they are reasons and no more than reasons, and one does not feed the heart with reasons. I do not want to die. No! I do not want to die, and I do not want to want to die. I want to live always, forever and ever. And *I* want to live, this poor I which I am, the I which I feel myself to be here and now.[7]

Fair enough, but perhaps instead of getting mad at evolution we should try to get even.

Can TECHNOLOGY do away with death altogether? For whatever it is worth, the tech powers need no convincing: the billionaires who pull the strings in the various Silicon Valleys of the planet are more keen on curing death for the few who can afford it than on making life easier to live for all. It is curious how the promise of a future eternal life helps one overlook present SUFFERING, especially of others. In its built-in shutting out of the POOR, the credo of salvation through high technology is worse even than the promises made by salvific religions: Unamuno's doomed crusade, at least, was fueled by a doctrine that promised eternal life to everyone.[8]

But MORAL considerations were never an obstacle to technological progress, which in this case too may well succeed. It may even succeed, for the chosen few, in doing away with the ravages of OLD AGE as well, thus avoiding a common pitfall in various mythical quests for immortality in which the hapless hero forgets to ask the gods also for eternal youth. Nominally, then, the battle would have been won, but the peace that would follow may not be to anyone's liking.

In the folklore of immortality, there are plenty of stories in which the immortal becomes "sick unto death" (to use Kierkegaard's phrase again) with EXISTENCE. One may argue that this would not happen to a well-adjusted person who is reasonably comfortable in his or her own skin and mind, but it is hard to anticipate what a few millennia, let alone half an eternity, of existence would do to a human psyche. If my self changes as it adapts to immortality, it may become so unrecognizable that the original me might just as well be dead.

In such a scenario, if I am subjected to gaslighting by a gradual change of personality, I may end up never acting on it (just like in real life elderly people who believe they have an "exit" prepared are overtaken by dementia or physical deterioration and end up in a nursing home or on life support). And if I actively and successfully resist change, would I also be able to resist *taedium vitae*, the profound weariness with life to which the really old are especially susceptible? In one of my favorite creation stories, *The Silmarillion*, Tolkien counts the mortal humans as blessed:

> Death is their fate, the gift of Ilúvatar, which as Time wears even the Powers shall envy.

Luckily, if I ever gain immortality through technology, I would always have an equivalent of The Switch at my disposal.[9]

Only in silence the word

Insofar as the human condition makes any sense, it is to be sought in stories that we tell ourselves. On one such story, death is what gives value and meaning to life. Here's the only surviving passage from *The Creation of Éa*—aren't creation stories invented by humanists the best ever!—which opens Ursula Le Guin's *A Wizard of Earthsea*:[10]

> Only in silence the word,
> only in dark the light,
> only in dying life:
> bright the hawk's flight
> on the empty sky.

Of related interest

To watch:

Ingmar Begman, *The Seventh Seal* (1957)

To listen:

Leonard Cohen, *You Want It Darker* (2016)

To read:

Jorge Luis Borges, "The Immortal" in *The Aleph and Other Stories, 1933–1969* ([1947] 1970d)

Ursula K. Le Guin, *The Farthest Shore* (1972)

Victor Pelevin, "News from Nepal" in *The Blue Lantern and Other Stories* (1997)

To go:

To the Farthest Shore and back (you may need the help of a dragon).

9 Empathy

To em or not to em. Us and Them. From ordinary household objects.

Faint to my ears came the gathered rumour of all lands: the springing and the dying, the song and the weeping, and the slow everlasting groan of overburdened stone.

—J. R. R. Tolkien, *The Lord of the Rings*[1]

To em or not to em

Some human cultures have a knack for making everything ultimately about the self—even empathy for others. As I was catching up with the recent research on the psychology of compassion, I discovered that about half of the papers published in the last five years on this topic focus on *self-compassion* or on compassion burnout.[2] At the same time, there seems to be no consensus among psychologists as to what empathy and compassion toward *others* actually are and what role they play in social behavior. Is empathy more of an emotion or a motive for ACTION? Is compassion a consequence of empathy, or a distinct mind state? Is emotional empathy a prerequisite for MORALITY, or would we be better off building ethics on a foundation of cognition and THINKING?[3]

The theoretical vacuum surrounding empathy helps explain the empirical focus on the self. Self-care is something that everyone understands. In comparison, feeling for others is a surprisingly muddled concept. Moreover, the POLITICS of deliberate ACTION motivated by declared and sometimes even sincere compassion "in the abstract" for the SUFFERING masses is what gave us some of the bloodiest episodes in human history: holy WARS waged in the name of salvation or enlightenment.

It must have been this lesson from history, particularly Russian history, that my father was trying to impress on my elementary-school self by repeating, on various occasions, "Мы им революций больше делать не будем" (We are not going to do any more revolutions for *them*). Young children not being in the habit of automatically empathizing with just anyone,[4] I was duly impressed at the time, and I remained so for decades.

Us and Them

The distinction between "us" and "them" in my father's proclamation is significant. A key shortcoming of emotional empathy as a basis for MORAL-ITY is that it typically only extends to "us"—to one's kin or to the handful of people who make up what in social psychology is called one's in-group. Moreover, reason, in the rare moments when it manages to attain a modicum of independence from emotions, has its own "cognitive" biases, so that reasoned compassion too tends more often than not to favor the in-group.

My father's life experience, which had included a Soviet takeover of his native country, a narrow escape from the Nazi invasion as the WAR broke out, and a stint in the Red Army, all topped by nearly a decade spent in the Gulag, is probably to blame for his later tendency to save his compassion for "us," his family. As to "them" . . . the docile Soviet citizenry he used to refer to as быдло, which means something like "plebs," but with a distinct connotation of "cattle." Empathy has many dark sides, of which this is one: disdain-by-default for those who are deemed unworthy of it.

From ordinary household objects

More damaging to personal and public welfare than such disdain is indifference: not caring one way or another. But even people who have learned not to care, so as to avoid being hurt, may feel themselves drawn back into the melee—because they too can still hurt, and because they realize that hurting together can be easier to bear than hurting alone.

This, in so many words, is the message of "The Little Black Box," a story by Philip K. Dick. It opens with the protagonist, an expert on Buddhism, being asked by the State Department to expound on the Christian concept of *caritas*, and culminates in her encounter, inside the virtual reality of an "empathy box," with a Christ-like figure "dying somewhere on a barren plain, surrounded by his enemies. Now I'm with him. And it is an escape from something worse. From you."

> She saw, around her, a desolate expanse. The air smelled of harsh blossoms; this was the desert, and there was no rain.
>
> A man stood before her, a sorrowful light in his gray, pain-drenched eyes. "I am your friend," he said, "but you must go on as if I did not exist. Can you understand that?" He spread empty hands.
>
> "No," she said, "I can't understand that."
>
> "How can I save you," the man said, "if I can't save myself?" He smiled: "Don't you see? There is no salvation."
>
> "Then what's it all for?" she asked.
>
> "To show you," Wilbur Mercer said, "that you aren't alone. I am here with you and always will be. Go back and face them. And tell them that."

Soon, she is wanted by the government, which has banned empathy boxes, for political agitation. She is on the run from the FBI. At the airport, she accepts a sample breakfast cereal box from a peddler. Inside, there is a piece of paper:

> HOW TO ASSEMBLE AN EMPATHY BOX FROM ORDINARY HOUSE-HOLD OBJECTS

Of related interest

To watch:

Wim Wenders, *Wings of Desire* (1987)

To listen:

Rare Bird, "Sympathy" (1969)

Crosby, Stills, Nash & Young, "Teach Your Children" (1970)

Pink Floyd, "Us and Them" (from *The Dark Side of the Moon*, 1973)

Leonard Cohen, "First, We Take Manhattan" (1988)

To read:

Philip K. Dick, "The Little Black Box" (1964)

Philip K. Dick, *Do Androids Dream of Electric Sheep?* (1968)

Vonda N. McIntyre, *Of Mist, and Grass, and Sand* (1973)

Arkady and Boris Strugatsky, *Трудно быть богом* (*Hard to Be a God*, [1964] 1973)[5]

To go:

Take Manhattan.

10 Emptiness

Einstein meets the Buddha. Enter Borges.

The world will be Tlön.

—Jorge Luis Borges, "Tlön, Uqbar, Orbis Tertius"

Einstein meets the Buddha

Although it may seem that any discussion of emptiness[1] would have to be self-undermining, this is not so. There is at least one thing that is worth bringing up in such a discussion: the ultimate TRUTH—

> The ultimate truth is, as we know, emptiness. Emptiness is the emptiness not of existence, but of inherent existence. To be empty of inherent existence is to exist only conventionally, only as the object of conventional truth. The ultimate truth about any phenomenon is hence that it is merely a conventional truth.[2]

Somewhat paradoxically, this ultimate truth does not seal our understanding of the world and of our place in it; rather, it opens it all up for inquiry. Even if all truths about the world are conventional, not all conventions were created equal, or else SCIENCE would long ago have been reduced to philosophy. Einstein, who was not averse to mixing the two, once wrote this about the nature of reality:[3]

> "The physical world is real." That is supposed to be the fundamental hypothesis. What does "hypothesis" mean here? For me, a hypothesis is a statement, whose truth must be assumed for the moment, but whose meaning must be raised above all ambiguity. The above statement appears to me, however, to be, in itself, meaningless, as if one said: "The physical world is cock-a-doodle-do." It appears to me that the "real" is an intrinsically empty, meaningless category (pigeon hole), whose monstrous importance lies only in the fact that I can do certain things in it and not certain others.

Insofar as this "monstrous" constraint on our ACTIONS is conditioned on our EXISTENCE, it is indeed merely conventional—but the only way to escape the strictures of physics[4] is for *us* not to exist. The world, whatever it is, sets the boundary conditions for our FREE WILL—a fitting straitjacket for our CONSCIOUS self, a ghostly presence in an illusory machine.

Enter Borges

The Buddhist doctrine of emptiness is central to its soteriology. It teaches that the realization of the ultimate truth is what brings salvation,[5] in the form of liberation from desire and attachment, and therefore from SUFFERING (there is also a bonus: eventual escape from the cycle of rebirth). Insight into the emptiness of the self is at the core of the requisite realization.[6]

We will never know whether or not Jorge Luis Borges's first published essay, "The Nothingness of Personality," which came out in 1922 when he was twenty-three,[7] had been driven by real insight into emptiness, as opposed to its mere intellectual acceptance. Be that as it may, to me the balance of Borges's long and glorious literary life suggests that he had attained liberation. More than that: for Borges, it took the unique form not of dispassion but of ardor for the world, the fading of which as he slowly went blind nonetheless failed to make him bitter.

A certain insight into Borges's feelings about life[8] is offered by aphorism #51 in his *Fragmentos de un Evangelio apócrifo*, which reads: *Felices los felices*—"Happy are the happy." It is hard to think of a better heading than this for an homage to Borges, such as the one offered by Jorge Aguilar Mora under this very title. Taking up Borges's 1969 collection *Elogio de la sombra* (*In Praise of Darkness*), which includes the "fragments" of the "apocryphal gospel," Aguilar Mora writes:[9]

> Su felicidad de entender el mundo como una ilusión y su escepticismo de no saber cómo vivirlo lo llevaron a una especie de culminación de la apuesta de Pascal, en la cual nada se dice sobre la fe y todo sobre la acción.

> (The happiness that he derived from understanding the world as an illusion and his doubts about how to live it led him to a kind of culmination of Pascal's Wager, in which nothing is said about faith and everything about ACTION.)

Of related interest

To watch:

Donald Cammell and Nicolas Roeg, *Performance* (1970)

To listen:

The Doors, *Celebration of the Lizard* (1970)

To read:

Jorge Luis Borges, *Elogio de la sombra* (*In Praise of Darkness*, 1969)

To go:

Into the shadow.

11 Evolution

The mountains and the monsoon. A universal history of iniquity. Definitely maybe.

Nothing in biology makes sense except in the light of evolution.
—Theodosius Dobzhansky

Evolutionary biology underlies all behavioral disciplines because *Homo sapiens* is an evolved species whose characteristics are the product of its particular evolutionary history.
—Herbert Gintis

We have learned that [subjective experience] in us has evolutionary origins in simpler forms and is seen today in unicellular forms of life.
—Peter Godfrey-Smith[1]

The mountains and the monsoon

People who practice RELIGION have a predilection for imagining being ruled by supreme beings that look just like themselves, even if their official theology says otherwise.[2] It is thus quite ironic that evolution, which is the real arbiter of our fate as a species, does not in the least resemble *us*. Evolution is not an object, and so necessarily not a being, in the sense that a human, a marmot, or a self-driving car is. We can brand evolution as faceless or malevolent or indifferent as much as we like, but taking these imputations of human qualities too literally would be a category mistake. Tempted as I am to write that evolution's invisible hand holds us on an invisible leash, a better metaphor is needed to do justice to its elemental force that shapes us and buffets us about.

Here's what evolution actually is: a set of abstract MATHEMATICAL constraints on the dynamics—that is, on the change of the collective state over time—of certain types of complex systems.[3] Earth's biosphere is just such a system, with an untold number of interacting parts. It consists of millions of populations of replicators, whose individual anatomy and physiology tend in turn to be exceedingly intricate. All of this makes for very complex dynamics.

Despite this COMPLEXITY, the general principles that govern population dynamics in systems of replicators are relatively well understood. These principles determine how various species, including humans, fare over time. By the same token, they also determine what the bodies and the brains of individuals in the successive generations get to be like, which in turn constrains their behavior. In addition to this biological evolution, there is the evolution of culture: of patterns of behavior that are learned and propagated by individuals, affecting their performance as biological replicators. Behavior also influences biology by modifying the species' niche, notably by means of material culture and technology. Because of this interdependence, evolution is really always *co*-evolution—of genes, culture, and environment.[4]

Because evolutionary dynamics has two distinct time scales—slow for biology and fast for culture—it may be likened to a river in a monsoon country. A good example is the Brahmaputra, which begins in southern Tibet as Tsangpo and crosses India's Assam and Arunachal Pradesh states and Bangladesh on its way to the Bay of Benghal. Brahmaputra owes its existence to plate tectonics: the fifty-million-year-old northward push of the Indian plate against the Eurasian plate. This push caused the still ongoing uplifting of the Himalayas, along with the fold that is the Tsangpo valley. The Himalayan range and the Tibetan Plateau play a critical role in bringing about the annual monsoon. And the river, especially during the monsoon-induced floods, changes the landscape, slowly reducing mountains to sand and silt and completing the circle of mutual influence. The interplay of slow tectonics, seasonal weather, and the fast flow of water shapes the landscape and steers the course of the river—just like the interplay of genes and culture, through slow and rapid changes, adds up to the evolution of us.[5]

A universal history of iniquity

Our brains, bodies, and behavior are the products of a long history of interplay among the many factors that have determined the course of life of each of our ancestors, going back billions of years. How those lives were lived is now water under the bridge. Out of each individual's entire life, the only thing of any consequence for evolution is the bottom line: their fitness, which is a measure of how effective their lineup of genes and their cultural repertoire are at replication.[6]

Neither bodily perfection, nor subjective well-being are optimized by selection based on fitness.[7] This simple fact should cut short any complaints about various deplorable aspects of our physique or about the paucity of HAPPINESS in our lives. Railing at evolution is as pointless as throwing a tantrum at the elements: one may end up as laughingstock for the ages, like Xerxes, the Persian king who ordered the waters of the Hellespont to be given 300 lashes and branded with red-hot iron for obstructing his invasion of Greece. Still, keeping a record of the iniquities that have been visited upon us by evolution makes sense: it may help us understand what we are and why, and perhaps eventually act on this understanding.

The list of regrettable traits that evolution has saddled us with runs long. Some of these—teeth instead of a nice beak; a wobbly stack of vertebrae instead of an exoskeleton—are mentioned in chapter 22, which is about OLD AGE, a condition that makes one really feel some of evolution's worst screw-ups. Quite a few others come to mind. On the bodily side, the list includes, in addition to teeth and the spinal column, the useless appendix and the inane anatomy of shoulders and knees. On the side of behavior and culture, I find particularly lamentable the traits that underlie discord between adolescent CHILDREN and their PARENTS, due in part to the evolution-sanctioned drive for territorial dispersal.[8]

A revealing illustration of how closely intertwined biological and cultural evolutionary processes are is the case of pain. It is commonly thought that pain signals tissue damage, but there is more to it. There are striking differences in how humans and other animals experience pain. A deer with a broken leg appears much less affected by it than a human with the same predicament (which I know from personal experience, having once broken a leg and, on another occasion, both clavicles). A compelling explanation of this difference may be found in our ultrasociality: humans, but not deer, have come to depend in their survival on help from their conspecifics. In the woods, a lame deer would do well to keep quiet, lest it attracts wolves; a human with a broken leg can reasonably hope to be carried away by the rest of the foraging party before the wolves arrive.[9]

Even if similar reasons can be found for other types of pain too, they would not *justify* our continued susceptibility to SUFFERING—neither with regard to our evolutionary fitness, nor with regard to our well-being or HAPPINESS. Our social environment and our TECHNOLOGY are now such that experiencing agony that makes us scream would appear to be unnecessary.[10] When I was lying on my back with two broken clavicles after flying off my bike, the driver of a passing car called an ambulance; any screaming on my part would have only interfered with the paramedics' work. On my solo hikes in the wilderness, where no one can hear you scream, I make a point of keeping my satellite communications device where I can reach it even after a fall.[11] And if my ache is mental, I know where to find help. And yet, I can hardly hope to be as serene as a deer in the face of pain or suffering.

Definitely maybe

In a nearly century-old satirical novel, *The Twelve Chairs*, which used to be universally read in Russia, there was a slogan on the wall of a rowing club: "Helping people who are drowning is a task for those people themselves."[12] Perhaps now that we have an inkling of how evolution works, we could try to do something about it?

One option that suggests itself is for us to go virtual. Once we become code, what could be easier than reaching in and editing out the undesirable parts? Unfortunately, there is zero chance that the minds of somewhat complex animals such as ourselves could be recast as "software" (as opposed to billions of parameters of a precisely and intricately wired brain-like web of computing elements). Even if an explicit program emulating a mind were available, the full import of any modification to it is virtually certain to be impossible to predict, as the theory of computational COMPLEXITY has demonstrated.

Any attempt to make improved humans by editing the human germline, which is within reach of the CRISPR/Cas9 TECHNOLOGY,[13] would face a complexity issue of a different nature. Most organismic traits are polygenically determined: they depend on a complex interaction of multiple genes, which, moreover, is compounded by a variety of interacting complex processes during development. Because the full consequences of playing around with the genome are so difficult to anticipate, doing so would amount to a mix of hubris and nearsightedness, if not outright STUPIDITY.

Sadly, humanity's record of intervening on the cultural instead of the biological side of its evolution has so far been less than stellar. All attempts to improve the human condition on a large scale by revolutionary means have resulted in massive SUFFERING and often in lasting changes to the worse.[14] We need not be surprised: societies are very complex systems, with all the implied difficulties of mapping the course of their evolution over time. Whatever hope there is for our POLITICS and our TECHNOLOGY to make up for some of our built-in faults lies in more modest interventions. In politics and in the social sciences, these could be in education and mental health. In technology, worthy and safe goals are perfecting medicine and making food, shelter, and energy freely available.[15]

Whether or not deflecting our evolutionary doom proves possible, we will always have the "what if" visions of what our society could have been like, if only we ourselves were different. The ones that I like the best have been dreamed by Ursula Le Guin, in whose invented Hainish Universe different planets are populated by versions of humans that differ in some key traits. There is the peaceful Chiffewar (name-dropped but never described); the gender-fluid Gethen (in *The Left Hand of Darkness*); the cultural stasis on Aka, where science was never discovered (in *The Telling*); and on Hain, 70,000 years of recorded history of a society in which some folks happily stick to the tradition of making a living by fishing from wooden sailboats, in full view of the planet's spaceport across the bay.

Of related interest

To read:

Michael Swanwick, *Stations of the Tide* (1991)

Greg Egan, *Diaspora* (1997)

To go:

The "Grand Canyon" of the Tsangpo.

12   Existence

A bit of Talmudic existentialism. I think, therefore I ache. The mindfulness ruse.

The Sages taught: For two and a half years, Beit Shammai and Beit Hillel disagreed. These say: It would have been preferable had man not been created than to have been created. And those said: It is preferable for man to have been created than had he not been created. [Ultimately,] they were counted and concluded: It would have been preferable had man not been created than to have been created.
—Talmud (Eruvin 13b)

Hence the sombre words of Sophocles "Never to have been born counts highest of all . . ." are well met by the old Jewish reply—"How many are so lucky? Not one in ten thousand."
—Bernard Williams, *Problems of the Self*[1]

A bit of Talmudic existentialism

As a precocious toddler, I had once publicly thanked my mother for having given birth to me, so that I could, in my own words, "live for a while in this world." As I eventually discovered, this transparent attempt to ingratiate myself with my PARENTS (a superfluous move, seeing that I was a pampered and doted-upon only CHILD) put me on the losing side of a famous disagreement between Shammai and Hillel, the two stellar authorities in Jewish halachic thought. The severe and strict Shammai and the liberal and lax Hillel used to argue about pretty much everything of any importance in the interpretation of the biblical law. In this case, the debate was about existence: whether to be ("to have been created") is better than not to be, with Hillel initially arguing that being is preferable over nothingness. In the end, Hillel conceded—quite surprisingly, given that his opinions prevailed in virtually every other case—and the two schools concluded jointly that it is not.[2]

The ending of this Talmud story shows that the Sages fully realized the predicament shared by all those who are alive: even if it is preferable for people not to have been created, this preference is entirely beside the point for self-aware humans, for whom existence is a *fait accompli*, so that the real question, like Hamlet's, is what to do about it now. It may seem that the responsibility for choosing what to do with one's existence can be easily dodged, perhaps simply by not thinking about it, but this is just self-deception: as pointed out by Sartre,[3] pretending that nothing needs to be decided here is in itself a decision. In any case, the Sages' answer to the "What now?" question is quite in line both with Shakespeare's and with Sartre's: seeing that man exists, he should "examine his actions." Unfortunately, that is easier said than done.

I think, therefore I ache

If contemplating one's existence and examining one's ACTIONS were easy or fun, we would not have needed all those spiritual and intellectual authorities urging us to do so (whether by presenting it as a divine commandment or by appealing to our sense of honor as humans). It is a cruel fact of life that although people do not enjoy such contemplation, they keep returning to it compulsively, even when they should by rights be perfectly happy "living the moment." A sign of this cycle of compulsion is the prevalence of mind-wandering—mental spacetime travel that we engage in, despite the anguish that is typically brought about by rumination about the past and ANXIETY about the future.

At any given moment during a person's waking life, there is an even chance that he or she is mentally absent from the here and now.[4] During these episodes of mind-wandering, people think about unrelated things, or replay in their head their past experiences, or imagine and plan for the future, all the while relying on automated, subconscious, and subpersonal cognitive processes to carry on their daily routine.

Although predisposition to mind-wandering sounds like it should be a serious EVOLUTIONARY handicap, it may actually confer an advantage, by making temporary, opportunistic use of brain resources, which are not needed for routine moment-to-moment functioning, for the purpose of evaluating the past and planning for the future. When attentional monitoring discerns that the present situation has ceased to be routine, the brain "snaps out" of the daydream and enters a crisis mode, only to drift away again as soon as the immediate needs are taken care of.

Mind-wandering makes us feel down. It detracts from our subjective well-being, which is a key component of HAPPINESS. The participants in studies whose mood is sampled at random times during the day report feeling worse off if they happen to be mentally elsewhere or elsewhen at the moment. These negative feelings are especially pronounced when people are caught in the middle of self-focused THINKING: ruminating over a past episode in which they feel they have underperformed, or fretting about an upcoming stressful situation.[5] And of course, pondering one's nonexistence or DEATH makes one feel even more terrible.

That mind-wandering and rumination make you feel worse than you normally do strengthens the idea that it is actually good for you in the evolutionary sense (otherwise why would we keep doing what we dislike?). This is not good news. Despite what "positive psychology" books or popular sentiments (such as "Man has been created for happiness like a bird for the flight")[6] may say or imply, people have *not* evolved, nor are they destined, to be happy: EVOLUTION is indifferent to happiness, misery, or any of life's other subjective qualities as such—the only thing that matters is the subjects' fitness.[7] But can we not outsmart it?

The mindfulness ruse

An obvious solution for dealing with listless mind-wandering and depressing rumination is to try and train your mind to stay put. Getting instruction, and much practice, in mindfulness meditation may help you develop the proper habits[8]—at a cost. For one thing, those of us who do not reside in a sheltered environment where our basic needs are taken care of, such as a catered retreat, can probably ill afford to neglect weighing our past deeds and planning for the future, which mind-wandering alone makes possible.[9]

There is also another downside to staying in the moment: by clipping your mind's wings to make it possible, you end up with bare existence—a life that has been pared down to literally nothing. Full of nothing is precisely what a mindful moment becomes, if you indeed succeed in stripping it of all conceptual connotations and pieces of your past, which your MEMORY dutifully keeps serving up. If such EMPTINESS of the mind is the price one must pay for the peace of mind, I would rather have my regular existence, with all the SUFFERING that is built into it.

Of related interest

To watch:

Federico Fellini, *8½* (1963)

To listen:

Gustav Mahler, *Symphony No. 1* (1889)

To read:

Jean-Paul Sartre, *Being and Nothingness* (*L'être et le néant* [1943] 1956); *The Roads to Freedom* (*Les chemins de la liberté*) trilogy (1963a, b, c)

Philip K. Dick, *Martian Time-Slip* (1976)

Kij Johnson, "26 Monkeys, Also the Abyss" (2008)

13 Fear

Where the wild things are. True grit. We have seen the enemy.

Camilla: You, sir, should unmask.
Stranger: Indeed?
Cassilda: Indeed it's time. We all have laid aside disguise but you.
Stranger: I wear no mask.
Camilla: (Terrified, aside to Cassilda.) No mask? No mask!
—Robert W. Chambers, *The King in Yellow*

I must not fear. Fear is the mind-killer. Fear is the little-death that brings total obliteration. I will face my fear. I will permit it to pass over me and through me. And when it has gone past I will turn the inner eye to see its path. Where the fear has gone there will be nothing. Only I will remain.
—Frank Herbert, *Dune*

One cannot abolish terror and retain civilization.
—Max Horkheimer and Theodor W. Adorno, *Dialectic of Enlightenment*[1]

Where the wild things are

The wild things are and have always been where you can't see them. As a snorkeler who often ventures far away from the shore, I find it unsettling when, having followed a turtle or a dolphin, I lose sight of the seabed where it drops off suddenly into the abyss. Double-checking that the knife strapped to my leg is still there in its sheath helps a little, as does sticking my head out of the water for a moment, to make sure that *my* world, where I can see all the way to the moon, is still there. Can't look up for too long, though: it's better to see even just a little way down than not at all.

The fear of the unseen—think of what you would experience if forced to swim in the murky and possibly piranha-infested waters of an Amazon tributary—is the price we pay for having good vision when and where it is not useless. We are so accustomed to being able to see danger from afar that a temporary loss of this sense can be terrifying. The nocturnal black ghost knifefish, whose home is in the Amazon and to which objects appear as disturbances in the electric field it generates, knows nothing of the terror of swimming in murky water (or so I hope, for the fish's sake).[2]

As our civilization picked up steam, we kept discovering, as well as inventing, new kinds of unseen terrors to supplement the old classic of being out in the thick of a forest on a foggy night. Some were real: deadly germs, lead pipes, an assassin's poison. Others we commissioned our media to amplify or invent for our own amusement, as if the visible terrors of real WARS[3] were not enough: the stalker, the lurking serial killer, the cloaked Romulan spaceships on *Star Trek*, the Predator (a space alien just like Ridley Scott's creature, but arguably scarier because literally invisible rather than merely hiding).

POLITICS, which feeds on all human traits, finds our weaknesses particularly delectable. POWER could always be gained, and money earned, by exploiting fear, but the fear of the invisible has proved the most potent of all. America's "war on drugs" was a major conceptual innovation, which allowed government military and paramilitary build-up and war profiteering to proceed in "peacetime," with minorities often being singled out for state violence and incarcerated in for-profit prisons. This, however, was completely outdone by the invention of the "war on terror."

The propaganda machine that used the Islamist terror acts of 2001 to jump-start and promote this idea—no matter that it aids the terrorists' cause—has convinced many Americans that they are in mortal danger at all times.[4] Importantly, the new enemies are invisible, because they look just like "us" (except when they commit the tactical mistake of wearing a turban, which "we" shun). This twist in the plot has managed to up the ante on our regular running fear of the "domestic terrorist"—a mentally unstable or merely sociopathic "real American" with a gun, who is also invisible until he acts. This fear of the invisible other can only be ratcheted any higher if someone spikes the water supply with a chemical agent capable of inducing in the general populace the Capgras delusion—the belief that one's acquaintances and family members have been replaced with strangers who look indistinguishable from the originals.

True grit

In patriarchal societies, timorousness or cowardice in an adult male carries a lot of stigma: *страшно в лесу, стыдно дома* (afraid in the forest, ashamed at home). To drive fear underground is, however, not the same as to make it disappear altogether. Overt fear may regroup and resurface as low-level ANXIETY, which may be easier to hide, but harder to live with over time.[5] I can only imagine the harm that can be inflicted upon CHILDREN by teaching them MORALITY by means of fear of divine retribution coming from an invisible but omnipresent source of POWER, of the kind that abound in theistic RELIGIONS.

How often does society make people repress their fear simply because it's cheaper and more convenient than attempting to remove its cause? Exhorting the public to show courage in the face of an invented WAR or praising the resourcefulness of "hardworking Americans" who endure POVERTY—propaganda typically carried out by people who themselves neither fight nor suffer hardship—is amazingly offensive. I will admit that to me the Litany against Fear, from Frank Herbert's *Dune*, still mostly sounds like a noble idea, but I do realize that it is only ever invoked there by temporarily inconvenienced noblemen—that is, by those with privilege.[6] For a regular citizen, constantly worried about making ends meet, harassed by the state, encouraged by the POWER elites to fear terrorists and immigrants, and expecting a new war to break out any day, the Litany is of little use, other than on the day of the revolution.

We have seen the enemy

It is too bad that all successful revolutions (and restorations) to date have merely replaced one set of sources of existential fear with another, while leaving certain fears in place. Instead of a violent revolution, we might just as well try to fix our POLITICS, seeing that as a species we now have the power to abolish all natural causes of fear except DEATH.[7] But it could be that fear is neither merely a politician's option, nor just the state's favorite tool,[8] but rather serves as the very foundation of civilized society:

> The noonday panic fear in which nature suddenly appeared to humans as an all-encompassing power has found its counterpart in the panic which is ready to break out at any moment today: human beings expect the world, which is

without issue, to be set ablaze by a universal power which they themselves are and over which they are powerless.

This gloomy passage from the *Dialectic of Enlightenment*[9] brings to mind a Soviet-era joke involving the famous, and fictitious, Q&A section of "Armenian Radio." Radio Yerevan was asked: "Will there be another world war?" Radio Yerevan answered: "In principle, no. But the struggle for peace will be such that not a single stone will be left standing."

Of related interest

To watch:

Ari Folman, *The Congress* (2013)

To listen:

Talking Heads, "Life during Wartime" (from *Fear of Music*, 1979)

To read:

Stanisław Lem, *The Futurological Congress* ([1971] 1974b)

To go:

On a solo night hike.

14   Free Will

Complications. Misapprehension. Chance. Necessity. Implications.

I believe with Schopenhauer: We can do what we wish, but we can only wish what we must.
—Albert Einstein

—Por eso estoy aquí—le dije.
—¿Aquí? Siempre estamos aquí.

("That is why I am here," I said to him. "Here? But we are always here.")
—Jorge Luis Borges, "August 25, 1983"[1]

Complications

The Sufi sage Khodja Nasreddin was strolling one evening on the outskirts of his village when he saw in the distance some riders rapidly approaching. Thinking that they might be robbers, Nasreddin climbed over the wall of the nearby cemetery and hid behind a tombstone. The riders, whose own suspicions had been aroused, followed him to the tomb and demanded that he explain his behavior. "You see," said Nasreddin. "It's complicated. I'm here because of you and you are here because of me."[2] The same can be said about your situation and mine: you're here on this page because of me and I am here writing it because of you.

Although we are, in a manner of speaking, on the same page, my "here and now" is not identical to yours and is in fact probably far removed from it both in space and in TIME. My writing can only affect you despite this separation because my present time is in your past *and* we are sufficiently close to each other in space so that information about my ACTIONS could have reached you, while traveling no faster than light. This last proviso is needed because, as Einstein has famously postulated, no information or causal influence can travel faster than light. In the technical terminology of Einstein's Special Relativity Theory, as far as causality is concerned, I am in your past "light cone" and you're in my future one.[3]

Complications arise, on a scale that transcends anything that Khodja Nasreddin might have imagined, because all causal influences that are not ruled out by Special Relativity are potentially ruled in.[4] Everything that has been happening in one's past light cone—which is a sizeable chunk of spacetime, extending all the way back to the Big Bang—may in principle have had an effect on one's present state of mind, and therefore on one's choice of next action. This means that for each of us the freedom of will is, at best, qualified.

Misapprehension

All the causal complications would be beside the point if one were free to override the influence of the past on one's choice of action. It certainly *feels* like I am free to either act on the information that reaches me from my past light cone, or to ignore it in favor of my own wishes.[5] Unfortunately, this commonsense notion of freedom of the will, which is rooted in how we feel about the choices we make, amounts to a fundamental misapprehension of what freedom means.

Consider what happens if I exercise the perfect freedom of completely ignoring my past in choosing actions. Such entirely uncaused choices are by definition uncorrelated—that is, necessarily *random*—with respect to everything, including my own experience and action history, as well as all the past events in the universe that might have been of influence. Complete freedom of choice is thus revealed to be the same as perfect randomness of choice—surely not what we intuitively mean by freedom in this or any other context.

Opting for partial freedom does not resolve this paradox. If I choose to ignore the influence of one particular event from my past, then my choice is still unfree with respect to all the other events, and is still random with respect to the one that I have resolved to ignore. Every inch of territory that we liberate from the thralldom of past causes is thus immediately taken over by the blight of chance.

It is important to realize that no amount of sophistication in action planning and control can make this problem go away. This is because the problem is conceptual: the commonsense concept of freedom of the will turns out to make no sense.[6] In place of the vaunted freedom we find merely a blend of chance and necessity.[7]

Chance

Given that resorting to chance is the only way to make a perfectly unconstrained choice, the possibility of such "free" (for the lack of a better term) choice depends on the availability of a physical mechanism that is truly random, which can be consulted in making decisions. A natural candidate for this purpose would seem to be the essential randomness at the heart of quantum mechanics—a physical theory that has been extremely successful in the sense of being unexcelled at capturing the behavior of matter at small scales. An agent facing a choice between two alternative actions can perform a quantum-mechanical equivalent of a coin flip— for instance, monitor an atom of a radioactive element for decay within a certain time window—and be assured that the decision based on the outcome would be random.

The notion that quantum-mechanical processes are inherently random is accepted by most physicists, but not by all of them. One notable dissenter was Einstein, who could not bring himself to accept that "God plays dice." According to the competing hypothesis, which he first advanced, the randomness of processes such as the radioactive decay of a heavy-element nucleus is only apparent. This semblance of randomness is blamed on imperfect knowledge: if we only had access to *all* the information about the state of the Universe, including the values of certain hypothetical "hidden variables," random events would be revealed as deterministic and predictable.[8]

A decades-long concerted theoretical and experimental effort aimed to refute Einstein's view on the matter has succeeded in demonstrating that randomness in quantum mechanics cannot be explained away by any so-called "realist" theory involving hidden variables—with one exception. The exception is the theory known as superdeterminism, according to which the state of the Universe at all times follows logically from the initial conditions at the Big Bang. Superdeterminism, if true, rules out the "freedom of will" rooted in randomness; if this is how the Universe works, it has no room for chance, only necessity.[9]

Necessity

There is a small catch with regard to superdeterminism: it cannot be tested experimentally.[10] Still, it is possible to advance a logical argument for it: if certain "design principles" for a universe apply, then the only way to build one that works is to make it act like a deterministic computer, which is seeded with a set of initial conditions and proceeds to compute how everything plays out over time, step by step.[11]

For superdeterminism, or any other "theory of everything," to stand, it must account for all the observable basic physical properties of the actual Universe—quite a tall order. As a would-be answer to some of the deepest questions of EXISTENCE, superdeterminism in particular is further burdened by the need to counter the deeply seated human intuitions about free will, which most human physicists tend to share. Still, despite the formidable challenges, this idea is being explored with some degree of success.[12]

If the scientific case for superdeterminism ever becomes overwhelming, it would spell the end to any pretensions to freedom of the will that humans have been nurturing for so long. Paraphrasing Hegel (something that I hate to do and usually manage to avoid, but in this case there seems to be no choice), freedom would then indeed prove to be the insight into necessity.[13]

Even if the Universe is entirely deterministic and ruled by necessity, it emphatically does *not* imply that the future is predetermined. Rather, it is being determined—that is, computed on the fly, as time goes by. The future is thus both subjectively and objectively open-ended (a realization that may bring some relief to those of us who do not tolerate unfreedom well). This feature of deterministic computer-like universes is a MATHEMATICAL consequence of certain fundamental COMPLEXITY-related properties of computational processes. If this is what the Universe is like, it *must* go through the motions—compute its future—for the future to become determined enough to merit being called "reality," even if it is all logically implied by the initial conditions.[14]

Implications

If we care at all about MORALITY,[15] we ought to be rooting for more rather than less causal structure and determinism in the Universe. Any consequences, good or bad, of choice that is based on perfect randomness are literally nobody's fault; for the concept of responsibility to apply, there must be a self—an enduring cluster of MEMORIES that affect behavioral choices (including occasionally resorting to a coin flip) and that can therefore be held responsible for the outcomes of those choices. Because selves that are embodied and embedded in the world are necessarily affected by their circumstances, this responsibility can only be partial, but as a foundation for societal cohesion and functioning, it is arguably better than no responsibility.[16]

If superdeterminism is true, morality as we know it would take on an entirely different meaning. How are we to judge a person's deed if they could not have done otherwise? Indeed, how could we then keep pretending to initiate any ACTION or to refrain from acting? The answer, such as it is, is merely an appeal to our humanity. Whether or not the Universe is really deterministic, in the universe that we inhabit, which is constructed by CONSCIOUSNESS and furnished by PERCEPTION, agency and actions feel real and their consequences give rise to emotions that really matter to those who experience them. The enlightened person, who directly experiences the unfreedom of the will rather than merely understanding intellectually the theory of superdeterminism or the doctrine of dependent origination,[17] may feel differently, but of course enlightenment by definition implies indifference to this or any other feelings. As to the rest of us . . . when all is said and done, we just might find ourselves slightly better off for having this insight into what we are and how the world works: [18]

Happy is he who was able to know the causes of things.

Of related interest

To watch:

Lana and Lilly Wachowski, *The Matrix Reloaded* (2003)

To listen:

Nina Simone, "I Wish I Knew How It Would Feel to Be Free" (1967)

Talking Heads, "Once in a Lifetime" (1982)

Daniel Kahn & The Painted Bird, "Freedom Is a Verb" (2017)

To read:

W. Somerset Maugham, *The Appointment in Samarra* (1933)

Jorge Luis Borges, "August 25, 1983" in *Collected Fictions* (1999a)

To go:

To the Source.

15 Happiness

Machineries of joy and sorrow. Happiness fast and slow. The dark side of happiness.

One must never look for happiness. One meets it by the way—always going in the opposite direction.
—Isabelle Eberhardt[1]

I could die now happy, I have been, I have seen. I have heard, I have smelt and I have felt, is that not enough?
—Mary Lange, "Voices from the Kalahari"

Если хочешь быть счастливым, будь им.

(If you want to be happy, be so.)
—Kozma Prutkov

Machineries of joy and sorrow

How can you tell whether a given country is a net exporter or importer of oil? Exporters typically have an oil minister, importers have a minister of energy.[2] A parallel distinction applies to happiness—a commodity that Americans pursue with almost as much verve as oil. If we ever build the shining city on the hill, it may well have a minister of happiness; in the meanwhile, we have self-help books and positive psychology.[3]

Ray Bradbury, a sci-fi writer many of whose works celebrate a kind of small-town America that might have just fallen out of a Norman Rockwell painting, once wrote a story with the wonderful title "The Machineries of Joy." Toward the end of that story, one of the protagonists, who is a Catholic priest, toasts the joy of space travel:

Somewhere did Blake not speak of the Machineries of Joy? That is, did not God promote environments, then intimidate those Natures by provoking the existence of flesh, toy men and women, such as are we all? And thus happily sent forth, at our best, with good grace and fine wit, on calm noons, in fair climes, are we not God's Machineries of Joy?

Although these questions are all rhetorical, I will take them up. The answer to the first one is no: although "the machineries of joy" sounds a lot like William Blake, he did not write these words. As to the questions that follow . . . it's complicated. At times it does feel, doesn't it, that we are being toyed with—by powers that derive their joy not from ours, but rather from the game itself, like a cat playing with a mouse it has caught, or the assorted gods playing with the heroes of the *Iliad*, the *Epic of Gilgamesh*, or the *Bhagavad Gita*.[4] To someone who does not share in the consolations of RELIGION, that kind of feeling doesn't bring much joy.

We can gain an insight into our occasional feelings of being at the mercy of fickle powers, as well as into our failure to be joyful at all times (for who in their right mind is?), if we rewrite the quote from Bradbury, substituting "evolution" for "God." EVOLUTION—which is the epitome of fickleness and also somehow of slow but inexorable force—can be said to be "provoking the existence of flesh," but it is definitely *not* in the business of promoting joy as such. All emotions are part of a behavioral regulation mechanism, which can only be effective if it embodies both up-regulation and down-regulation: joy and sorrow are two sides of the same coin. It takes hard drugs to get more than one's natural share of joy, and even that route is not sustainable, for reasons that have as much to do with the physiology of addiction as with the economics of feeding it.[5]

Happiness fast and slow

People were on to the inevitable ups and downs of happiness long before SCIENCE has had a look at the brain's machinery of joy. Here's what Blake did write about it:

He who binds to himself a joy
Does the winged life destroy
He who kisses the joy as it flies
Lives in eternity's sunrise

The "winged life" evolved to be skittish, though, and so often enough it evades us; yet we are doomed to commit to MEMORY all the attempts to catch up with it, both the successes and the failures. The running tally of those is what determines how we feel about our lives in the long run.

The upshot of this is that happiness comes in two shapes. The first one, joy, is an emotion that we share with all other animals; the second one, life satisfaction, involves much explicit and deliberate THINKING and as such is peculiar to humans. Given how unlikely it is to be perfectly satisfied with one's life, our ability to ponder such things and our compulsion to do so make for a rather mixed blessing. On the one hand, there is the warm feeling of recalling success; on the other hand, failure breeds ANXIETY in YOUTH and, in OLD AGE, REGRET.

What if joy in the moment is so intense as to eclipse completely all other feelings? Short of freezing the moment—not a good idea, in light of what we know about the nature of EXISTENCE in TIME and of CONSCIOUSNESS—there seems to be only one recourse:

> Now more than ever seems it rich to die,
> To cease upon the midnight with no pain,
> While thou art pouring forth thy soul abroad
> In such an ecstasy!

These lines, by John Keats, point to an unimpeachable, if extreme, way to act upon the old dictum that proclaims: "Count no man happy until he be dead."[6]

The dark side of happiness

Although people in real everyday life do sporadically experience the kind of dramatic "ecstasy unto DEATH" that European Romantics wrote about, such experiences are rare enough and in any case are not seen as particularly desirable (although the preferences in these matters differ across cultures).[7] I would therefore rather focus here instead on unremarkable garden-variety happiness. Apparently, that too can have negative consequences—perhaps not so drastic as those of an ecstatic experience that makes one wish for immediate death, but significant nevertheless. For instance, a chronic up-regulation of happiness may push people toward risky behaviors, while feeling happy at inappropriate times may reduce their ability to deal with challenging situations.[8]

And what of the complement of the everyday type of happiness: the unremarkable, garden-variety SUFFERING? Arguably, it is so prevalent in the world that we have built for ourselves that a reduction of misery becomes a more worthy goal than the pursuit of happiness. In one regard, this makes things easier: equating happiness with the absence of suffering happens to be one of the main tenets of the practical philosophy of Epicurus (who has been widely misrepresented as a hedonist). In another regard, the problem of misery gives rise to a question that is as hard as any of those posed by life: What should we do about the suffering of others?[9]

It would seem that amidst misery one can only be really happy as long as the plight of others is kept out of sight and banished from CONSCIOUSNESS. Most of us, myself included, are really adept at looking away from the suffering of others while trying to focus on our own happy thoughts. That happiness nevertheless remains elusive is a possible sign of that great rarity, cosmic justice. Perhaps if we take it to heart, things could be made slightly better all around.

Of related interest

To watch:

Nacer Khemir, *Bab'Aziz—The Prince That Contemplated His Soul* (2005)

Andrei Tarkovsky, *Stalker* (1979)

To listen:

Violeta Parra, "Gracias a la vida" (1966)

Nusrat Fateh Ali Khan, "Munadjat de Jalaluddin Rumi" (1998)

Midnite (Vaughn Benjamin), "Jah in dem" (2003)

To read:

Ursula Le Guin, "The Ones Who Walk Away from Omelas" in *New Dimensions 3* (1973)

Alan Lightman, "The Center of Time" in *Einstein's Dreams* (1993)

To go:

To the Well at the World's End (and back).

16   Home

No home. No homeland. No rest. No end.

Wo gehn wir denn hin? Immer nach Hause.

(Whither are we going? Ever homewards.)

—Novalis, *Heinrich von Ofterdingen*

You can go home again, . . . so long as you understand that home is a place where you have never been.

—Ursula K. Le Guin, *The Dispossessed*

Где ж лучше?—Где нас нет.

(Where is it better, then? Where we are not.)

—Aleksandr Griboyedov, *Горе от ума (Woe from Wit)*[1]

No home

In my hometown, winter meant snow. Snow would come in late November and stay on the ground through March. After a particularly heavy snowfall, the janitors on each block in the Khrushchev-era projects[2] where we lived would venture out to clear a path to the bus stop. The janitors being Soviet-state employees (motto: "You pretend to pay us and we pretend to work"), everybody always had to walk on some packed snow. The only snow-free spaces were immediately over the underground pipes that carried central-heating steam from the local power plant to each apartment building, criss-crossing the town like ley lines.

With the fall of the USSR, a favorite slogan of Lenin's, later made infamous by Khrushchev—"To catch up with and overtake" (Догнать и перегнать[3]) the capitalist West—became reality in at least one respect. In the "developed" country where I now live, extreme urban POVERTY and homelessness can always serve as a reminder for the passers-by of their own good luck. Growing up in a big city in the USSR, I had never ever seen a homeless person—thanks in part, as I now realize, to my privilege-induced selective blindness—until the very day on which my family left the country, never to return. In the waiting hall of the tiny border train station, a dirty-looking man was sleeping on a bench, his head on a small bundle. A militiaman came in, saw the sleeping man, and commenced prodding him until he got up and left. It turns out that keeping millions of homeless out of sight had been one of the rare public welfare tasks that the Soviets did excel at.[4] Nowadays, though, the denizens of the old Soviet housing projects too can share in the Western experience of relative privilege—their local homeless are newly visible, huddling in winter in makeshift sheds built over the steam lines.

Against the dark background of literal homelessness, it seems wrong to complain about any metaphorical kind, but of course complain is what people, myself included, nevertheless do—often in inverse proportion to the apparent significance of the grounds they cite for their disaffection.[5] Still, dismissing such complaints out of hand would be a bit like blaming people for not being happy when it seems like they ought to be. In matters of HAPPINESS, judging others makes little sense, because happiness is by definition subjective. Similarly, the concept of home has little about it that is objective, except perhaps the distinction between home and shelter. Nobody pretends that the homeless who are put up in a shelter thereby also gain a home: a place is only a home if it *feels* like home.

No homeland

For some, home is by choice not a place at all, but a certain activity or company. Paul Erdős, the famous itinerant MATHEMATICIAN, spent his life on the move, staying for a few weeks at a time with each of his hundreds of collaborators in many countries.[6] Like Erdős, people who voluntarily identify with a traditional nomadic culture do not need a fixed abode—a tent or an improvised RV works better. This way of living is, however, rapidly disappearing, surviving mainly in desert places where intensive agriculture is infeasible. Whereas regular WAR often leaves settled people homeless, what the nomads lose in this final stage of their age-old conflict with the settlers is their peculiar brand of homelessness. No longer free to roam, the nomads find themselves being forced into resettlement projects or urban slums by the prevailing nation-state POLITICS of territorial imperative.[7]

The POWERS that control people's fates in a nation-state have always liked to have it both ways. The settled society disdains and punishes those who do not have a home, yet does nothing to guarantee that every person who wants a home can have one; and it casts out entirely those whose conception of home differs from the "consensus" one. A dilemma faced by this last kind of people, the outcasts, is perfectly reflected in the shifting fortunes of the ethnic minority into which I was born, Russian Jews—a group whose ancestors had been nomads much like the Bedouin and whose last memories of settled existence in a "national home" of their own were a couple thousand years old by the time I arrived on the scene.

In the Russian Empire and its successor, the USSR, as in many other countries of the Jewish diaspora, those who refused to assimilate were resented by the "locals"; but those who wanted to assimilate were at best kept at an arm's length. A case in point is the official campaign against the "rootless cosmopolitans" (безродные космополиты, a code phrase for "Jews") organized during Stalin's waning days. Collectively branded as likely traitors, and allowed neither to blend in nor to emigrate, Soviet Jews could hardly feel at home in a country they have been living in for centuries—just like the Roma, but occupying a different set of cracks in the foundation of the empire.

In 1972, after Cold War politics forced the USSR's hand, Soviet Jews were allowed to leave. Those of them who, like my family, went to Israel found themselves elevated from the status of rootless sojourners to that of ruthless landlords: in their newly regained "historical homeland," their old role was played by the Palestinian Arabs. Those who chose instead to emigrate to the United States also received a status boost, their share in the white privilege having been all but secured by the hard work of the great waves of Jewish immigration fifty and more years earlier. In light of this history, it is puzzling how so many of them could be so anti-immigrant, especially now that they are again being accused of dual loyalty and are being reminded of their imperfect whiteness by the fascists newly admitted into the mainstream of American POLITICS.[8]

No rest

The nagging feeling of not belonging joins the usual economic and political reasons in prompting people to pull out their roots, such as they are, and seek their fortune elsewhere. Strangely enough, there are people who are willing to give up a certain privilege—from having a home to having a share in a homeland—in search of a life that might, or might not, be better in ways that matter more. Such people are sometimes perceived as strange, or even vaguely dangerous to the settled folk from whose midst they come; as the Russians say, "Как волка ни корми, он всё в лес смотрит" (However much you feed the wolf, it still looks to the forest).[9] A wolf's existence, even in a pack, is, however, no picnic, and a person who has found the strength once to pull up the roots may find it difficult to strike roots in the new place.

Insofar as a true home is a place where we want to be and where we will continue to want to be, presumably indefinitely, it is something that belongs to the future at least as much as it does to the present. But what then about the possibility of getting truly home by following the road that one is still in the middle of? It is difficult for people to decide whether or not they will like a place before they even get there; and it is difficult, to say the least, to decide whether or not they will REGRET moving there as TIME goes by. It seems prudent not to indulge in too much hope on that front.

In the end, it may not matter. The feeling of being stuck in a place and wanting out can make up for the scarcity of hope that one might have for finding the rainbow at the end of the road. The final twist in my family's debate on whether or not to leave the USSR and go to Israel that I remember most vividly had to do with just such a feeling. Our tiny apartment had such narrow doors that when my grandmother passed away, her coffin had to be taken out through the window of the largest room (which I had been sharing with her for years). She had been ill for a while and it was her passing that allowed us to consider emigrating. My young self was champing at the bit, but to the grown-ups it was clear that we were taking a huge chance (going to a country at war, with no language, no money, no relatives). And then my father said, "What I *don't* want is to live out my life here only to go out through the window in a coffin."

No end

The condition of endless restlessness that no amount of rest can allay—existential migration[10]—is hard on the migrants, yet some of them would be reluctant to give it up. These are the ones who do not *want* to permanently settle down, nor do they *want to want* to do so.

In one's YOUTH, it is easy to get excited by the prospect of an open road: "You but arrive at the city to which you were destin'd—you hardly / settle yourself to satisfaction, before you are call'd by an / irresistible call to depart"; but of course Walt Whitman could make pretty much everything sound exciting.[11] It is somewhat more surprising that such sentiments inconveniently tend to grow stronger in one's OLD AGE. Perhaps this is because the concept of home acquires by then a frisson of finality. It is not for nothing that Robert Louis Stevenson's lines "Home is the sailor, home from the sea, / And the hunter home from the hill" are part of an epitaph, in a poem whose title is "Requiem." But there's at least one renowned old sailor who would have nothing of that. It is the aged Ulysses of Dante and of Tennyson, who, having just made it back to Ithaca, declares his intent to leave again:[12]

> My purpose holds
> To sail beyond the sunset, and the baths
> Of all the western stars, until I die.

Of related interest

To watch:

Chantal Akerman, *News from Home* (1977)

Tony Gatlif, *Latcho Drom* (1994)

To listen:

Paul Simon and Art Garfunkel, "Homeward Bound" (1966)

Georges Moustaki, *Le Métèque* (1969)

Janis Joplin, "Me and Bobby McGee" (1971)

To read:

Arthur C. Clarke, "Rescue Party" (1946)

Alice B. Sheldon, "The Women Men Don't See" (1973)

Edward W. Said, "Reflections on Exile" (1984)

Ursula K. Le Guin, *Always Coming Home* (1985)

Robyn Davidson, *Desert Places* (1996)

To go:

To Ithaca, then west.

17 Language

The tentacles of intent. The Ring of Fire. Gaming the Game. Big Two-Hearted River.

מָוֶת וְחַיִּים בְּיַד לָשׁוֹן

(Death and life are in the power of the tongue.)
—Proverbs 18:21

Ce qui n'est pas ineffable n'a aucune importance.

(That which is not ineffable has no importance.)
—Paul Valéry, *Mon Faust*

The tentacles of intent

Had the King James translation of the Bible been more literal, its version of Proverbs 18:21 would have placed death and life not "in the power" of the tongue, but rather in its *hand*. In the original Hebrew, יַד לָשׁוֹן "the hand of the tongue," is an entirely unremarkable idiom, which follows the common use of "hand" to signify agency: one is said to be surprised *at the hands of* the weather when caught in the rain without an umbrella. In English, in comparison, such usage can give one a pause: the metaphorical hand of the tongue made me think just now of slender, writhing tentacles of the speaker's intent, each crowned with a little cluster of fine tendrils of nuance, reaching into the listener's brain.[1] Of course, if squid had language, this would come across as quite natural to them.

There is a certain irony to all such metaphors for ACTION or POWER. Hands are what we use to engage with the physical world, by handling ("manipulating," from the Latin word *manibus* for "hand") things. At the same time, language, which we use to engage with the social world, by telling and being told things, can pack more punch than a fist. Indeed, some of us are so positioned that things that we say can recruit enough hands to literally move mountains. (It so happens that in Hebrew, דבר, *davar*, can mean either "thing" or "word.") And over those who are especially close to us—our PARENTS, our CHILDREN—our words can have altogether too much power . . . remember what words the Queen of the Night in Mozart's *Magic Flute* flings at her daughter Pamina to bend her to her will:

> Fühlt nicht durch dich Sarastro
> Todesschmerzen,
> So bist du meine Tochter nimmermehr.

> (If Sarastro does not through you feel
> The pain of death,
> Then you will be my daughter nevermore.)

Using language to move things around by moving the minds of others may have been the one critically important function of language that made its EVOLUTION possible: on one intriguing theory, the use of proto-language in the teaching of stone toolmaking could have created a self-reinforcing alliance between signalling abilities and a key fitness-boosting skill.[2] As it became richer and its structure more intricate, language proved useful for other purposes as well: referring to things (including those not present at the moment); conveying and inducing emotions; socializing with people; and thinking and talking—and writing—about thinking and talking.[3]

That people can produce, and sometimes even comprehend, paragraph-long sentences, which must be positively packed with information, is an extremely impressive behavioral feat, which is also uniquely human. The structural sophistication of complex language suggests that it encodes equally sophisticated meanings, whose copying from one brain to another is thereby made possible. It is easy, then, to get the impression that the balance of language use is communicating information.

Yet, to conclude that language is primarily or essentially a system for message-passing would be a blatant disregard of human nature. As a species that excels in making tools and WAR, we were bound to have made the most of the opportunity to wield an instrument as powerful as language, which we proceeded to weaponize. And what we use this ultimate weapon for is to sway, and perhaps gain control of, the thoughts and deeds of other people.[4]

The Ring of Fire

In any attempt to put together the story of the nature and uses of language, resorting to fictional examples is more readily forgivable, seeing that such examples themselves necessarily consist of language, which is being used to tell a story. I can thus with a clear conscience point out that *The Lord of the Rings*, a story that easily passes for a war epic, can also be seen as a parable in three volumes on how the word can prove stronger than the sword. In *TLotR*, the fate of Middle Earth is decided not in the clash of armies but in the clash of words wielded by its power brokers. On one side, there are the "lies of Mordor" and the "Voice of Saruman"; on the other, the subtle stratagems of Gandalf, who tells Frodo early on that he, Gandalf, is not in the business of ordering people about:

> "Why did you let me keep it. Why didn't you make me throw it away, or, or destroy it?"
>
> "Let you? Make you?" said the Wizard. "Haven't you been listening to all that I have said? You are not thinking of what you are saying."

Gandalf's "long labors" were all about getting people to resist evil—a noble cause (as long as there is no doubt about what evil really is). His means were honorable, too: always persuasion, never coercion (except with orcs, who only understand force). But his words still *made* people do things. In one of the last chapters of *LoTR*, it is revealed that he was the keeper of Narya, the Ring of Fire and a mover of people's hearts, which in the end proved more potent even than the One Ring, a ring of POWER.[5]

In real life too, in seeking mastery over people's wills, the soft power of persuasion is definitely the way to go—ideally, persuasion that is not perceived as such. This is why so much of the language that is bandied about in public amounts to demagoguery that is dressed up as straight talk; and propaganda, bullshit, and lies that masquerade as the TRUTH. When duly propitiated and pandered to, STUPIDITY itself can be made to preen at its own perspicacity and common sense.[6] The tentacles of intent extending from other people, whose good will we can trust but rarely, reach deep inside our skulls. But these are also the bonds that keep human society from falling apart—without language, the world as we know it would not exist.

Gaming the Game

We are drawn into the Game of language willy-nilly at a tender age. Our only chance to flourish in the society whose collective EXISTENCE depends on this Game is to learn to play it as well as we can. All humans come with the requisite learning mechanisms preinstalled, but apart from that, we are each of us on our own. The task is daunting: to learn many tens of thousands of patterns of usage—combinations of sounds or gestures that make sense to the learner and have somewhat predictable and desirable effects on the listeners.[7]

The ability to put together and utter a sentence has much in common with managing other types of complex ACTION.[8] Imagine yourself walking from home to the corner store to pick up some lunch, and then on to the park, while keeping to the shady side of the street, avoiding puddles from last night's rain, dodging some people, exchanging handshakes with others, and all the while trying not to get run over by an electric bike while on the sidewalk, or by a car when crossing the street—doing all this is a lot like writing or reading about it. But there is much about the language faculty that *is* special.

For one thing, it takes a lot of sheer MEMORY. After figuring out that in English one typically says "life and death" as opposed to "death and life," along with many thousands of similarly arbitrary distinctions, the learner must remember them all (I love it that one of the words for "language" in Spanish is "idioma"). Most people on the planet get to memorize two or more sets of trivia like that, one for each language they master (being monolingual is an exception, not the rule, on this planet).

Every learner's success depends on sleuthing and inference skills that would make Sherlock Holmes proud—all deployed by babies without a visible effort or an awareness of the nature and the immensity of their undertaking. One kind of challenge that they routinely meet is learning that "rabbit" is the noise that is used to refer to rabbits, as opposed to an infinite number of other conceivably relevant entities or events—an impressive feat, given that neither the noise nor the concept is made known to the learner ahead of time.[9]

Another Holmesian challenge is picking up and using complex patterns. Here, the objective is to string various noises together, so that they join forces in doing your bidding. The little band, marching in more or less the proper order, becomes a one-off verbal tool for pointing at the world, for expressing yourself, or for making others do your bidding—a sense; a sentiment; a sentence. The ad hoc coalition is then disbanded: the probability of a long utterance being ever repeated verbatim is vanishingly low.

The single most important thing about the language Game is that it is neither learned nor played alone. PARENTS actively help CHILDREN to get established in it; and for players of all ages, participating in banter feels much more natural than engaging in soliloquy. This, by the way, is why writing well is hard: when committed to a permanent medium, even well-crafted language ossifies and begins to grate (I can only imagine you reacting to these lines as I am cobbling them together on the screen).[10]

What with all these challenges and difficulties, not all the players of the Game can hope to reach the level of Wizard. For many people, hope is thwarted by things that are beyond their control. The eventual richness or poverty of one's language is determined to a large extent by the lottery of birth, as is economic POVERTY, to which poor language skills contribute so much: CHILDREN born into poor households may have less than half of the experience with language than rich kids, and the amount and quality of social engagement with absent or distracted or depressed PARENTS are lower.[11] But if deprivation and inequality drive people down into the dens of the orcs, it is of no concern to POWER, which is only interested in securing a steady supply of slaves.

Big Two-Hearted River

To the extent that language acts on people's brains by putting to use contents and abilities that are already there, it serves to make those who already are intellectually and emotionally rich even richer, and the poor poorer. The same utterance can obviously have widely different effects on listeners, depending on the mindset that they bring to the conversation, on their familiarity with the concepts it evokes, and on the patterns that the speaker makes use of.

A master storyteller can work wonders here. When I first read Hemingway's short story "Big Two-Hearted River," I took it at face value: a slightly wooden account of a fishing trip, along the lines of "What I did last summer." Having discovered much later that Hemingway had intended it to be about WAR, although war is not mentioned in it, I reread it and had a minor epiphany (my army service, such as it was, must have helped). *Of course* war did not have to be invoked by name: being always explicit is for writing appliance manuals.

In any case, what is really important may well be ineffable. BEAUTY would seem to be, although deft manipulators of words keep finding ways of dealing with such stuff that should make stage magicians green with envy. If it can be helped at all, it is best to leave most of the work to the readers' imagination, as Stanisław Lem did in one of his cyberfables, *The Princess Ineffabelle*, which manages to have it both ways. Ursula Le Guin once wrote, "The artist deals in what cannot be said in words. The artist whose medium is fiction does this *in words*. The novelist says in words what cannot be said in words."[12] Whoever first came up with the notion that a picture is worth a thousand words could not have been a serious student of language. Photographs of carnage in World War I trenches or of a World War II beachhead battle may move us deeply, and "Big Two-Hearted River" does run to many hundreds of words, but a properly prepared mind can be rattled by a single word raising a vast spectre of hell: Verdun; Dunkirk.[13] And reading a good story is a kind of experience that even the best filmmakers aspire to match—by using their own genius to create a visual story out of the language of the script.

Originally a tool that served other, very much down-to-earth purposes, language has become for us an essential window into the sublime. A significant part of human culture resides in the millions of stories that have been told and recorded and in the billions of them that are being played out by speakers and listeners every day. All of us partake in and contribute to this titanic artifact, which we have made and which has made us into what we are. And as with all our other creations, it is being constantly subverted for use in the unending war that we fight with ourselves.

Of related interest

To watch:

The Monty Pythons: "Literary Football Discussion" (from *Monty Python's Flying Circus*, series 1, episode 11, recorded in 1969)

To listen:

Wolfgang Amadeus Mozart (with libretto by Emanuel Schikaneder), *The Magic Flute* (1791)

To read:

Ursula K. Le Guin, *The Telling* (2001)

Laurent Binet, *The 7th Function of Language* (2017)

To go:

Visit the Pyramids. Sneak into the Library of Babel.

18   Love

What a lovely way to burn. Che cosa e amor. Tuqburni.

סַעַר וָדֹמִי צַהַל וּבֶכֶה
פָּצַע וְצֹרִי אֹפֶל וָאוֹר

(Tempest and stillness, laughter and tears,
Hurting and balm, darkness and light.)
—Rachel, "A Song"

Felices los amados y los amantes y los que pueden prescindir del amor.

(Happy are the beloved and the lovers and those who can do without love.)
—Jorge Luis Borges, "Fragments of an Apocryphal Gospel"[1]

What a lovely way to burn

The tale of "Julnar the Sea-Born and Her Son King Badr-Basim of Persia,"
which is part of *The Book of Thousand Nights and a Night*, places the reader at
a rather peculiar risk: that of falling in love with a fictional character (note:
to avoid exposure, do *not* read the quoted excerpt that follows). In the story,
Julnar and her brother Salih decide that it is time for young Badr-Basim to
be married, but only "to one who is his equal in beauty and loveliness and
wit and piety and good breeding and magnanimity and dominion and rank
and lineage."[2]

Salih has the uniquely suitable girl in mind, but is reluctant to speak
of her, lest Badr-Basim overhears "and his heart be taken with her love
and maybe we shall be unable to win to her." As Badr-Basim appears to be
asleep, Salih goes on to tell Julnar of the Princess Jauharah ("jewel"):

She is prime in comeliness and seemlihead of face and symmetrical shape of perfect grace; her cheek is ruddy dight, her brow flower white, her teeth gem bright, her eyes blackest black and whitest white, her hips of heavy weight, her waist slight and her favour exquisite. When she turneth she shameth the wild cattle and the gazelles and when she walketh, she breedeth envy in the willow branch: when she unveileth her face outshineth sun and moon and all who look upon her she enslaveth soon: sweet lipped and soft sided indeed is she.

At that point, what we had been led to suspect would happen, happens: it turns out that Badr-Basim has only been feigning sleep—

When King Badr Basim heard the words of his uncle Salih and his mother Julnar, praising the daughter of King Al-Samandal, a flame of fire burnt in his heart full sore and he was drowned in a sea which hath nor bottom nor shore.

The spectacular consequences of the carelessness on part of his mother and uncle take eighteen Nights to describe. Now, the notion of love "at first hearing" may appear fantastic. To me, it reminds of the Monty Python skit about a joke that is so potent that it is fatal to anyone that hears it.[3] But is it really more far-fetched than love at first sight?

Che cosa e amor

Romantic love is unique among human emotions in its absolute focus on a single individual at a time—its object—to the exclusion of all others.[4] The focus may all of a sudden switch to another object (as when a new infatuation makes you forget your old flame), but if there *is* no obsession, then it ain't love. And for as long as your love is true, you are at the mercy of your beloved.

Just how far the lover's obsession with the beloved can go is amply illustrated by the story of Layla and Majnun, the most famous pair of star-crossed lovers of the Muslim cultural orbit.[5] If you know even a little Arabic or colloquial Israeli Hebrew, you will recognize מג'נון, *majnun*, as a common word for "crazy" (literally, "possessed by the Jinn"). Majnun, whose real name was Qays, earned his nickname by acting in increasingly strange ways after having been denied Layla's hand in marriage by her father. In some versions of the story, it was Majnun's crazy behavior while trying to woo Layla that caused him to be turned away by Layla's family in the first place.

The details of the story of Layla and Majnun may be largely fictional, but the mutual effects of romantic relationships and mental health on each other are real and by now well-documented. One intriguing finding reveals just how unfortunate being turned away must have been for Majnun: it looks like improving romantic relationships improves mental health, but the other way around—not so much. Speaking of mental health, romantic love is now increasingly understood as a kind of addiction. It needs not be negative if the love is reciprocated and "appropriate,"[6] but true love that is unrequited is hard on one's heart.

Romantic love, which lets one live such a range of strong positive and negative emotions, is our species' original extreme sport. If you're really into free solo rock climbing, you would not pass over an opportunity to scale some walls in Utah just because California was so great last time around. Likewise, it is possible to be in love not with a particular person but with love itself, as Cherubino appears to be in Mozart's *Le Nozze di Figaro*, as he sings:

Non trovo pace
notte né dì,
ma pur mi piace
languir così.

I find no peace
By day or night,
Yet to languish thus
Is sheer delight.

Of course, Cherubino has the many privileges of YOUTH[7] (as do most free solo climbers). One of these privileges is having the drive and the daring to play with fire. Keep doing that, though, and you risk getting burned and being left with a lifelong MEMORY of the experience:

Plaisir d'amour ne dure qu'un moment,
chagrin d'amour dure toute la vie.

The pleasure of love lasts only a moment,
The grief of love lasts a lifetime.

Tuqburni

There is another sense in which romantic love is like playing with fire: if things go wrong, lovers may end up without issue, a fate that is not looked upon kindly by EVOLUTION. Being but once removed from actual procreation, love must be recognized (to the chagrin of the romantics) as evolution's sharpest tool. And because raising human CHILDREN has come to be such an expenditure of time and energy, parenthood is both easier and more effective if taken on with a long-term partner. This calls for a lasting attachment—a more temperate kind of love.[8]

Love for one's lifelong companion is beautifully expressed by an Arabic phrase, *tuqburni*, which in the Shami dialect means literally "You bury me." Wishing to DIE before one's partner, so as to be spared the grief of separation, may be somewhat inconsiderate of the partner's own feelings, but the sentiment is still moving, and very human. And if the wish is reciprocated and fulfilled—in the fullness of time[9]—then the two old lovers will at the end have lived the tale of Princess Jauharah and King Badr-Basim:

> And they ceased not from living the most delectable of life and the most solaceful of days, eating and drinking and enjoying every luxury, till there came to them the Destroyer of delights and the Sunderer of societies; and this is the end of their story, may Allah have mercy on them all!

Of related interest

To watch:

Claude Lelouch, *Un homme et une femme* (*A Man and a Woman*, 1966)

Jacques Demy, *Peau d'âne* (*Donkey Skin*, 1970)

Bernardo Bertolucci, *The Sheltering Sky* (1990)

Eytan Fox, *Ha-Buah* (*The Bubble*, 2006)

Susan Youssef, *Habibi, rasak kharban* (*Darling, You're Not Right in the Head*, 2011)

To listen:

Georges Moustaki, "Ma liberté" ("My Freedom," 1970)

Bob Dylan, "Sara" (1975)

Leonard Cohen, "Ain't No Cure for Love" (1988)

The Decemberists, "We Both Go Down Together" (2005)

To read:

Ivan Bunin, "Тёмные аллеи" in *Dark Avenues and Other Stories* (1949)

Robert Sheckley, "The Language of Love" (1972)

Emil Draitser, "Это непростое дело" ("It's Not a Simple Thing," 1984)

Junot Díaz, "The Cheater's Guide to Love" (2012)

To go:

To the secret walled garden.

19   Mathematics

Unreasonable effectiveness. Ineffectiveness of reason. But time and chance happeneth to them all.

Raffiniert ist der Herrgott, aber boshaft ist er nicht.

(Subtle is the Lord, but he is not malicious.)
—Albert Einstein

"Surety you crave! Sauron gives none."
—J. R. R. Tolkien, *The Lord of the Rings*

"Look at that!" the mathematics greeted her. "We could *go* there. Or look, *there*. We could go anywhere. Let's go somewhere!"
—M. John Harrison, *Light*[1]

Unreasonable effectiveness

I have a complicated relationship with mathematics. Having been brought up by my PARENTS (both physicians and quite innocent of any mathematical knowledge or skills) to admire mathematics and its heroes, I willingly went along with the fantasy that perhaps one day I also might become one. I must have suspected early on, though, that this was much easier said than done, and so I set my sights on SCIENCE instead (physics), but not for long. In the end, I decided to pursue one of the holy grails of practical parenting—electrical engineering (by that time, I had years of experience building from scratch shortwave radios and other such contraptions).

When it came to choosing a graduate program, though, I fell right back under the spell of mathematics, a siren whose song I could not resist, yet whom I could never hope to get ahold of. I owe my choice of computer science—a discipline whose very name is a misnomer, as it is actually a branch not of science, but of mathematics—to a 777-page volume that eventually became known as "the book that launched a thousand careers."[2]

My knowledge of mathematics, such as it is, leaves me neither confident in my ability, nor anywhere near satisfied with its level. Instead, I am full of admiration, and not a little envy, for the abilities of others in my field. Out there, there's a lot of room for improvement for literally everybody: as Einstein wrote in a letter to a high school fan, "Do not worry about your difficulties in Mathematics. I can assure you mine are still greater."[3]

As a matter of principle, even a little math is better than none, though. It's disingenuous to express pride, as many people of culture do, in refusing to follow even the simplest mathematical argument, seeing that math *is* a brand of culture. Basic math literacy requires some effort, but no special talent. In this, it is just like mastering reading and writing. Curiously, though, while illiteracy is not something that people like to advertise about themselves, never opening a book is—just like hating math.

This suggests that professing an anti-math stance is simply a variety of the "know-nothing" social signaling behavior, which serves to unite those who engage in it against the "eggheads."[4] From the standpoint of POLITICS, this taking ownership of STUPIDITY is particularly dangerous. Because the culture of mathematics values clear THINKING above everything else, publicly shunning it is the same as declaring an aversion to reason, which in turn has implications for the know-nothing's MORALITY. Insofar as sides must be taken in the resulting standoff, the connection between math and thinking is, for me, reason enough to like math. It is the reason singled out by Ulrich, the protagonist of Robert Musil's *Man without Qualities*, who "loved mathematics because of the people who could not endure it."[5]

Our species' relationship with mathematics has, however, grown in significance far beyond the primate-style group dynamics that surrounds it. Our survival has come to be entirely dependent on bending the physical universe to our needs—arguably, a not entirely positive development (see chapter 13), but one that cannot be rolled back. This requires that mathematics continue to be used as a tool for furthering SCIENCE and TECHNOLOGY. Its "unreasonable effectiveness" (to use Wigner's phrase[6]) in that task is a mysterious foundational property of the universe, and as such is inconvenient for anyone who expects human reason to replace all mystery with knowledge and understanding.[7]

Ineffectiveness of reason

The mystery of the foundational role of mathematics in the universe cannot be resolved by empirical means alone, that is, by doing more science: one must in a sense step outside it. This is quite literally what some mathematicians—or rather, metamathematicians—see themselves as doing: "Physical scientists study our structural universe from bits and pieces observed from the inside, whereas mathematicians study structural universes formally as complete systems from the outside."[8]

The ultimate success of such "mathematical universe" projects depends on how good a job can be made of discovering systems of interrelated abstract structures that are, on the one hand, complex and therefore expressive enough to describe our actual universe and, on the other hand, free of internal contradictions that would cause a universe to break (in this connection, see the second epigraph to chapter 1).

The creation of new structures in mathematics, which are all relational, proceeds by deduction (see chapter 34), that is, by formally perfectly-constrained logical reasoning from premises, which are the axioms and the previously constructed relations. The axioms, on which everything else rests, are supposed to be both self-evident and self-consistent.

Geometry was the first front on which this line of defense against conceptual chaos was breached. In the nineteenth century, Karl Friedrich Gauss, János Bolyai, Nikolai Lobachevski, Bernhard Riemann, and others showed that Euclid's Fifth Postulate was independent of the other four, and that modifying it in various ways led to the development of non-Euclidean geometries, some of which were subsequently put to use in physics. Soon after, set theory, a branch of mathematical logic established by Georg Cantor, which studies collections of items and had been considered by many as the proper foundation to all of mathematics, saw one of its axioms questioned and was shown to be riddled with paradoxes.[9]

The twentieth century put a quick end to the most ambitious undertaking to date of placing all of mathematics on an axiomatic basis—an attempt that, had it been successful, would have brought about the possibility of automatizing all of math and therefore all of SCIENCE. The project was summarized in Alfred North Whitehead and Bertrand Russell's *Principia Mathematica*, published in 1913; in 1931, Kurt Gödel put that dream to rest in a short paper titled "On Formally Undecidable Propositions of Principia Mathematica and Related Systems."[10]

Gödel's First Incompleteness Theorem, whose proof was contained in that paper, applies to formal systems (a formal system is a set of axioms assumed to be true, along with rules by which further truths can be deduced from the axioms). Gödel proved that for any sufficiently expressive formal system—such as the proposed *Principia*, but also any of much more modest scope, such as arithmetics—there exist statements that are true, yet unprovable within that system.[11] The implications of this astounding result for the nature of TRUTH, the role of creativity in mathematics, and the capabilities of THINKING systems, natural and artificial, are still being debated.

Meanwhile, the turmoil in the foundations of mathematics created by this and related developments due to Alfred Tarski, Alonzo Church, Emil Post, and Alan Turing continues apace.[12] While it makes the study of meta-mathematics more appealing than ever, it also implies that the hope of developing a single formal framework encompassing all of mathematics, and perhaps by extension also the grand pattern of our reality, had been misplaced.

But time and chance happeneth to them all

Luckily, in cognitive science and AI, formal logic has in any case long been demoted from playing the first violin, which is now in the hands of statistical methods. Indeed, in the sciences of the mind, "rational" now means, to many people, "statistical."[13] Many developments contributed to this conceptual-methodological shift. One of them was the apparent irreducible randomness of quantum mechanics (one of the most numerically precise theoretical frameworks in physics, which moreover serves as the foundation to all modern electronic TECHNOLOGY).[14]

Since its inception in the Industrial Age, statistics was thought of as a means for estimating collective or average characteristics of populations whose individual members are ruled by random "chance" in the sense of Ecclesiastes 9:11, as per the title of this section. More recent developments in statistics and probability theory produced methods for both quantifying and managing uncertainty, making the most out of whatever patterns that hide in random-looking data. In human sciences such as psychology and sociology, statistics can now do much more than describe collective behavior:

it has become a powerful tool for making sense of the computational processes that comprise an individual mind.

Still, as Warren McCulloch once noted, "the stochastic horses of [data] drag no chariot to absolute certainty."[15] Moreover, the provably intractable mathematical COMPLEXITY of many of the key problems faced by a complex control system such as the human mind forces controllers to resort to "good enough" approximations that depend on their history and circumstances. The resulting irreducible apparent randomness implies that the behavior of an individual person in a given situation is much more difficult to predict than a group average. This is surely a letdown for those in POLITICS who aspire to full control over each person's every ACTION.

The inherent stochasticity and complexity of behavior regulation is also something of bad news for those individuals who strive for full *self-control*. There is a passage in the Mishna[16] that offers a curious answer to an important question:

> Who is mighty? One who conquers their impulse to evil, as it is written, "One who is slow to anger is better than the mighty, and one who rules over their spirit than one who conquers a city" (Proverbs 16:32).

Ben Zoma, the sage who made this pronouncement, was on to something: the mathematics of running around with a sword is surely easier than the calculus of cause and effect that rules the sword-bearer's spirit.

Of related interest

To watch:

David Malone, *Dangerous Knowledge* (2007)

To listen:

Johann Sebastian Bach, *The Well-Tempered Clavier* (1722)

To read:

Douglas R. Hofstadter, *Gödel, Escher, Bach: An Eternal Golden Braid* (1979)

Greg Egan, "Luminous" in *Luminous* (1999)

Neal Stephenson, *Anathem* (2008)

To go:

Wherever the mathematics proposes to take you.

20 Memory

The waters of Naihe. Some work of noble note. Across the universe. The Time Warp again. All memory and fate.

Entonces descendió a su memoria, que le pareció interminable, y logró sacar de aquel vértigo el recuerdo perdido que relució como una moneda bajo la lluvia, acaso porque nunca lo había mirado, salvo quizá, en un sueño.

(Then he descended into his memory, which seemed to him endless, and up from that vertigo he succeeded in bringing forth a forgotten recollection that shone like a coin under the rain, perhaps because he had never looked at it, unless in a dream.)

—Jorge Luis Borges, "The Maker"

Yo no hablo de venganzas ni de perdones; el olvido es la única venganza y el único perdón.

(I do not speak of revenge or forgiveness; oblivion is the only revenge and the only forgiveness.)

—Jorge Luis Borges, "Fragments of an Apocryphal Gospel"[1]

The waters of Naihe

Would you give up all the memories of your life as the price of admission into Paradise? Let me warn you up front that the question as posed is subtly biased. To see how so, look up this painting: *The Waters of Lethe by the Plains of Elysium*. There is a throng of people there—all of them dead, judging from the title—and they are waiting to cross the river of forgetfulness. They look European, but the connection between DEATH and forgetfulness is not specifically so: for one thing, the Greco-Roman myth of Lethe has a parallel in a place in South China, where people used to believe that the dead cross the River Naihe by a bridge on which Old Lady Meng ladles out a soup of forgetting.

The conceit behind my phrasing of the opening question should now be apparent: in stark contrast to the happy souls who dance on the far side of the Lethe, those who are waiting to enter the waters look distressed, or mournful, or resigned. For them, memory is not something that one grudgingly gives up (as my use of the word "price" would suggest), but rather a great burden, which they can't shed soon enough.[2]

The other assumption that I sneaked into my question is that crossing into Elysium requires that *all* memories be given up. We know what memory brings: it brings diamonds and rust, as the memorable line in that song by Joan Baez goes. If we decide to forget—assuming that we can at will—does it have to be everything? There is at least one reason it better be (which may exonerate me from one count of bias in phrasing). The reason is this: even if we could hold on to just the diamonds, it would not avail us, because it might serve, at least on bad days, only to sharpen the nostalgia for that TIME when diamonds were there for us to pick.[3] It is almost as if memories had a way of getting at us regardless of whether they are positive or negative.

That all memories have the potential to inflict pain may be why the Greeks hoped that the chosen few who are destined for Elysium are first relieved of the burden of memory. What about the ordinary people who, having failed to merit an afterlife of peace and pleasure, were instead thought to be doomed to roam dark Hades as insubstantial shadows? They too upon dying were supposed to pass through the waters of oblivion—a surprisingly humane belief, which reflects well on the conception of MORALITY in classical Greece. Imagine how cruel it would be instead for a RELIGION to preach a hell, whose inmates not only suffer bodily torments, but also recall and contemplate both their sins and the happy moments of their bygone lives, for all eternity.[4]

Some work of noble note

Having learned something about memory from the role it plays in the mythology of *dying*, we may now better appreciate the modestly heroic task that we are all saddled with: *living* with memory ("DEATH closes all: but something ere the end, / Some work of noble note, may yet be done").[5] It all begins innocuously enough, with the bright memories of childhood (for those of us who manage not to have been born into POVERTY or WAR or abuse or neglect). As our encounters with the world multiply, the accumulated memories become more of a mixed bag, which keeps growing, even as some of its contents are lost along the way.

What is remembered and what is forgotten depends on many things, including likely utility—"likely" as far as EVOLUTION is concerned, not our conscious wishes regarding what we would like to remember and what to forget.[6] For better or for worse, sheer memory capacity is not an obstacle: in animals like ourselves, the size of the brain correlates with longevity, the longer-lived species having more room for remembering their lives.[7] And so, as we grow OLDER, our burden of memory grows heavier.

The first of the two predicaments that arise out of this accumulation of memories over a lifetime I have already noted: more memories means more good memories and also more bad ones—and both the good ones and the bad ones can be difficult to deal with. The second predicament has to do with the one thing that is common to remembering and forgetting. If memory is so much of a burden, it would stand to reason that oblivion would bring relief—but no, that too can be hard, as long as we, unlike those who have passed through the waters of Lethe, remember that there are things that we may have held dear and have now forgotten.[8]

Across the universe

It would be a mistake to conceive of memory as a sack of odds and ends on the back of an itinerant peddler. It's more like a sackful of slumbering cats, which occasionally wake up, a few at a time, claw their way out, and demand attention. When that happens, hold on to your hat: indulging awakened memories causes the body to be put into autopilot mode, while its resident CONSCIOUSNESS goes off wandering in a virtual reality constructed by the brain.[9]

Memories coming to the fore of conscious experience do not merely trigger mind-wandering: without them, there would *be* no virtual world to wander in. Everything about it—"The baseless fabric of this vision, / The cloud-capp'd towers, the gorgeous palaces, / The solemn temples, the great globe itself, / Ye all which it inherit"—is made of memory stuff. The same goes for imagination, both the mundane variety, which we use in making plans for the future, and the fancier kinds that underlie creativity and invention.[10] The virtual world is not there for our entertainment: along with memory that makes it possible, it serves our most basic existential needs.

The Time Warp again

The slightly strange thing about mind-wandering is that even as people's CONSCIOUSNESS is being hijacked, they are typically unaware of being away from the here and now, unless jerked back to reality.[11] This can happen because of some real-world event that requires an immediate intervention, or because the mind-wanderer notices the spacing-out.

While suppressing mind-wandering altogether would seriously impair one's regular human EXISTENCE, learning to detect, and intervene on, one's own mind trips can be useful. A memory trip that loops back on itself tends to be self-perpetuating, and because memory is inseparable from emotions, getting caught in a loop amounts to rumination. This is never any good: if focusing on the past, rumination engenders REGRET, and if on the future, ANXIETY.[12]

All memory and fate

It seems, then, that human memory is a Gordian knot of contradictions and complications. It is a vast storage space for the trophies and the detritus of one's life, into which some stuff disappears without a trace, yet much persists, scheming behind your back and spawning monsters that lurk, waiting to pounce on you unawares. It is a combination time machine and teleportation booth, which would have been pure fun were you to exert a better control over it. As an infant, you're mostly just a bundle of reflexes and genetic predispositions; the longer you live and the more memories you amass, the more sense it makes to call those memories *you*.[13]

Let me now offer you my own answer to the question with which I opened this chapter: *I* would not willingly give up *any* of my memories—not even in exchange for a ticket to Elysium. Not permanently, that is. Temporarily is an entirely different matter. I really wish I were able to retain a memory of everything that I have ever done or that has happened to me, to be recalled or banished at will—temporarily:

Yes, to dance beneath the diamond sky with one hand waving free
Silhouetted by the sea, circled by the circus sands
With all memory and fate driven deep beneath the waves
Let me forget about today until tomorrow[14]

Of related interest

To watch:

Michel Gondry, *Eternal Sunshine of the Spotless Mind* (2004)

To listen:

Bob Dylan, "Mr. Tambourine Man" (1964)

Joan Baez, "Diamonds and Rust" (1975)

To read:

Shimon Edelman, *Beginnings* (2014)

To go:

To the happiest point in your spacetime, then back to the here and now.

21 Morality

Silentio Dei. On the genealogy of morals. Human, all too human. Away from Omelas.

> Deus é o silêncio do universo, e o homem o grito que dá um sentido a esse silêncio.
>
> (God is the silence of the universe, and man the cry that gives meaning to this silence.)
>
> —José Saramago

> Right action is its own end. Dharma without karma.
>
> —Ursula K. Le Guin, *The Telling*[1]

Silentio Dei

The indifference of the universe is, for human affairs, its most consequential quality.[2] The weight of the world's silence in matters of morals is especially hard to bear. The challenge of explaining it within the strictures of a RELIGION (theodicy) seems to affect ordinary people's faith but little, while keeping professional philosophers and theologians busy.[3] Free thinkers are worse off: for them, once the cosmic indifference is perceived, there is no ultimate consolation in faith. Not only are we left to our own devices in regard to what matters to us the most[4] (as in all other regards), but also, in any attempt on our part to fill this void, success or failure can only elicit a merely human approbation or opprobrium.

Combined with the developing understanding of what we humans really are, this situation can be deeply unsettling. Just how much so, I came to appreciate only relatively recently. I was teaching an introduction to cognitive science, whose foundational insight is that minds are what brains compute. To one of the students who came to my office hours, the realization that she, along with everyone else, was basically a meat computer somehow implied an unraveling of all morality. "If we are merely bundles of computations," she asked me, "what prevents me from taking a machine gun and killing everyone?"

Why, I replied, does it always have to be about gunning people down? But I was not really in a position to complain about such leaps of moral imagination. I should have known better than pretending for years that one could do, or teach, SCIENCE of the mind in the abstract, while leaving mundane matters such as morality to others. The textbook that I had written for my course actually did have a section on morality. I refrained from assigning it, because I thought it would take the already overworked students too far afield. That proved to be a mistake (luckily, not a fatal one). And of course, dismissing morality as tangential to science is in itself a moral stance.[5]

Ethical behavior, like any other human behavior, is, or should be, a matter of reason.[6] Admitting the deep reach of moral questions empowers science—the paragon of reason—rather than limiting its purview. Such an admission also strengthens the case of reason against dogma, helping it elevate humanism over the sundry organized RELIGIONS, each of which claims a monopoly on morality. And it makes for some great philosophy: Hilary Putnam, who has argued persuasively for the inseparability of facts, theories, and values, noted, "The case for the idea that facts and values are deeply entangled draws on some of the best philosophical work of the last hundred years."[7]

Most people, however, do not explicitly engage in philosophical investigations or in a scientific study of morality;[8] nor, if they are religious, do they necessarily know much about their denomination's theology and the morals that it is set to enforce. And yet, most people manage to conduct themselves for the most part in a manner that would not get them censured by their peers, or even by their clerics. What kind of moral knowledge can ordinary people be said to have? And how do they come by it?

On the genealogy of morals

In the Old Testament, moral knowledge and the meting out of justice based on that knowledge are both exclusive prerogatives of the supreme being. Adam and Eve's very first run-in with the law got them expelled from Eden, and for what? For wanting to know for themselves what the law actually says. The Snake's insinuation that eating the forbidden fruit would confer the knowledge of good and evil was never denied by the authorities.

A lot can be learned about human societies from their creation myths. The biblical story makes it painfully obvious that we fashion our gods after ourselves: it is ever the case with our species that POWER gets to write the laws. The legend of the Fall also hints at another truth: the path to power, guarded so jealously by "the Man," begins with the very intention on the part of the underclass to learn for themselves what is what.

Myths aside, it is the drive to learn and the ability to do so, not ready-to-use knowledge, of good and evil or of anything else, that EVOLUTION equips us with. Ironically, even our biblically commanded fear of snakes is neither innate nor universal. To be sure, it is real and widespread enough, but that's only because infants are very quick to associate grown-ups' aversive behavior with the sight of a long and thin undulating shape. If you grew up, like I did, in a city where encounters with snakes are vanishingly rare, or if the people who raised you had no fear of snakes, it is very likely that you, like myself, do not recoil at the sight of one.[9]

In the cities for sure, but also in their natural habitats, snakes have now reasons to be afraid of us more than we are afraid of them. This sad fact of life in the Anthropocene leads to the well-known moral question: Whose side are you on? If it's one species against another, you'd think that speciesism would win hands down. However, as it sometimes happens in moral judgment, what is for one person an open-and-shut case is, for another, a difficult dilemma, and for a third one, a no-brainer again, but stood on its head. As Edward Abbey quipped on the case at hand, "I'm a humanist; I'd rather kill a man than a snake."[10]

Another sign of the Anthropocene is that the largest study of human moral leanings at the time of this writing had subjects (millions of them, in 233 countries) make life-or-death decisions in simulated scenarios in which self-driving *cars* faced dilemmas of the "Should I run over that male executive or this homeless person?" sort.[11] Striving to quantify how people perceive driving dilemmas is commendable, but even large amounts of data are no substitute for an understanding. In any case, focusing on artificial (in more than one sense) situations is tangential at best to the understanding of morality in natural social interactions.[12]

A mark of our natural social dynamics, which sets us apart from most other species, is our readiness to cooperate. Intuitive mores are the prime candidate for serving as society's tool for nudging its members into cooperation. Conveniently, internalizing morality can spare everyone the need to keep an eye on each other at all times. There is at long last some real SCIENCE behind these ideas. One particular ethnographic study has identified seven common types of unforced cooperative behavior in all sixty societies that were looked at: helping kin, helping the group, reciprocating, being brave, deferring to superiors, dividing disputed resources, and respecting prior possession.[13]

In that study, respect for property was observed in significantly more societies than bravery, or respect for persons, or fairness. This would seem to be a win for those conservatives, whose POLITICS prioritizes property over people and who also like to pretend that *is* implies *ought*. Fairness, in turn, proved to be rarer than all other types of moral behavior. Such poor showing for fairness[14] is likely to be a little disquieting all around: even capitalists would rather be seen as having won fair and square at the economic game that we, as social animals, are all forced to play.

Imperfect as human cooperation may be, accounting for its scope and stability has always been a challenge for EVOLUTION science. Cooperation is *the* key to the co-evolution of our species and our culture. And yet, as realized already by Darwin, a predisposition to cooperation is a trait that undermines the fitness of the individuals who carry it, by encouraging them to spend valuable resources on helping others. One way of preventing selfish cheaters and free-loaders from condemning cooperators to oblivion is for cooperation to be limited to kin, which people do not necessarily do. For cooperation to work for groups of unrelated individuals, there must be a mechanism that compensates them, as a group, for their susceptibility to cheating, or a means for cheaters to be caught and punished.

A variety of candidate mechanisms that can stabilize cooperation have now been identified and the general principles that govern its evolution are coming into focus.[15] This puts the genealogy of morals within the reach of science. At the risk of infinite regress in making a value judgment about a system of values, I would say that the picture painted by the emerging scientific understanding of human morality is uninspiring.

Human, all too human

A bleak truth regarding the fundamental nature of human moral knowledge and moral behavior is the banality of it all. Hannah Arendt famously noted that evil can be commonplace and unremarkable, so it is not outlandish to expect the opposite of evil to be like that as well. We may find the concept of the "ordinariness of goodness"[16] heartwarming, but perhaps only because things could have been much, much worse. Instead of drowning in ordinary evil, humanity manages to keep afloat—just barely—by clinging to jetsam of ordinary good.

The ordinariness of most of the good that we are liable to come across consists in its lowly origins and often questionable reliability. The banality of morality underwrites the cynicism of Willie Stark ("the Boss") in Robert Penn Warren's novel *All the King's Men*. Stark is asked: "If, as you say, there is only the bad to start with, and the good must be made from the bad, then how do you recognize the good? Assuming you have made it from the bad. Answer me that." His reply is "You just make it up as you go along. . . . What the hell else do you think folks been doing for a million years, Doc?"[17]

Quite. The technical term for "making it up as you go along" is "reinforcement learning," the most general computational formulation of learning from experience.[18] Reinforcement learning needs only one bit of information in a way of feedback about each ACTION: thumbs up or thumbs down. This is how a species, taken collectively, learns over evolutionary time. This is also how individuals learn—on the fly and often pretty much from scratch—how to fit into the cultural niche where they find themselves at birth or after a move to a new country. If we all make it up as we go along, there is no call for acting scandalized as we stand back and take in our made-up morality. The existence of patterns of cooperation documented across societies, which I mentioned earlier, does not imply that one can predict with absolute confidence what the moral choice would be on the part of a given individual in a given situation. There is no absolute and universal scale of moral values, whether or not one feels that there *should* be one. Instead, values are loosely constrained by biological and cultural EVOLUTION, in ways that differ among individuals, families, and groups. The Latin root of "morality" is, after all, *mores*, that is, customs.

Evolution and reinforcement learning reward (or rather refrain from punishing) success, which in a limited-resource setting is subjective. Because of this, morality's dependence on evolution and learning implies a kind of anthropic principle: —What is good (for the winner)? —Whatever works. This inconvenient truth is appalling to many of us, but not to all. Cynics will be quick to observe that the level of indignation here can be regulated by playing with the definition of "winner." Among cooperators, it is the group that wins or loses—or rather the *in*-group individuals (a group, being an abstraction, knows no SUFFERING or HAPPINESS). What we call informally "ethical behavior" is, then, merely the behavior of people whose in-group is broader than the average. And the in-group encompasses all of humanity only for true saints and other fictional characters big on EMPATHY, such as Tolkien's Gandalf, who professed pitying "even Sauron's slaves."

Against this backdrop, telling others what to do from a self-proclaimed moral high ground is a risky business. A special place in the hell of public opinion is reserved for those who are caught at not practicing what they preach (although in POLITICS it seems that literally anything can be forgiven by one's in-group). As Judith Shklar wrote, "Hypocrisy remains the only unforgivable sin even, perhaps especially, among those who can overlook and explain away almost every other vice. However much SUFFERING it may cause, and however many social and religious rules it may violate, evil is to be understood after due analysis. But not hypocrisy, which alone is now inexcusable."[19] You'd think even hypocrites should be forgiven, though, as only a saint would be in a position to cast the first stone at one. Still, stones fly.

Away from Omelas

In Ursula Le Guin's imaginary domain of Omelas, all citizens are thriving, and happy, and complicit in an act of terrible cruelty. A rite of passage for every adolescent is a visit to a dark cellar, where a small child is held in chains, cold, hungry, and miserable. It is explained to the visitor that the city's peace and prosperity are predicated entirely on the child's continued captivity. Most youths then return home to a life of pleasure and plenty; but some walk away from Omelas and never look back.[20]

"The Ones Who Walk Away from Omelas" is a constant presence on the reading lists of seminars that I teach (as it is on many other campuses). But what can I realistically expect from those who read this story? Most of my students, friends, and family, myself included, acquiesce to living in a society where the well-being of some depends on the misery of many. From a utilitarian point of view, the condition of this society is even worse than that of Omelas. The SUFFERING may not be as absolute, but the sufferers are many and the HAPPINESS that is bought so dearly is intermittent and imperfect. And of course the reason for the suffering is not an ordained need to propitiate an inhuman Fate, but merely human POLITICS.

Because morality is culture-dependent and is learned anew, and transformed, as young people are socialized[21] and in turn socialize their elders, this state of affairs might perhaps be fixable. Le Guin's own life work was to chip away at the foundations of Omelas by telling stories.[22] Are there any cracks in the wall surrounding our fortress of Looking-The-Other-Way where a moralizing wedge has a better chance of going in?

One opening would seem to be offered by EMPATHY. Pity is, however, forgetful and is ineffectual when its object is out of sight. It also tends to stop at the in-group/out-group divide. Gandalf may pity the orcs, but his protege Aragorn omits them from his list of the kindreds who should be trusted: "Good and ill have not changed since yesteryear; nor are they one thing among Elves and Dwarves and another among Men."[23] And if orcs are to be given the benefit of the doubt, how are we to recognize them when they're not conveniently "ill-favored" but look just like everyone else?

Would reason, which came up in the beginning of this chapter, be a better tool for opening people's eyes than compassion? In expert hands, it can be extremely effective, but not necessarily in a sense that deserves to be unconditionally endorsed. For whatever it is worth, Aragorn's inspired appeal quoted just now happens to be pure demagoguery: as he knows, the lore of Middle Earth abounds with examples of such amoral behavior—including murderous strife between and within the "free peoples," Elves, Dwarves, and Men—as would make an orc blush.

In real life too, people argue in bad faith and generally do not reason well. Bad reasoning—part bad THINKING and part bad use of LANGUAGE—opens up the way to violations of moral norms, especially on the part of those whose STUPIDITY makes them blind to hypocrisy. As Voltaire reflected, those who make you believe absurdities, can make you commit atrocities.[24]

Perhaps those who left Omelas should just raise an army and lead it back home to raze the dungeon, free the child, and punish its captors? As the Russian saying goes, "Клин клином вышибают" (You can only drive a wedge out with another wedge). History suggests that this will not work. For change to be effective, it has to be systemic. It also must involve a coordinated change of heart of an entire generation, for which a conquest by force is the least effective means. Not even an Elven Queen with a magic ring can help us in this matter, as Sam Gamgee had to be told by Galadriel:[25]

"I wish you'd take his Ring. You'd put things to rights. . . . You'd make some folk pay for their dirty work."

"I would," she said. "That is how it would begin. But it would not stop with that, alas! We will not speak more of it. Let us go!"

Of related interest

To watch:

Stephen O'Regan, *They're Made Out of Meat* (2006; based on a short story by Terry Bisson)

To listen:

Midnite (Vaughn Benjamin), "Due Reward" (2001)

To read:

Ursula K. Le Guin, "The Ones Who Walk Away from Omelas" in *New Dimensions 3* (1973)

To go:

Away from Omelas, then back—when you know what to do.

22 Old Age

Comfortably numb. Catabasis. Cassandra's golden years. Volver.

Старость—не радость.

(Old age is no fun.)

—Russian proverb

Old age should burn and rave at close of day,
Rage, rage against the dying of the light.

—Dylan Thomas, "Do Not Go Gentle into That Good Night"

Al andar se hace el camino
y al volver la vista atrás
se ve la senda que nunca
se ha de volver a pisar.

(As you go, you make the way
and when you turn and look back
you see a path that you'll never
return to step on again.)

—Antonio Machado, "Caminante, no hay camino"

Comfortably numb

There is a state of human EXISTENCE so terrible that just catching a glimpse
of it can become a life-changing experience—at least for those whose sense
of EMPATHY can rise to the occasion. In the old Pali Canon, there is a story
about the Prince Vipassī, who was brought up sequestered in a palace spe-
cially built for him by his father, "with no male attendants, surrounded by
female musicians, and he never left that palace." (The female musicians, it

goes without saying, were all young.) One day, the Prince decided to go for a drive:

> And as he was being driven to the pleasure-park, Prince Vipassī saw an aged man, bent like a roof-beam, broken, leaning on a stick, tottering, sick, his youth all vanished. At the sight he said to the charioteer: "Charioteer, what is the matter with this man? His hair is not like other men's, his body is not like other men's."
>
> "Prince, that is what is called an old man."

Having seen, on subsequent outings, a sick man, a dead man, and an ascetic on a quest to find the cause of SUFFERING, the Prince resolved to leave the palace and become an ascetic himself. Eventually, he fulfilled the quest and came to be known as the Buddha Vipassī.[1]

Old age—the first of the "Four Sights" that together shattered the future Buddha's youthful obliviousness to suffering—is at the root of the other three. An old person is more likely than a young one to get sick, to die—or to become an ascetic. What keeps the less Buddha-like among us from dropping everything and going off on a search for a radical cure for life at the first close encounter with old age is, presumably, our merely human level of empathy.

What empathy there is, is not distributed evenly: young people feel less for the elderly than the other way around (this is why it is quite safe even for younger people to be reading this chapter). What could otherwise be seen as a negative trait actually makes a lot of sense from the standpoint of the "terror management theory" of emotional well-being maintenance.[2] The young should be thankful for it, for their turn to be old will come soon enough.

Catabasis

Mick Jagger and Keith Richards of the Rolling Stones (a hugely popular band in the 1960s and 1970s) were both twenty-three in the year they wrote the line "What a drag it is getting old." I was two thirds that age when I first heard it. I now realize—as I am sure they do, too, now that they are over 75—that I had at the time no idea just much of a drag getting old really is.[3]

Here's how things might have been: you feel fine for three score and ten years, then you keel over on the spot and die.[4] What happens instead is constant, steady descent into decrepitude—gaslighting by *normal* bodily physiology (remember, "normal" is what the "N" in "SNAFU" stands for). I mean, what's the deal with the lower back? And who needs teeth? I wish I had a chitinous exoskeleton and a pair of mandibles instead! Or a beak. A beak instead of teeth would be great.[5]

A lot of writing has been devoted to rounding up arguments to the effect that getting old is not bad as it would seem and that its advantages may outweigh its disadvantages.[6] Each of those arguments has some merit, although I don't find them entirely convincing. Myself, I can think of a few more, but if they are any better, it is at the expense of not being very nice. For instance, the schadenfreude over the universal inevitability of aging is kind of mean—it would be more noble of me to rage over my own decline than to gloat over that of others. The least offensive case that I can make in favor of old age is that it makes people, little by little, so weary of life that eventually they no longer mind DEATH.

Cassandra's golden years

Death came to Cassandra, who had been shunned by her people for fore-telling bad things, in captivity and exile, when she was still young.[7] Had she lived to an old age, her candor would have made her even less popular, and more miserable. Imagine facing, or being, a woman who not only sees the unpleasant future, but is also ready to explain to you how and why it has been shaped by what you have done, or failed to do.

Unlike Apollo's gift (or curse) of prophecy, understanding how the world works is a real skill, which many can master. As a key ingredient of wisdom, it is something that those who can, gain with age. Those inconvenient truths that *everybody knows*—as per Leonard Cohen, "everybody knows the deal is rotten"—are perceived most clearly by someone who has been around for a while. Indeed, aging does not blunt one's perception of the world's sorry state: it makes it more acute.[8] This is the real-life Cassandra's curse.

Volver

One of the classical purported consolations of old age is a lifetime's worth of fond MEMORIES ("We will always have Paris"). It seems to me, though, that as *I* go through life, all my significant experiences with places or people have two sides to them: from each one I take away a page for my memory album, and in exchange, with each place or person I leave a piece of my heart. As I get older, I find it harder and harder to retrace my steps to where many of those pieces are; some are already forever out of reach.[9]

I only became fully aware of this bind on a recent hiking trip to Death Valley. The path on the way to the summit that I had set my sights on that day kept growing steeper and trickier by the minute, so much so that I would have been unable to go on, were it not for my poles. Because going down a steep and slippery path is always harder than going up, I was pondering whether or not to quit while I was ahead and turn back. I went on. The view from the pinnacle was mind-blowing (I shall not attempt to describe it),[10] but my enjoyment of it was diluted by an anticipation of the pending descent. For the first time ever on a hike, it crossed my mind that once I left my just-attained destination, there would be no returning to it.

No matter—as the next window of opportunity for a hiking trip got closer, I was at it again, poring over the topo maps. What is better than a mountaintop? Another mountaintop that you haven't stood upon yet.[11]

Many a "special" place can be revisited even if it is difficult to get to, if one has time and money. You cannot go back to your YOUTH, but at least, for whatever it is worth, you may be able to go back to the place where you were young.[12] Not so with people you were young with. Seeing a friend after a decade or two of separation is as terrifying an experience as, I imagine, seeing your reflection in the mirror would be, had you spent a couple of decades in a world without mirrors.[13] The only way to avoid sharing such an experience with a friend is to never lose sight of each other by growing old together.

Of related interest

To watch:

Yasujirō Ozu, *Tokyo Story* (1953)

Ingmar Bergman, *Wild Strawberries* (1957)

To listen:

Gustav Mahler, *Symphony No. 5* (1904)

Leonard Cohen, "Everybody Knows" (1988)

Penelope Cruz, "Volver" (from Pedro Almodóvar's 2006 film by the same name)

To read:

Freya Stark, *Perseus in the Wind* ([1948] 2013)

Ernest Hemingway, *Across the River and into the Trees* (1950)

Vladimir Nabokov, *Ada, or Ardor* (1969)

Joseph Brodsky, "Песня невинности, она же опыта" ("A Song of Innocence, Also of Experience,"[14] Part II, 1972)

Walter M. Miller Jr., *Saint Leibowitz and the Wild Horse Woman* (1997)

To go:

The place where you grew up; a mountain you have not yet climbed.

23 Parents (The Liberation from)

Be good. Be you. Be back.

וְהֵשִׁיב לֵב־אָבוֹת עַל־בָּנִים וְלֵב בָּנִים עַל־אֲבוֹתָם

(And he shall turn the heart of the fathers to the children, and the heart of the children to their fathers.)

—Malachi 3:24

You can go home again, . . . so long as you understand that home is a place where you have never been.

—Ursula K. Le Guin, *The Dispossessed*[1]

Be good

As we all discover sooner or later, the people who have the POWER to hurt us the most are those whom we hold dearest. You can play it cool and spare yourself, and perhaps others, some SUFFERING by choosing to shun romantic LOVE and to refrain from having CHILDREN (although both are choices that may be deeply REGRETTED when it is too late). But there is one type of love-related peril about which we have little choice, being first exposed to it when we're young and weak and inexperienced. It is our war of independence from our beloved parents.[2]

Attachment to a parent, in the technical sense professed by Western psychology, may or may not be a human universal, but every child's survival and flourishing depend entirely on the support of their family and social circle. This dependence is an EVOLUTIONARY given, which of course is modulated and molded by the specific practices of the culture in which we grow up and which co-evolves with our biology.[3] And insofar as humans perceive extreme dependence as unfreedom, the motivation on the part of human CHILDREN, as they grow up, to redress the balance of power is clear.

As in any asymmetrical conflict, those on the weaker side must bide their time and build their strength, and so do children in contending with their elders. Children conform and learn the ropes while still small, test their bonds periodically, and finally assert their independence or not, if the particular family power structure and the personalities involved come down on the side of stability.

Even if the revolution never happens, it does not mean that the underclass holds no resentment toward the bosses. My mother, eighty-six years old at the time of this writing, still occasionally recalls her dad making her return a pair of sandals that her mom had bought her, just because he was not consulted about the purchase. As far as I know, she was a very compliant child, but I like to think that the sandals episode partly motivated her decision, a decade later, to jilt her family-approved fiancé in favor of my future father—a wild card, a political prisoner just back from Siberia, who gave her parents the jitters.[4]

Be you

I recently learned from my mother that my father later repeatedly urged her to forgive her dad's despotic slips ("He's an old man," he would say, "just let it go."). Her parents, for their part, continued to meddle even after she was married. You'd imagine that starting a family of your own should convince your parents to treat you as an equal, but it doesn't always work like that. And of course it takes two sides to make peace and only one side to keep the animus alive.

A bit like Aeneas fleeing from the fall of Troy with his father Anchises on his back and his son Ascanius in tow, I myself have by now had a chance to play both sides in this game.[5] One lesson suggested by this experience is that it is easier to advise others on how to manage their parents and their children than to put one's own house in order. Another one is that it need not take longer than a minute to burn through an amount of good will that could otherwise have lasted for years. One day when I was in grad school, my father, whom I always adored, shared with me a joke—as it turned out, a rather tired one, which even I had already heard. On a piece of paper (he never mastered email), he had written: "BS: bullshit; MS: more shit; PhD: piled high and dried."

A couple of decades later, in one of the last lucid episodes before he died, my father said to me that the years I had lived at home were the happiest in his life. I cherished the MEMORY of that moment for many years, until, with a little help from a friend, it connected in my mind with the old grad school joke. The years that I spent at home were also the years during which I mounted no challenges to my father's authority, or to his self-esteem.

I still love my father very much—perhaps even more now that more of his human side has been revealed to me. But of course now is too late to have a conversation with him. And back then—I can't remember responding in any meaningful manner. Punching upwards takes more spirit than I could apparently muster at the time. At least I think I never made fun of my own children's career aspirations, but who knows what else I may have said or done for them to resent and remember. And so it goes.

Be back

It may be instructive to consult the Book of Malachi, from which I took the epigraph for this chapter (and for the one on children), regarding who it is that "shall turn the heart of the fathers to the children": the Prophet Elijah, the forerunner of the Messiah. Religious Jews pray daily for the coming of the Messiah, but in modern Hebrew slang, the expression "when the Messiah arrives" means something like "when hell freezes over." Until then, it is up to the fathers and the children in each generation to stop and perhaps reverse the drifting apart of their hearts.

Truly, it is a task cut out for a Messiah or a mythical epic hero. Having a heart-to-heart talk with one's parents can be hellishly difficult, more difficult even than having it with one's CHILDREN. Here too, REGRET can serve as a great motivator: a foreboding of future regret about not having tried to talk when there was still time. In any case, the willingness to negotiate need not imply capitulation. Assuming that there is someone on the other side who is worth talking to (a far from foregone matter), "the talk" is best attempted after we have not only asserted ourselves but also proven our mettle: left HOME, made it "out there"—on our own terms and in our own eyes—and made it back. And perhaps finally standing up to and making peace with our parents can help us truly understand what it is that Joseph Campbell's "hero with a thousand faces"—one of them ours—is up against in taking on the world:

> The problem of the hero going to meet the father is to open his soul beyond terror to such a degree that he will be ripe to understand how the sickening and insane tragedies of this vast and ruthless cosmos are completely validated in the majesty of Being.

Of related interest

To watch:

William Shakespeare, *King Lear* (1606)

Yasujirō Ozu, *An Autumn Afternoon* (1962)

To listen:

Bob Dylan, "The Times They Are a-Changin'" (1964)

Pink Floyd, "Mother" (from *The Wall*, 1979)

To read:

Joseph Campbell, *The Hero with a Thousand Faces* (1949)

Donald Barthelme, *A Manual for Sons* (1975)[6]

To go:

Away, then back home for a visit.

24   Perception

Use your illusion. Umwelten. How things really are.

It's always night or we wouldn't need light.
—Thelonious Monk

To those who see [the world] clearly and properly, the separation between that which perceives and that which is perceived ceases.
—Laṅkāvatāra Sūtra

Things are not as they are seen, nor are they otherwise.
—Laṅkāvatāra Sūtra[1]

Use your illusion

It's always night inside my skull—yours too, unless there are actual gaping holes in it. This proposition would be unremarkable, were it not for my visual experience, which often suggests otherwise. What it suggests right now, with me being awake and aware and my eyes open, is that the place from which *I* look out at the world is just behind the bridge of my nose. Even more strikingly, I see what I see through what appears to be a large oval hole in the front of my head. But when I feel around with my fingertips in search of it, I find that all is well with my face. This can only mean one thing: that the sensory reality that I inhabit is virtual. To put it less gently, I am living a lie.[2]

That the lie is being perpetrated by me on myself is something of a solace, as is the realization that it fits right into the bigger picture of what CONSCIOUSNESS is. And I know I can—praise be to EVOLUTION—by and large trust my perception not to lead me into grave error, such as stepping off a cliff, or overlooking a pair of watchful eyes in tall grass, or otherwise messing with my chances of having and raising CHILDREN. The perceived world is an illusion, but it is a useful one.

The predicament of the brain, confined to the perpetual darkness inside the skull, is, after all, not as dire as it sounds. The senses gather and make good use of enough information about what is happening on the outside to keep the virtual reality rig alive and kicking. If there is still any unease left, it comes from too much THINKING, and too much worrying, about far-out things like ultimate TRUTH. One such worry that arises out of thinking about perception is this: given that *everything* we perceive is a virtual construct, how can we keep believing that our senses reveal to us the world as it really is?

Umwelten

The realization that the perceived world is virtual immediately leads to another one: that what it looks like should depend on the kind of virtual reality engine that one employs. Things are likely to look very different for species whose brain, body, and ecology all differ from the human "standard." The same goes even for humans who happen to have special abilities. A useful, if fictional, prop for thinking about these matters is Zatōichi, the hero of a long-running action film series in Japan, whose prowess with a sword was not in the least impaired by his blindness. The trope, which the viewers loved, was that the Blind Swordsman leveled the playing field against sighted opponents by making better use of his remaining senses and his other skills. (He did not always play fair: in some fight scenes, he would first cut off the wicks of the candles, plunging everything into darkness.)

A key insight into Zatōichi's situation is that *light* is of no use to him, nor is it even present as such in his perceptual world; and yet he acts as if the scene were brightly lit. Imagine this: Zatōichi and a sighted human walk into a barn. Make it a dark barn. Inside, the two of them meet a bat and an owl. There are now four qualitatively different kinds of perceptual worlds in play; five, if we count the mice scurrying on the floor; six, if the cat wanders in. Jacob von Uexküll, the ethologist who was among the first to realize the inevitable idiosyncrasy of each "lived world," or *Umwelt*, remarked that "the dog is surrounded by dog things and the dragonfly is surrounded by dragonfly things." When a human and a dog go for a walk, the leash between them has each end in a different virtual world.[3]

How things really are

If different species, or even different individuals belonging to the same species, inhabit different perceptual worlds, what can we know about what the *real* world is like? Clearly enough to make ACTION possible; apart from that, not much. Amazingly, the more basic a question about that real world seems, the more difficult it is to get a definitive answer to it. Is it dark at night? The sense in which it is for us is of little concern to a bat, and of no concern to a mole. Is air thick? Not really to us, but sufficently so for a swallow to push against during its aerial acrobatics. Is water wet? Not to a duck or a water strider. In the face of such differences, it seems silly to insist that our perceptual world is somehow privileged or that what we perceive is how things *really* are.[4]

How things look and feel depends not only on who is doing the looking and feeling, but also on what ACTION or other purpose it serves, as well as on the perceiver's experiential history (and therefore on MEMORY) and bodily and emotional state. I may see a rock outcropping encountered on a hike *as* a human face or *as* a battering ram, depending on where my mind was wandering as I was walking up to it (arguably, the best hiking experience requires that the hiker practice *just seeing* instead of *seeing as*).[5] When I am hungry, a mountain track that I am facing looks steeper than right after a meal. The prospect of jumping at six o'clock in the morning into the indoor pool, in which the water is kept cool to prevent lap swimmers from overheating, feels discomforting to different degrees, depending on whether it is summer or winter outside, as I found out, having been doing this three times a week for many years. Luckily, it helps to think about other matters while swimming. For example, anticipating how the chapter that I am working on is going to end literally warms me up: it distracts me from the initial feeling of cold and I also swim faster, so that it takes me a couple of minutes less to do my usual 3,200 yards.[6]

As we find ourselves compelled to doubt the very notion of objective truth about what the world is like, can SCIENCE help? Yes, as long as we don't expect it to do the impossible. Whatever the world is "really" like, evolution has been clearly successful—in an endless variety of strange and beautiful ways—in coming up with effective means of dealing with the world. Science, which operates on much the same principles of variation and selection, can be at least equally successful. But evolution has no use for questions of ultimate TRUTH and scientists too are supposed to shun them. In some disciplines, they have learned to do so. Is the electron really a wave or a particle? Quantum mechanics, an epitome of theoretical and practical success in physics, rightly refuses such questions.

The COMPLEXITY of the human brain greatly exceeds that of any other physical system that we know of, so that in perception science it is even more important not to waste time on arguing about absolutes. What color is this banana? Purple (it's my favorite variety from Costa Rica), but there is no matter of objective fact about this observation, because color has no physical definition: it is entirely the construct of the observer's visual system in its interaction with the environment.[7] At least as far as color is concerned, things are neither as they seem, nor otherwise.

There is a philosophical tradition out there that holds this—the essential EMPTINESS of all things—to be an ultimate TRUTH in its own right; indeed, the only ultimate truth. Some find this notion liberating—the religious tradition that is built around that philosophy holds this to be the only liberating notion. Others, like the reluctant hero of Ursula Le Guin's *The Lathe of Heaven*,[8] find it hard:

> There is a bird in a poem by T. S. Eliot who says that mankind cannot bear very much reality; but the bird is mistaken. A man can endure the entire weight of the universe for eighty years. It is unreality that he cannot bear.

But now that we have seen it, bear it we must.

Of related interest

To watch:

David Loxton and Fred Barzyk, *The Lathe of Heaven* (1980)

David Cronenberg, *eXistenZ* (1999)

David Lynch, *Mulholland Drive* (2001)

To listen:

David Bowie, "Sound and Vision" (1977)

To read:

Philip K. Dick, *Ubik* (1969)

Greg Egan, *Diaspora* (1997)

Victor Pelevin, *Buddha's Little Finger* (originally *Чапаев и Пустота*, [1996] 2001)

To go:

To Inner Mongolia (see Pelevin, above, for directions).

25 Politics

The tools of the trade. A shining city on the hill. Into the catacombs. News from Nowhere.

Car le siécle est tout noir
En chapeau haut de forme
Et pourtant nous courons

(Because our age is all in black
It wears a tall top-hat
And still we continue to run)
—Guillaume Apollinaire, "Un son de cor . . ."

The individual cannot bargain with the State. The State recognizes no coinage but power: and it issues the coins itself.
—Ursula K. Le Guin, *The Dispossessed*[1]

The tools of the trade

If politics is, as Bismarck saw it,[2] an art, it is one that has more to do with craftiness than with creativity. The tools of this craft turn out societies that are infinitely diverse in their details, yet strikingly consistent in condemning most of their members to a life of scarcity and suffering, while ensuring that they are kept oblivious to the very possibility of change, or unwilling to countenance it, or incapable of bringing it about.

There are about as many tools in the toolkit of politics as in a Swiss army knife:

- eroding and distorting TRUTH
- amassing and exercising POWER
- preaching and subverting MORALITY

- cultivating and harnessing RELIGION
- promoting and exploiting STUPIDITY
- generating and directing FEAR
- instigating and perpetuating WAR

And then there is a special tool, which contains all the others—think of a Swiss army knife that has a button which, when pressed, releases a Jinn armed with an identical Swiss army knife—

- turning people into tools of POLITICS

As an ultrasocial species, we all depend on each other in many ways, sometimes absolutely. The political process—a system of cultural practices ranging from semi-innocuous rituals to thinly disguised psy-ops instruments—capitalizes on the basic human predisposition to cooperate. In doing so, it creates stable social units that keep propagating themselves despite member turnover. In a sense, it is these communities, over and above particular people such as Bismarck, or your current president, or their bankrollers, that effectively wield the tools of politics.

A shining city on the hill

I live in one type of community like that. It consists of a few hundred million people, surrounded by a fence. The system that we created and that keeps it all going teaches us to fear and distrust those on the other side of the fence. Just to keep everyone on their toes, it also encourages us to fear and distrust those on the inside who look different from us. It teaches us to take ignorance as a sign of authenticity and to distrust learning and inquiry. It teaches us to revere power and especially money, helping us to decide which of the two candidates to vote for every few years. It expects us to render unto Caesar the things that are Caesar's, and unto God the things that are God's. And it forces us to pay (preferably, enthusiastically) for wars, which aim to convince people in other corrals that they should give up *their* ways of life (or at least give us their oil).

To be sure, billions of people have to endure more than mere hypocrisy and venality on the part of their ruling class.[3] In politics, as in any domain of human endeavor that contributes to what I called in chapter 32 "unnecessary" SUFFERING, it is always difficult to pick a case to denounce that cannot be immediately eclipsed by a more outrageous one. Comparing cases is, however, tricky. Are liberal democracies categorically better than theocratic and other authoritarian political systems? My political situation is much better than that of an apostate living in a theocracy or a dissident in a totalitarian state. But this is not necessarily true of all my fellow citizens—nor, arguably, even of the majority of them; witness the ubiquity in the liberal democracies of socioeconomic inequality and the extent of its human toll.[4]

It is a grave insult to the intelligence and the moral sense of the multitudes who find themselves trapped in the underclass in a liberal democracy to hear it being extolled as not only the best political system in the world but also the best conceivable one. It is sad that any apologetic spin on the liberal West's politics is not universally rejected as sham. Just now, I was planning to write "even the best-intentioned liberal scholars are complicit in this failure" when I realized that this phrasing tacitly assumes that "liberal" is synonymous with "good." While this assumption is just fine by some people, I wonder if there's more to it than a knee-jerk reaction to fascists, who cannot imagine a deadlier insult than "liberal."

Judith Shklar once singled out a "bare bones liberalism which, having abandoned the theory of progress and every specific scheme of economics, is committed only to the belief that tolerance is a primary virtue."[5] I am receptive to the idea that tolerance is a virtue, but it cannot be an unconditional one. As Karl Popper has noted, in a book that came out the year the Nazis were defeated in World War II, "if we extend unlimited tolerance even to those who are intolerant, if we are not prepared to defend a tolerant society against the onslaught of the intolerant, then the tolerant will be destroyed, and tolerance with them."[6] A case can be made, however, that Nazis (past and present) are not the only ones who do not deserve to be tolerated. Always and everywhere, they have been cultivated by the POWER elites as a tool against attempts to advance economic and social justice.[7]

When the political system itself in liberal, nominally democratic states becomes a tool for preserving inequality and injustice, is it any surprise that popular support for democracy wanes? In Europe, this is happening now not only in the traditionally economically disadvantaged South, but also in the social-democratic, prosperous North.[8] Not only do the democratic *ideals* appeal less now to the masses: the actual process of governance in many established democracies, such as France and the United States, has been recently rated as "flawed."[9] It looks like the system that has been and still is being peddled to the masses as democracy is unable to deliver even on its own pandering slogans. And so the rich, who used to poll as more pro-democracy than the working class, are now more pro-army rule.[10] How else would they protect their wealth and their privilege when the dam bursts?

Into the catacombs

If the political-economic situation at HOME becomes impossible,[11] it may be best to pull out the roots and leave before it is too late. Where should newly homeless economic migrants and political refugees turn? In the last century and a half, the nation-states' monopoly over border control has meant that migrants typically have few, if any, options, none of which may be particularly attractive. A story is told of an old Jew in the Soviet era, who received permission to emigrate, an unheard-of thing in the "communist" earthly paradise.[12] To help him decide where to go, he was given a world map on a globe. After spinning it for a while, he frowned and asked: "Do you maybe have another globe?"[13]

If you feel politically and intellectually oppressed, but your economic situation is not unbearable, there is one option at your disposal that does not require physically leaving home: inner emigration. You shut out the news, avoid political discussions, and retreat into your little world, where bad things don't happen. While the phrase dates back to the French revolution of 1830, the pattern of behavior that it stands for is as old as politics. It was adopted in response to RELIGIOUS persecution by crypto-Jewish Marranos in medieval Catholic Spain; by Christians in imperial Rome and in Soviet Russia; by atheists in Sunni and Shia Muslim theocracies in the Middle East and South Asia; by Muslims in China's Xinjiang—the list is long.

With the emergence of states founded on totalitarian atheist ideology, such as the Soviet version of communism, members of the secular intelligentsia too learned to THINK not only for themselves, but *to* themselves (the Russian word for "dissident," инакомыслящий, means literally "one who thinks otherwise"). Growing up in the USSR, I was taught from an early age not to repeat at school what I heard being said at home. Eventually, I came to understand why. And then the Soviets found it to be politically expedient to let some of their Jews go, and my parents and I emigrated for real.[14]

Years later, I moved countries all over again (more than once, actually), now with a family of my own in tow. Only then I finally got the joke about the old Jew and the globe.

Once the only way for certain people in totalitarian states to stay sane, inner emigration is now being rediscovered by millions of disaffected citizens in Western "democracies."[15] Unfortunately, this trend benefits the political establishment. Worse, the dynamics of disaffection favors the deepening of the hole that the dissidents find themselves in. People who, instead of going into internal exile, choose to engage with the political reality are the only hope for eventual change to the better. However, the political reality being what it is, engaging with it necessarily involves publicly expressing a very negative view of the status quo—an attitude that can lead to cynicism and eventual retreat into the inner world.

To people who conform because they don't know better, vocal dissent appears to be a kind of insanity.[16] At times, even the dissidents themselves can be persuaded that something is wrong with them. In a society that fetishizes HAPPINESS, no matter how strained, a widespread undercurrent of vague disaffection creates a market for self-help books that promote anodyne "positive psychology."[17] A much more lucrative market exists for psychological and pharmacological treatments of disaffection. The medicalization of dissidence is a powerful tool for self-preservation on the part of the political system.[18] The system also has at its disposal subtler tools for channeling disaffection. A case in point is an opinion piece that appeared recently in the *New York Times* under the title "How Loneliness Is Tearing America Apart: When people have a hole in their life, they often fill it with angry politics." In politics, if you want to find out the true intent behind a public declaration, ask *cui bono?*—who benefits?[19] In this case, the answer is out there in the open: the author of that article, a regular contributor to the *Times*, is the president of the American Enterprise Institute, a propaganda engine of the oligarchy.[20]

News from nowhere

The inconvenient truth behind politics is that neither of the choices that are available to us at present is workable. To live alone is impossible: to do so, one "must be either a beast or a god," as Aristotle wrote in *Politics*. But when we band together and form a state—a *polis*—it takes on a life of its own and, with active participation of many of its citizens, becomes an instrument of oppression of everyone else.

There is no political system in existence under which every citizen would be perfectly *autonomous*, that is, governed by his or her own laws. Oppression through the denial of autonomy is always there; only its extent varies. This is obviously true for authoritarian regimes, but isn't there also an obvious alternative to those? Robert Paul Wolff, who offers a most concise and clear analysis of our political predicament, does not reject this alternative out of hand: "There is only one form of political community which offers any hope of resolving the conflict between authority and autonomy, and that is democracy." This, however, only holds for unanimous direct democracy. Once voting is delegated to the citizens' representatives and majority rule is instituted, democracy becomes flawed at best and an empty slogan at worst.[21]

Democracy's fundamental flaws are a thorn in the side of all those who deplore being subjected to laws to which they did not consent. Wolff refuses to move one inch until this problem of "heteronomous minority" is resolved: "Perhaps, as Winston Churchill once remarked, democracy is the worst form of government except for all the others; but if so, then the "citizens" of America are as much subjects of an alien power as the Spaniards under Franco or the Russians under Stalin. They are merely more fortunate in their rulers." As we saw, however, even this consolation is not available to those who are oppressed not only politically but also economically. Indeed, the very distinction between politics and economics is untenable.[22]

As the roots of the problem at hand run so deep, the solution to it must be radical indeed. If, as Wolff puts it, "the just state must be consigned the category of the round square," then a precondition for justice, political and economic, is the abolition of states, that is, anarchism.[23] Although to some "anarchism appeals as an ideology partly because we now live in an age of diminished hopes and dreams,"[24] others see it as our only hope.[25]

To appreciate anarchism's appeal, one could start with good old utopian fiction, such as *News from Nowhere; Or, An Epoch of Rest* by William Morris, published in 1890, but still surprisingly readable. Worlds away from Morris's post-revolution pastoral England, yet closer to Earth in many regards, are the twin planets, Urras and Anarres, of Ursula Le Guin's *The Dispossessed* (subtitled *An Ambiguous Utopia*). One is home to a very recognizable capitalist "democracy" and the other, just a short space flight away—is the refuge of a breakaway anarchist collective.

It would be easier then to learn to think about real politics in terms of what Eric Olin Wright called "real utopias"—ambitious, yet feasible alternatives to dominant political and economic structures.[26] For this kind of thinking to become common enough to make eventual change possible, education is key.[27] But what hope is there for a post-change community of truly autonomous agents to exist without devolving into . . . no, not anarchy!—barbarism?

There are hardly any historical precedents of anarchist politics being practiced on a large scale (one exception is the anarcho-syndicalist control of Barcelona, along with much of Catalunya and Aragón, in 1936–1938).[28] Insights from history and from political science, such as they are, suggest that stable extended cooperation without coercion is possible, but not guaranteed.[29] As one might expect, the critical factor seems to be economics.

The case of Barcelona workers who "refused to produce without a monetary incentive" proved to be something of an embarrassment for the socialist-anarchist experiment.[30] Such stumblings may be excusable under the circumstances:[31]

> Now, quite apart from the fact that . . . socialism[32] suffers the devastating liability of only exhibiting internal contradictions when you are trying to use it as an adjunct to your own STUPIDITY (unlike capitalism, which . . . happily has them built in from the start), it is the case that because Free Enterprise got there first and set up the house rules, it will always stay at least one kick ahead of its rivals.

It just might be possible to render the "house rules" irrelevant, though. Imagine a society in which a revolution in production has led to such material abundance that all economic concerns have disappeared along with the need to work for a living or even for a life of luxury.[33] Such a revolution would have to rely on TECHNOLOGY—a notoriously unpredictable transformer of societies. Still, it may be less utopian than hoping to change human nature on a massive enough scale and over a short enough time to allow a society free of oppression and exploitation to take root and persist. We know that when attempted on a small scale, things tend not to end well, as suggested by the historical lessons of the Paris Commune, suppressed by the French Army, and of the Spanish Second Republic, overrun by Franco's fascist rebels aided by Nazi Germany.

In this regard too, the solution may end up having to be somewhat technological—the same, in fact, as it was in Le Guin's ambiguous utopia. We may have to leave here, leaving everything behind, and go build a new home and a better society elsewhere, perhaps in the asteroid belt. And if we ever look back toward the inner planets and the distant Sun, we will remember why we did what we did:

> We took nothing. Because there is nothing here but States and their weapons, the rich and their lies, and the poor and their misery.[34]

Of related interest

To watch:

Bernardo Bertolucci, *1900* (1976)

To listen:

Daniel Kahn & The Painted Bird, "Inner Emigration" (2011)

Stephen Marley, "Rock Stone" (2016)

To read:

William Morris, *News from Nowhere; Or, An Epoch of Rest* (1890)

Ethel Voynich, *The Gadfly* (1897)

Edward Abbey, *Good News* (1980)

To go:

Nowhere.

26 Power

The great chains of being. The invisible hand. Beyond Freedom and Dignity.

Grasshopper always wrong in argument with chicken.
—Malaclypse the Younger, *Principia Discordia*[1]

The great chains of being

When was the last time you made a moderately consequential decision without any regard to what others may have to say about it? Probably never—not even if you're a childless orphan, raised by the wolves and living alone in the wilderness (surely your lupine foster PARENTS would have enforced *some* discipline). If so, then other people have had, and likely still have, power over you.

That some people, individually or as a group, have on some occasions power over the decisions of others is a human universal, found in all past and present societies.[2] Power differentials are so common in our social life that many of them escape attention. The use of power may go unnoticed by a habitual wielder; in some situations, even those on the receiving end may be oblivious to it—a condition snubbed by ostentatious power-hungry fools, but appreciated by professionals.

All this would have been of much less concern if power were equally distributed—but it is not. Nor is it symmetrical. B. F. Skinner, who advocated social engineering through behavioral control, points out that "the relation between the controller and the controlled is reciprocal," yet the list of examples he then offers stands his point on its head: "In a very real sense, then, the slave controls the slave driver, the child the parent, the patient the therapist, the citizen the government, the communicant the priest, the employee the employer, and the student the teacher."[3]

Persistent inequality in the distribution of power across individuals implies hierarchy, and there are in fact at least three distinct ones: a universal dominance hierarchy based on age; another, nearly universal in the ordering it imposes, based on gender; and a third induced by social constructs that are culture-specific. These and other categories of power are all intersectional: there are many combinations of individual circumstances and social identities that carry power—and disempowerment, so that a person may, occasionally or even routinely, end up with the short end of several sticks at once.[4]

The complexities of power imply that it depends on context no less than on the person.[5] A privileged character, who is used to having his way without giving it a second thought, may find himself constrained or coerced by someone with more, or a different kind of, clout. And even those who have nothing to lose but their chains sometimes get a chance to take it out on others.[6] There is always a bigger fish than your present oppressor, and always a smaller one than you. This, however, is a paltry consolation. And can the SUFFERING of one powerful person make up for that of the object of another's power? The chains of power crisscross families, organizations, and societies, binding all of us together, even as some of us amass rank and dominance, while others lose what little control they have over their lives.

The invisible hand

The end of CHILDHOOD brings about a remarkable realignment of power in one's life. Leaving behind the nuclear family (or, as it may be, the wolves' cave), people find themselves beset with new demands and constraints. The hand that occasionally yanks one's chains is now for the most part invisible. It is also much more impersonal. You hang out with some new friends and a change comes over you, so that your old friends barely recognize you—how did that happen? Your social credit rating goes down and you're banned from buying a train ticket—what did you do to offend the system? You have plans to study but are instead steered—by whom?—into juggling several dead-end jobs. (It has to be several, because one doesn't even cover the rent—why?) And just then, your elected representatives vote to fund another WAR overseas.

Power that is hard to trace back to its source is difficult to defy, in particular if it is so well camouflaged that the pressures it exerts are not even recognized as such. Power is relational; and because the position of every regular individual member of society is defined simultaneously by many social relations, patterns of power rarely resemble a fixed pecking order. Rather, power takes the form of a complex, dynamic web.[7] The structure of power thus matches that of the other aspect of human existence that has to do with causes of behavior: our so-called FREE WILL. The web of power that we all spin and in which we are trapped sets the social boundaries for our freedom of will.

Beyond Freedom and Dignity

The indispensability of the concept of power in understanding human nature is rivaled only by that of EVOLUTION. With all due respect to biological and cultural evolution, though, are we not capable of rational THINKING? May reason not prevail over the dynamics of power, even if the latter has been ordained by evolution?

One question here is whether or not reason *should* prevail. Reason itself suggests some inconvenient answers to this normative question. For one thing, CHILDREN cannot reason as well as adults. Then there is STUPIDITY, the consequences of which power can greatly amplify. This is an unfortunate fact of life, which afflicts also our POLITICS. It holds both for autocracies and oligarchies, in which political power is the prerogative of a select few, and for democracies, in which the minority has by default less power. Finally, even sound reason is no substitute for sound MORALITY—a complex and tricky notion in its own right, which we don't really know what to make of. It seems, then, that subjugating power to reason might not be the solution we want, after all.

The other big question is whether or not power *can* be subjugated to reason. There have always been voices in philosophy, and more recently also in SCIENCE, in favor of this idea.[8] It too, however, faces an inconvenient truth: unless power is entirely abolished, any attempt to exercise it runs the risk of hurting someone's feelings (over and above their physical well-being). Exactly how a particular act of power would affect an individual's dignity is up to the context, the subjects' emotions, and, in the final account, their personal perception. People's feelings—especially about their freedom—are complex, easy to offend, and hard to predict.

In the face of these formidable obstacles, it has been proposed that righting the human condition requires that we, as a society, move "beyond freedom and dignity."[9] To the humanists, though, such a move would be tantamount to a doctor venturing to cure a patient by killing him.

A less extreme solution to the problem of power might be patterned on the one that has been proposed for that other notoriously intractable problem, SUFFERING, which cannot be eliminated—only reduced, by doing away with its "avoidable" causes, such as POVERTY and disease. If we settle for merely reining in power, it might be possible to prevent at least its excesses. Given that too much power in the hands of a few people can cause many others to suffer, pulling on the reins might gain a little more dignity for the many, at the expense of a little less freedom for the few.

Of related interest

To watch:

Sergei Eisenstein, Броненосец Потёмкин (*Battleship Potemkin,* 1925)

Mira Nair, *Monsoon Wedding* (2001)

Pedro Almodóvar, *La mala educación* (*Bad Education,* 2004)

Guillermo del Toro, *El laberinto del fauno* (*Pan's Labyrinth,* 2006)

To listen:

Radiohead, "You and Whose Army?" (2001)

To read:

J. R. R. Tolkien, *The Lord of the Rings* (1954)

To go:

To Orodruin (make sure you have the One Ring with you).

27 Poverty

Cui bono? Double double jeopardy. UBI bene?

Унтер-офицерша налгала вам, будто я её высек; она врёт, ей-богу, врёт. Она сама себя высекла.

(The sergeant's widow lied to you that I flogged her; she's lying, by God, lying. She flogged herself.)

—Nikolai Gogol, *Ревизор*

I want to see everyone, concluded he, all creeds and classes pro rata having a comfortable tidysized income, in no niggard fashion either, something in the neighbourhood of £300 per annum. That's the vital issue at stake and it's feasible and would be provocative of friendlier intercourse between man and man. At least that's my idea for what it's worth. I call that patriotism.

—James Joyce, *Ulysses*[1]

Cui bono?

It would have been quite convenient for everyone involved if poverty were demonstrably the result of some character flaw, maybe laziness, on the part of the poor. The rich could then assuage their occasional guilt by reminding themselves that the poor's SUFFERING is self-inflicted.[2] And the poor themselves might seek solace in the knowledge that justice is being served, and also that they can always leave poverty behind, as soon as they roll up their sleeves and get serious about work.

Because MORAL attitudes are by definition opinions, which need not be grounded in a TRUTH, it does not matter that the poor in fact work longer hours on the average than the well-to-do.[3] As long as one is committed to "system justification"[4] (a mainstay of conservative POLITICS), there is no need to be distracted by facts. And then, of course, there is the convenience for the employers of having an inexhaustible pool of workers on hand, all of whom are highly motivated to compete with one another in the race to the bottom of the wage pyramid.[5]

It would seem that only those who benefit from the prevailing economic system should be motivated to justify it. Perversely, though, those who get the short end of the stick do so too, in a way. By convincing the poor that they are to blame for their own condition, the system helps perpetuate itself, by turning what could have been indignation and anger into guilt and shame.[6] But the iniquity does not end there.

Double double jeopardy

There are two faces to the SUFFERING that comes with poverty. One is physical privation: hunger and extremes of cold or heat. The other is mental misery: shame and guilt, but also, first and foremost, constant ANXIETY about the ability to make ends meet, especially in the face of sudden illness or other unexpected expenses.[7] It would seem that it is better to be rich and healthy than poor and sick.[8]

There are also two faces to the dynamics of poverty. The first one comes out of its defining characteristic—financial hardship. With even regular meals being uncertain, the chances of ever being able to come up with extra means to get ahead and climb out of the hole are small. And then there are poverty's effects on the brain. A young protagonist in one of Orhan Pamuk's novels argues passionately that "mankind's greatest error, the biggest deception of the past thousand years is this: to confuse poverty with stupidity."[9] The cruel truth is that the very condition of being poor has a mind-numbing effect, not only robbing people of the energy needed to think clearly, but also impairing their ability to do so.[10] What might have otherwise been a temporary predicament becomes a trap.

This dynamics ensures that, just like inherited wealth, poverty is a condition that runs in the family. For the mistake of being born to poor parents, children pay for the rest of their lives.[11] The societies that get to be like that are both stable and distinctly stratified—by POWER and HAPPINESS, by income and wealth, by education and employment, by health and longevity—pyramid-like temples to the little gods of greed.

UBI *bene?*

Unlike pyramids built of stone, these products of our cultural EVOLUTION cover the face of the earth—no technological society has been spared. Both adult and child poverty exist even in the "welfare states" of northern Europe,[12] and even there, sadly, the future of the social safety net is not guaranteed, for the usual POLITICAL reasons.

This marks socioeconomic inequality as a *systemic* problem, which may have to do with the basic structure and dynamics of modern human societies.[13] Nothing short of a systemic solution can make it go away. Meanwhile, sporadic demands for at least a partial remedy such as a living wage are met by those in POWER, if not literally "в штыки"—with bayonets at the ready, as the Russians say—then with legislative obstruction, backed up by militarized police with guns and tear gas.

It defies understanding how someone could object to people being paid for their labor a living wage—in the words of James Joyce's epic hero, Leopold Bloom, "a comfortable tidysized income . . . if you work."[14] It's not like they would be paid for possibly doing nothing, which is what one actually radical idea, universal basic income or UBI, would allow.[15]

In light of the entrenched opposition on the part of POWER to the eradication of poverty, my guess is that any systemic solution to it would have to be even more radical than UBI. Until the people are ready to conceive of and put in place such a solution, those of us who side with change are stuck with Stephen Daedalus's reply to Bloom: "We can't change the country. Let us change the subject."

Of related interest

To watch:

Charlie Chaplin, *Modern Times* (1936)

Walter Salles, *The Motorcycle Diaries* (2004)

To listen:

Eugène Pottier, "L'Internationale" (1871)

Joe Hill, "The Preacher and the Slave" (1911)

John Lennon, "Working Class Hero" (1970)

To read:

Anton Chekhov, Мужики (*Peasants*, 1897)

Barbara Kingsolver, *The Bean Trees* (1988)

To go:

To organize for change.

28 Regret

Nothing, really? The ledger. Fools and heroes.

If I followed that road to the end,
I would come to the sea of death, they told me,
and so from halfway along, I turned back,
being me, weak and rational.
Since then all the paths I have roamed
were entangled, and crooked, and forsaken.
—Yosano Akiko, "Cowardice"[1]

Nothing, really?

Whether or not an unexamined life is worth living is a foundational question in philosophy, one that still generates debate.[2] In real life, though, it has been moot ever since EVOLUTION bestowed on our ancestors the ability to experience regret. Whether we want it or not, our lives are examined, in detail, by critics who are both knowledgeable and strict: ourselves. An integral part of everyone's daily EXISTENCE is scrutiny of past opportunities for ACTION, whether taken up or passed over. Except in people blinded by STUPIDITY or narcissism, the outcome of this self-examination is rarely self-laudatory.[3]

Of the many faces of regret, two stand out. The first is disappointment in oneself for not living up to one's goals and aspirations, as reflected in one's conception of the ideal self. The second one is shame about not having behaved as one ought to, in terms of the perceived moral duties and responsibilities. People's tendency to be more susceptible to ideal-related compared to ought-related regret[4] suggests that success in personal pursuits is generally valued higher than adherence to public mores—unless the person is the kind of saint whose entire self is centered on MORALITY, such that its personal and public pursuits are one.

Because one's self—the authority that commissions the regret-generating inquests—has access in principle to the perfect information about each case, making one's regrets public can be very revealing. The same goes for what one professes not to regret—an act of defiance that is often perceived in a sentimental light, even if it applies to life choices that have nothing to do with romantic LOVE. It was love that Édith Piaf sang about when she performed "Non, je ne regrette rien"; but she also dedicated her recording of it to the fabled mercenary service of a fading empire, the French Foreign Legion (which promptly adopted it as its parade song). This choice on Piaf's part no doubt makes sense to some people (probably the same ones who find running away to join the Foreign Legion romantic). To those on whom the Legion waged WAR, as well as to many others, it appears questionable, to say the least. Tell me what you don't regret and I'll tell you who you are.[5]

The ledger

It is useless to try to minimize regret by refraining from ACTION. Not only do people regret inaction too, but also regrets over a failure to act are actually more common, and more compelling, than regrets over action.[6] Regret is especially poignant when the missed opportunity is known to have been unique, as in a once-in-a-lifetime professional break or a chance meeting with a mysterious attractive stranger.

A well-worn ledger of regrets is a common fixture of OLD AGE. Eventually, you discover which of its entries are written in indelible ink. If knowledge is POWER, so is self-knowledge, and a particularly prized kind of power, too; and thus the ledger is not without its uses. "You will live to regret it" may come across as a warning or a curse (which are one and the same if FREE WILL is an illusion, as it well might be). Imagining this phrase being addressed to you by your future self makes it a possibly useful advice.

You may dislike such advice and choose to ignore it (as Cassandra's prophecies were all doomed to be), but in doing so you would be turning a blind eye to a unique perspective on the decisions you're facing. In the science of decision-making, this perspective has been codified as the Minimax principle: choose the option that avoids the maximum possible anticipated regret.[7]

The computational COMPLEXITY of estimating the anticipated regret quickly gets out of hand as the number of options grows. Faced with such "tyranny of choice," the decider is forced to choose suboptimally, resulting on the average in more regret, and less HAPPINESS, compared to situations where the number of options is small.[8] The proliferation of choices is not something that is often encountered "in the wild": we owe it to our TECH-NOLOGIES, whose development is driven more by considerations of profit than by real needs.

But even without technological assistance, the ability to experience regret can be a damn nuisance. Insofar as the evolutionary function of the MEMORY of past events and actions is to optimize future behavior,[9] regret that one feels in old age is the mark of a rather senseless aspect of the tyranny of TIME. The ledger keeps filling up as one gets older, but the future, for the sake of which it is supposedly kept, gets shorter, and the regret more pointless.

Fools and heroes

Pointless cruelty happens to be also one of the horns of a strange dilemma arising from the theory that regret's evolutionary role is to hone future decision-making. If our sense of FREE WILL in choosing how to act is an illusion (a possibility that I discuss in chapter 14), SUFFERING the pangs of regret is all for nothing. This very insight, however, should then suffice to silence the regret and abolish the suffering. The other horn of the dilemma is sharper: if free will is real, it means that one *could have done better*, making any regret-induced suffering well deserved.

Note, however, that "doing better" in this context is a concept that is underwritten by evolution, and as such it does not necessarily align either with one's ideal self or with one's ideal MORALITY. If by doing what I think is right I put my evolutionary fitness at risk, the mechanisms of regret will kick in. To keep them in check, all I can do is hope that what I think is right *is* right, and try to live up to the honor of being a rebel for the right cause, even if it carries little hope. For inspiration, and a measure of comfort, one can always go to the classics: William Empson, writing of the tragic figure of Satan in John Milton's *Paradise Lost*,[10] echoes Sir Walter Raleigh's remark that Satan's "very situation as the fearless antagonist of Omnipotence made him either a fool or a hero, and Milton is far indeed from permitting us to think him a fool."

Of related interest

To watch:

Akira Kurosawa, *No Regrets for Our Youth* (1946)

Ang Lee, *Crouching Tiger, Hidden Dragon* (2000)

Richard Linklater, *Before Sunset* (2004)

To listen:

Édith Piaf, "Non, je ne regrette rien" ("No, I don't regret anything," 1960)

To read:

Ivan Bunin, *Ида* (*Ida*, 1949)

Vladimir Nabokov, *Ada, or Ardor* (1969)

Michael Swanwick, *The Changeling's Tale* (1994)

To go:

To Wŭdāng Shān.

29   Religion

A rose by any other name. Hanging onto the tiger's tail. The heart of a heartless world. Pride and prejudice.

Feliz el que no insiste en tener razón, porque nadie la tiene o todos la tienen.

(Happy are they that do not insist they are right, for nobody is or all are.)
—Jorge Luis Borges, "Fragments of an Apocryphal Gospel"

Religion is the sigh of the oppressed creature, the heart of a heartless world, and the soul of soulless conditions. It is the *opium* of the people.
—Karl Marx, *Critique of Hegel's Philosophy of Right*

—Что же он велел передать тебе, раб?
—Я не раб, —всё более озлобляясь, ответил Левий Матвей,—я его ученик.
—Мы говорим с тобой на разных языках, как всегда,—отозвался Воланд,—но вещи, о которых мы говорим, от этого не меняются. Итак . . .

(—What, then, did he command you to tell me, slave?
—I am not a slave,—replied Levy Matthew with growing anger,—I am his disciple.
—You and I speak different languages, as always,—replied Woland,—but the things we speak about are not thereby changed. So . . .)
—Mikhail Bulgakov, *Мастер и Маргарита* (*The Master and Margarita*)[1]

A rose by any other name

What distinguishes a moralizing religion from mere "spirituality" is not so much the faith it demands as the dread of doubt and dissent. This distinction is quite general: it is true of any other ideology that prescribes and proscribes behavior. Religious fervor is thus often found in POLITICS, both left and right.

It is quite telling that Karl Marx, who insisted, correctly I think, that "the criticism of religion is the prerequisite of all criticism," was apparently oblivious to the irony of trying to shield his own theory of political economy from any doubt:[2]

> My views . . . are the outcome of conscientious research carried on over many years. At the entrance to science, as at the entrance to hell, the demand must be made:
>
> *Qui si convien lasciare ogni sospetto*
> *Ogni viltà convien che qui sia morta.*

The two lines that Marx quotes are from canto 3 of Dante's *Inferno*, a paean to the Christian Hell: "Here needs must all misgivings straight be check'd; / all craven scruples needs must here be dead." This passage happens to be a gloss (offered by Virgil, Dante's guide through the Inferno) on the famous slogan over the Gate of Hell: *Lasciate ogne speranza, voi ch'intrate*—"Abandon every hope, you that come in."[3]

This motto is nearly universal in its applicability to various special places in our species' collective cultural-historical Hell. It would be equally in place over the gates of Junípero Serra's missions in the Spanish California, where thousands of forcibly converted and enslaved Native Americans have perished,[4] or over the entrance to the Gulag camps, where the bolsheviks incarcerated dissenters (and the clergy).

One may object that the Spanish missionaries had good intentions: saving the souls of the natives from eternal damnation. It is true that past events should be judged in their proper historical context. It is equally true, though, that we should learn from history; and that can only happen if past atrocities are universally recognized as such—first and foremost by the heirs of their perpetrators. The canonization of Serra in 2015 suggests that no such recognition is forthcoming.[5] The lessons of the past have not been learned. Until they are, it will be very difficult to tell apart good intentions—with which the way to Hell is paved, as Marx happens to have remarked in *The Capital*[6]—from STUPIDITY, malice, or a mix thereof (see chapter 31).

Hanging onto the tiger's tail

To the extent that religion makes us stupid, it is generally for our own good. Imagine there is a heaven, into which only those who believe in it are admitted, and a hell, which is reserved for everyone else. Now spread the word about it and see how belief can make a multitude of people accept a life of hardship and hard work for the benefit of a few strangers; how it makes those few feel entitled to their privilege; and how all believers become united against the rest of the world. Everyone is reasonably happy, except the heretics, and who cares about *them*?

It may seem that a prophet is needed to set the wheel of dogma in motion, but cultural EVOLUTION can do it and keep it rolling all by itself, if the belief system is adaptive. Religions often are, in several ways. By promoting in-group cohesion and cooperation against out-groups, a religion can help its adherents compete better.[7] By mitigating discontent among the underprivileged (for instance by promising the faithful an eventual reward), it can stabilize the class system. And by offering to the privileged system justification, it can make them less prone to disillusionment and defection. Unlike merely POLITICAL institutions, which can be short-lived and are easy to subvert, a typical well-tuned religion—especially one that has access to CHILDREN—is long-lived, tamper-resistant, and virtually impossible to stamp out by force.

To pick up a specific example, clinging to their religion is what helped the European Jews to survive and even flourish for centuries in a consistently hostile environment. For Andrew Marvell, writing in the 1650s, the conversion of the Jews was as remote and hypothetical a future event as the biblical flood was a legendary past one: "I would / Love you ten years before the flood, / And you should, if you please, refuse / Till the conversion of the Jews."[8] The proverbial refusal to convert on the part of the Jews, even of those who are not very observant to begin with, may be a kind of halo effect of Judaism's core rituals: as every school kid in Israel is taught, "Far more than the Jews have kept the Sabbath, it is the Sabbath that has kept the Jews."

When fact-checking for this chapter, I realized that I did not know the source of this phrase. Was it some famous rabbi? It turned out it was written by Asher Zvi Hirsch Ginsberg, who went by the pseudonym Ahad Ha'am. In Hebrew, this means "one from the people," or more colloquially "a random guy"—quite the opposite of what Ginsberg actually was: a public intellectual, a writer, and one of the founders and early ideologues of secular political Zionism.[9]

The Zionist movement has always placed a higher value on the survival of the ethnos than on the separation of religion from state—a choice that was only strengthened by the terrible loss sustained by the Jewish people in the Holocaust. When Israel declared independence in 1948, public observance of the Sabbath, along with other key components of Judaism (notably, rabbinical oversight over marriage), was made into law.

What seemed at the time like an innocuous move on the part of the secular, nationalist, and nominally socialist ruling Labor party, intended to make the new state less of an abomination for the orthodox, proved in the long run fateful. Seventy years after independence, a majority of Israel's population self-identifies as religious or traditionalist, while religious parties have gained a stranglehold over Israel's POLITICAL process.[10]

In Israel and elsewhere, politicians often consider their own public policy statements as mere rhetoric, to be owned up to or brushed aside as convenient. In particular, for politicians who make a point of appearing observant, political expediency can easily trump sincerity in matters of both theology and religious praxis, as it does for so many religious leaders who enter politics.[11] It is hard to decide what is sadder: a crooked shepherd abandoning his flock to the wolves, or a true believer falling for his own spiel and getting eaten along with the other sheep. Be that as it may, using religion as a political tool is like trying to hang onto the tail of the proverbial tiger: the would-be rider is likely to end up sprawled on his back, with the tiger's paw across his throat.

The heart of a heartless world

It may serve a wolf in a sheep's clothes right to have its throat ripped out, but what of the real sheep? Even if, as Marx wrote, rejecting religion is the only way toward emancipation, taking it away from those people for whom it is the only solace—in Marx's own expression, "the soul of soulless conditions"—is unspeakably cruel. To hell with emancipation, then—if religion is an effective enough antidote to SUFFERING, well and good then.

Religions differ in their attitude toward suffering as such and in the degree of their concern with its causes. Buddhism, for instance, holds the ubiquity of suffering, *dukkha*, to be the first of its Four Noble Truths. The realization of these leads to the Eightfold Path—a prescription for proper behavior (*dharma*) that brings about salvation. This consists in the abolition of suffering through ending the cycle of rebirth. In this life, suffering may be minimized by following the precepts of the doctrine. This focuses exclusively on the individual sufferer, who is urged to let go of attachments and desires and such. In other words, if you're hungry because you are not paid a living wage, just suck it up.[12]

Catholicism too teaches the poor to expect the real reward only after DEATH (unless the wretch is also a sinner, who deserves everlasting hellfire). Strangely enough, POVERTY itself is praised and extolled as some kind of exalted condition rather than a soul-crushing trap collectively constructed and maintained by the society. Given that Marxism too identifies the poor—the proletariat, the have-nothings—as the spiritually most privileged class, it was only a matter of time before some Catholics and Marxists had a meeting of minds, which came to be called liberation theology. Unfortunately, all that the proponents of this idea have to show after decades of work with the poor is that in practice it boils down to a lot of theology and virtually no liberation.[13]

What good is religion, then, for the regular guy—for "ahad ha'am" who finds it hard to buy into the theology, which is the only ticket to solace, such as it is, that religion offers? There is universal humanistic value to religion—or rather, the world's many religions[14]—which directly inspired some of the best art, literature, and music ever created.[15] Much of this legacy, however, is of little concern to those of us who lack leisure and the means to enjoy it. What everyone, the rich and the poor, do have within easy reach is wonderful cathedrals and temples (built with the people's own hard-earned money, *ad maiorem Dei gloriam*), where they can sit in the same pew and forget, for a while, their divisions, their little worries, and the crushing weight of their EXISTENCE.

Pride and prejudice

Of course, I could be dead wrong in my doubts about theology (to be more precise, the correct theology, whatever it is). This would be a grave mistake, for which I might eventually suffer a terrible fate at the hands (metaphorical or literal, depending on how anthropomorphic the true pantheon is) of the supreme being or beings, should he or she or it or they be inclined to vengeance. Letting the probability, however small, of eternal and therefore infinite agony outweigh the inconvenience of becoming observant for the finite duration of one's life—Pascal's Wager—is not, however, a decision that makes sense to me.

Instead of rehearsing here the rigorous philosophical take-downs of Pascal's Wager,[16] I would like to confess that for as long as I remember, my own rejection of it has been motivated by pride, which in my book is not quite a mortal sin. For one thing, mine is milder than classical Greek hubris: rather than aspiring to fight the gods, I merely refuse to play by their rules—should there *be* any gods that set rules and care to enforce them.

I may be predisposed to this species of pride by the strong prejudice that I have against totalitarian regimes (I had the misfortune, and also the fortune, of having been raised under one) and against their leaders. In Bulgakov's great novel *The Master and Margarita*, it is hinted that Woland, who is Lucifer, had exiled himself from the presence of God because of his disgust with God's authoritarianism—a dig at Stalin, the tyrant who had Bulgakov persecuted to the death.

In a universe where God is like Stalin, I would rather do my poor best to side with Woland. A supreme being that demands blind faith and obedience on the pain of a fate worse than death would be the epitome of MORAL depravity. In the face of an absolute POWER that is absolutely evil, the only proper course of action is disobedience. By refusing to play along here and now, I am merely getting a head start on it.

Of related interest

To watch:
Joel and Ethan Cohen, *Hail Caesar* (2017)

To listen:
The Nooran Sisters, "Dama Dam Mast Kalandar" (2016, live in Dhaka)

To read:
Jorge Luis Borges, "The Approach to Al-Mu'tasim" in *Ficciones* ([1935] 1962a)

Stanisław Lem, "Non Serviam" in *A Perfect Vacuum* ([1971] 1999)

To go:
To Jerusalem; to Rome; to Mecca and Medina; to Bodh Gaya; to Amritsar; to Bubastis; to Karbala; to Teotihuacan; to Balkh; to Ayodhya; to Lhasa; to Varanasi; to Kyoto; to Sinai; to Rub' al Khali; to Arrakis.

Truth to power. The two towers. Power-proofing science.

Lastly, let none be alarmed at the objection of the arts and sciences becoming depraved to malevolent or luxurious purposes and the like, for the same can be said of every worldly good; talent, courage, strength, beauty, riches, light itself, and the rest. Only let mankind regain their rights over nature, assigned to them by the gift of God, and obtain that power whose exercise will be governed by right reason and true religion.

—Francis Bacon, *Novum Organum*[1]

Truth to power

Once upon a time, there lived in a remote galaxy, in a perplexing and secretive universe, a species blessed with curiosity and a sense of enterprise, whose members also had an appetite for POWER. A few of them, who already had more than their share, figured out gradually that even more could be gained by getting hold of more and better knowledge, preferably exclusive of the competition. Then they hit upon a new trick: how to make the universe yield some high-quality knowledge, and how to reinvest this interest to make the principal grow. What could go wrong?

If Francis Bacon, who described the new trick in 1620, sounds modern to our ears, it is because our science, and with it our modernity, are built on the methodological foundations that he helped put in place. The prerequisites of the runaway pursuit of power enabled by science are all there in his *Novum Organum*. On the one hand, there is the identification of knowledge with power: "Human knowledge and human power meet in one." On the other hand, there is the observation that science is self-accelerating: "[The] art of invention can be made to grow with the inventions themselves."

The new method explicitly aimed "to overcome, not an adversary in argument, but nature in action." Bacon's AMBITION had no bounds:

> It will, perhaps, be as well to distinguish three species and degrees of ambition. First, that of men who are anxious to enlarge their own power in their country, which is a vulgar and degenerate kind; next, that of men who strive to enlarge the power and empire of their country over mankind, which is more dignified, but not less covetous; but if one were to endeavour to renew and enlarge the power and empire of mankind in general over the universe, such ambition (if it may so be termed) is both sounder and more noble than the other two.

In hindsight, this passage, like the one in the epigraph, comes across as a piece of exemplary naïveté bordering on STUPIDITY (unless, of course, it is pandering to power). Bacon brands the pursuit of local power as "vulgar and degenerate" and imperial aspirations as "covetous"; yet he extols the idea of domination over the universe as "noble"—as if those who are capable of the latter would willingly give up the former. The concept of "mankind in general" was an empty abstraction in 1620; and the four centuries' worth of POLITICS since then did nothing but demonstrate time and again that it still is.[2]

Science's quest for power over nature soon came to be described in rather violent terms. No less a luminary than Leibniz wrote in 1696 of "the art of inquiry into nature itself and of putting it on the rack—the art of experiment which Lord Bacon began so ably." Two hundred years later, Durant thought he was quoting Bacon himself in resorting to the language of torture, the ultimate exercise of POWER, in describing the mission of science: "We 'put nature on the rack and compel her to bear witness' against herself."[3]

Were science as ineffective as torture in getting at the TRUTH of the matter under investigation, it would have been merely one of the many human flights of fancy, perhaps another RELIGION.[4] However, imperfect as it is,[5] science does occasionally yield testable, enduring, and even useful truths, which are assimilated into a growing body of knowledge that has long since exceeded any individual human's capacity for understanding.

This in itself makes many people resentful: we do not like giving up our opinions, even in the face of overwhelming evidence and the expertise of others.[6] And of course any new truth can prove to be a thorn in the side of vested interests and existing power structures.[7] But the situation is under control. The truth shall only make you free if it is both seen and thoroughly understood by you, and real truths, which are too inconvenient to accept, are often easy to hide and in any case too complicated to grasp when revealed.

The two towers

In light of scientific TRUTH's potential for wreaking havoc in the established order, one wonders how science has been allowed to build and keep its castles, the research universities (science's outposts in corporate research pursue primarily applied TECHNOLOGY). Not only is academic science founded on an explicit disdain of POWER, as per the Latin motto *nullius addictus iurare in verba magistri* (not obliged to swear allegiance to a master);[8] the university also shelters that other notorious source of inconvenient truths—the humanities. And most puzzling of all is the power elites' eagerness to send their children to be educated by the unreliable types who teach there.[9]

All this makes sense if power, in its tower of iron, has not so far felt sufficiently threatened by what is going on in the proverbial ivory tower of academe. The continued gain from new TECHNOLOGIES, much of which depends on letting universities be, must have justified whatever danger they present. Not that the danger is too dire: if the universities look like hotbeds of free THINKING and dissidence, it is because there is so little of that stuff on the outside.

In its administrative structure, the university is actually both conservative and conforming to society-wide practices. The ultimate authority, which can fire even tenured faculty, is the board of trustees. In the best corporate tradition, it consists of "business leaders" and rich alumni (hence the constant pressure on the administration to run the place like a business and to starve the humanities). Academic units are ruled by university-appointed deans—former faculty members with a penchant for control, who spend most of their time fundraising and tend to side with the administration in all practical matters. Discretionary budget can only be obtained by seeking extramural funding from government agencies, corporations, or foundations, whose respective agendas are determined by considerations of POLITICS, profit, and the founder's reputation—not science or scholarship for its own sake.[10]

Those faculty members who can make do without external funding may enjoy an amazing amount of freedom, if they have the good luck to be tenured at a progressive university that still manages to adhere to its charter despite political and corporate pressures.[11] Most such faculty seem content working and teaching within the boundaries of their discipline. In research, transcending these boundaries is praised in principle but discouraged in practice through withholding of support.[12] As to teaching, while engagement with "difficult" topics such as politics and social justice is tolerated and may even be encouraged, it is probably because the real world is left unchanged by it, as the students who have experienced the thrill of intellectual subversion in a seminar or two in their senior year head on to Wall Street.

Power-proofing science

Meanwhile in the remote galaxy, some members of the enterprising and knowledge-hungry species that discovered science become uneasy with how all the knowledge it generates seems to get commandeered by enterprise. The difficulty, they realize, lies in their very nature: without their lust for power or their drive for knowledge, they would not be who they are. But isn't science just the thing for dealing with even the hardest problems that the perplexing and secretive universe throws their way? They get down to work. After a while, success!—science discovers a way to make itself power-proof. And they all live happily ever after.[13]

Of related interest

To watch:

Stanley Kubrik, *Dr. Strangelove or: How I Learned to Stop Worrying and Love the Bomb* (1964)

To read:

Arkady and Boris Strugatsky, *За миллиард лет до конца света* (*A Billion Years before the End of the World*; published in English as *Definitely Maybe*, 1978)

To go:

To CERN.

31 Stupidity

Human, all too human. An eclipse of common sense. The wages of folly.
Worse than a fool. The stupidity of crowds. The unholy trinity.

In order to give a proper outline of the concept of stupidity [Dummheit] it is
first of all necessary to dispose of the notion that stupidity is merely, or mainly,
a deficiency of the intellect.
—Robert Musil, "On Stupidity"

Mit der Dummheit kämpfen Götter selbst vergebens.

(Against stupidity the gods themselves contend in vain.)
—Friedrich Schiller, *Die Jungfrau von Orleans*, act 3, scene 6

Простота хуже воровства.

(Simplemindedness is worse than thievery.)
—Russian proverb

Human, all too human

Putting one's thoughts in writing and offering them to the public is generally a risky business. As Clement of Alexandria noted in the preface to his
Miscellanies, published around 200 AD, doing so is like "reaching a sword
to a child": written words are easy for a reader to misunderstand but not
easy for the author to explicate or defend. Writers of fiction can try to hide
behind a sense of superiority or the artist's privilege (as did Faulkner, who,
when told that some people can't understand his writing even when they
read it two or three times suggested that they read it four times[1]). This
defense on the part of the author is, however, less effective in the case of
nonfiction; and when the topic is stupidity, it becomes self-undermining.

Writing about stupidity puts one in a double bind. On the one hand, to diagnose stupidity in others, I myself must not be afflicted with it too strongly; on the other hand, denial of one's own stupidity is one of the most reliable symptoms of this malaise. If I were smart, I would therefore refrain from writing about stupidity—indeed, from writing altogether, if I were *really* smart.[2] These very lines are thus a case in point with regard to the topic of stupidity. In taking it up, my hope is to make some sense of folly, starting with my own, as well as to be able to add to what my betters, such as Robert Musil or Stanisław Lem, had to say on such matters. If this turns out to be a fool's hope, then at least the stupidity of biting off more than one can chew will have been roundly demonstrated, and I will have proved my practical, if not analytical, qualifications for bringing it up.

An eclipse of common sense

The concept of stupidity that I am concerned with here has little to do with how much one knows or how good or quick one is at putting two and two together. I can therefore safely avoid discussing the psychological traits of erudition and intelligence, on which so much has been written.[3] The kind of stupidity that interests me is defined not by one's traits, but rather by one's behavior: in Forrest Gump's words, "stupid is as stupid does."

Conceiving of stupidity in this manner has useful implications for interpersonal dynamics. Calling someone stupid to put them down may help me feel better, but is unlikely to make them smarter or to make them behave better. Better call out their stupid ACTION instead, on the off chance that it would help them see the situation in a more constructive light, especially if I am polite about it and if it is understood that anyone, including myself, may have acted equally stupidly under the circumstances.

Focusing on actions instead of traits helps one avoid the double bind I mentioned earlier: it can be possible for me to discern stupidity in others, in some respects and on some occasions, even if in other respects and on other occasions I myself behave quite stupidly. Encouraging others to call out one's folly makes sense also in light of people's well-documented obliviousness to their own flawed character and performance—the Dunning-Kruger effect. Just like the scratching of one's back, the assessment of one's own limitations, including operational stupidity, works best when done by others.[4]

Unfortunately, people's aversion to being perceived as foolish—even if it's clearly a matter of a temporary eclipse of common sense rather than a systemic lack thereof—is such that candid comments intended for the better are often ineffectual and may well backfire. This in turn discourages potential commenters, as I can attest, in retrospect, having held often enough onto each of the two ends of this stick. Hindsight is the key in this matter: my two biggest REGRETS in life are not to have attained insight into operational stupidity early enough for it to really matter, and not to be able to keep it in mind at all times after attaining it.

The wages of folly

In a just world, a stupid act would have consequences only for the actor. Stupidity, which Musil saw as "not so much of a lack of intelligence as its failure," would then be a kind of pratfall, at times perhaps even amusing. In reality, though, we should not be hasty with schadenfreude, lest the joke in the end be on us. The consequences of stupidity on the part of the people in our social circle—family, friends, acquaintances, public figures—are likely to affect us, and rarely in a good way.[5]

Come to think of it, the entire business of stupidity is altogether too dismal to joke, let alone be glad, about. If the fool of the moment could not have known better because he or she is not smart or educated enough, it would seem that our MORAL duty is to EMPATHIZE, not condemn (ourselves we are ready to pity without having to be prompted). Now, pity is an emotion that is difficult enough to call up on demand; and it takes a saint to feel pity toward someone who harms you—even if they do so unwittingly (as in "lacking the wits not to"). So Jan Hus, while being burned at the stake for his RELIGION (by the adherents of a variant of the very same religion), exclaimed, upon seeing a peasant woman add a little brushwood to the fire, "sancta simplicitas"—holy simplicity.

The Russian proverb in the epigraph has less patience for simplicity, which it proclaims to be worse than thievery. I like to read this not as moral condemnation but as a statement of practical indignation: someone has acted like a damn fool, and now we have to suffer the consequences. Withholding condemnation is hard, though—especially after sustaining collateral damage from a stupid act of someone who is smart and well educated and thus *should have known better* than act like a fool.

Worse than a fool

Another Russian saying—"Что хуже дурака? Дурак с инициативой" (What is worse than a fool? A fool with initiative)—subtly recognizes stupidity as a blind force of nature, by using the impersonal "what" instead of "who." One can easily extend this line of thinking. Consider that people with AMBI-TION and initiative, including those who happen to be not occasional but habitual fools, are more likely than the rest of us to advance to a position of POWER, where a stupid act is, in turn, likely to have much more far-ranging repercussions. Consider also that a smart person is more likely to fall into the hubris of believing, without a good reason, to know what's better for someone else or for the general public. And when the stupidity arising out of hubris is amplified by power, we all better run for cover.

The stupidity of crowds

We ain't done yet: the potential for harm from the stupid acts of a hubristic potentate is more than matched by that of a crowd of ordinary people—that is, of people who occasionally behave stupidly, and who have been united by some common cause, such as a political party or movement, imperial aspirations, or a nation-state.[6] Robert Musil noted the link between POLI-TICS and stupidity, in an address delivered in 1937—a bad year, when the Nazis were preparing to take over his native Austria, when Guernica was bombed, when Stalin's mass murder campaign was at its peak, when the Imperial Japanese Army massacred the citizens of Nanking, when Domini-can Republic troops killed thousands of Haitians, when Italian fascists com-mitted the massacre of Addis Ababa, and when the Chicago police shot at and killed unarmed strikers.

Although the rest of the twentieth century is nothing to be proud of either, it looks like its contribution to the march of folly will be outdone by the century that followed it. Stupidity assisted by TECHNOLOGY has always been more damaging than in the state of nature, and in the case of mili-tary technology, not just more damaging but also more deadly. With the development of globe-spanning instant communication technology and the social media that it supports, the effects of individual and mass stupid-ity are primed to grow exponentially. I do not need to recount them here; for some recent examples, refresh your newsfeed.

The unholy trinity

Let's not get carried away, though, with indicting stupidity alone for the ills of the age. The question that needs to be asked is "Cui bono?" (Who profits?)—a staple of Roman jurisprudence. Who profits from stupidity in politics and the public sphere? Not the stupid themselves: Carlo Cipolla, who was an economist, held that stupid people are those whose acts leave themselves, as well as others, worse off. And what traits characterize those who would want you to think that only stupidity, as a trait, is to blame? A reasonable guess would be intelligence and malice.

The reasons behind this guess are straightforward: because malice needs cover, because intelligence can provide it, and because the best defense strategy is not to deny wrongdoing but to shift blame. Musil remarks that the combination of intelligence with malice leads to the worst kind of behavior and, for the victims, the worst outcomes. I would like to elaborate on this observation: intelligence and malice are at their worst when they have stupidity to take advantage of. This leads to my variant of Hanlon's Razor: never attribute to stupidity or malice alone what is best explained by an intelligent exploitation of stupidity by malice.

What hope is there of keeping this hybrid monster, which is wholly our own creation, at bay? Because stupidity is ubiquitous and is not going anywhere, the best bet may be to make people more aware of it, while chipping away at the alliance between intelligence and malice—in short, by teaching benevolence and humility. If there ever was something that's easier said than done, this just might be it.[7]

Of related interest

To watch:
John Boorman, *Zardoz* (1974)
Robert Zemekis, *Forrest Gump* (1994)
A mirror
To listen:
The news
Any national anthem

To read:

Robert Musil, "On Stupidity" ([1937] 1979)

John Brunner, *The Compleat Traveller in Black* (originally *The Traveler in Black*, [1971] 1982)

Stanisław Lem, *The Star Diaries* (1981)

Any issue of *Mad Magazine* (https://www.madmagazine.com/)

To go:

To the pyramids.

32 Suffering

Mindsets. Varieties. Mechanisms. Options.

In the beast, suffering is self-confined; in man, it knocks holes into a fear of the world and a despair of life.

—Peter Wessel Zapffe, "The Last Messiah"

Durch Leiden Licht

(Through suffering, light)

—Venedict Erofeev, *Москва-Петушки* (*Moscow to the End of the Line*)

Dichosos los que saben que el sufrimiento no es una corona de gloria.

(Blessed are those who know that suffering is not a crown of glory.)

—Jorge Luis Borges, "Fragments of an Apocryphal Gospel"[1]

Mindsets

If indeed there is nothing glorious about suffering, the proper attitude toward it is the stoical one: acknowledge its dominion, perhaps under protest, but without dignifying the faceless oppressor with complaints. One can hardly go about it better than Borges has done, in a passage dedicating his famous essay on TIME to his great-grandfather: "He died in exile; like all men, he was given bad times in which to live."[2]

For better or for worse, the notion that in life one must not complain too much if at all has been impressed on me by my father. The closest it came to having been made explicit was in two classical stories that he told me when I was eight or nine. The first one was Roman, from the sixth century BCE, about one Gaius Mucius, who came to be called Scaevola ("left-handed") after thrusting his right hand into a fire to impress his Clusian captors. The second story, which I later found in Plutarch's *Lycurgus*, told of a Spartan schoolboy who smuggled a fox into class under his cloak and suffered it to gnaw through his side rather than reveal its presence to the teacher.[3]

It must have been for a reason that neither story has anything to do with "natural" suffering, of the kind inflicted by hunger, disease, heartbreak, or disillusionment. My father must have placed a higher value on preparing me for dealing with adversity—to the extent that sticking through without flinching can be considered dealing with it—than on teaching me to recognize WAR propaganda, be it Roman, Spartan, or modern; EMPATHY wasn't even mentioned. He himself certainly practiced what he preached: he never complained about anything in his past. This, as I eventually learned bit by bit, included not only having fought the Nazis in World War II, but also imprisonment on a political charge by the Soviets, followed by nine and a half years in the Siberian forced labor camps. Never discussing any of that stuff spared him the sympathy of others, as well as the need to sympathize in return.

The nature and scope of human suffering is such that, no matter how hard *you* have it, it is a virtual certainty that there are people out there who have it harder. In my father's case, when the authorities found out that he had completed a couple of years of medical school before being drafted, he was sent to work in the labor camp's sick bay, which probably saved his life. Instead of having to chop and haul wood in subzero temperatures on a starvation ration, he was tasked with triaging inmates who collapsed overnight, separating the nearly dead from the slowly dying: the sick, the exhausted, the ones hanging by a thread. Only after he passed away, I learned from my mother that he had nightmares about this until his last days.

Such horror stories, an unlimited supply of which from all over the world is made available by the "news" TECHNOLOGY, can have a numbing effect on one's perception of suffering, both one's own and that of others. If that's what life is like, I better harden my heart against EMPATHY before it overwhelms me. And my conscience need not bother me as long as I include myself among those whose misery I manage to overlook.

It may take a very long time for such numbness to pass. When I first picked up Ursula Le Guin's *The Dispossessed*, in my twenties, her hero Shevek's musings[4] seemed to me dishonorable and deplorable:

> Suffering is the condition on which we live. And when it comes you know it. You know it as the truth. Of course it's right to cure diseases, to prevent hunger and injustice, as the social organism does. But no society can change the nature of its existence. We can't prevent suffering. This pain and that pain, yes, but not Pain. A society can only relieve social suffering—unnecessary suffering. The rest remains. The root, the reality.

Hadn't I just escaped injustice, by leaving Soviet Russia for the "free West"? And doesn't hunger only ever happen to others? As to pain . . . pain is not something that should be brought up in polite society (a STUPID notion, which also runs counter to a key EVOLUTION-sanctioned human trait[5]). I sold my copy of *The Dispossessed* back to the secondhand bookstore.

Years later, a changed me decided to give it another chance (having read everything else that Le Guin wrote may have helped the change along). I found myself in tears over one passage after another—so much easier than lowering my shields altogether, yet maybe better than nothing. There is gloom out there, but keeping one's eyes shut plays into the hands of a deeper darkness.

Varieties

A universal catalog of human suffering, should one ever be compiled, might arrange its varieties along two continua: social to personal, and unnecessary (in Le Guin's phrasing) to unavoidable.[6] On the social side, there are the preventable ravages of POVERTY: hunger, illness, ignominy, humiliation. They hinge on the POWER of the rich and the passivity of the poor (excepting those who are brainwashed and beaten into submission from birth and thus cannot be blamed for their condition). In comparison, there are kinds of social suffering that appear to be unavoidable, such as the pain of someone who is rejected for being different (there is no historical precedent for a perfectly tolerant society).

On the personal side, much of the suffering seems preventable (or would be, if POWER were not so deeply invested in the status quo). The combination of progress in medical SCIENCE, proper education, and attention to mental health would go far in helping people make the best of their lives. There are, however, ways of suffering that no amount of progress can touch, because they arise out of the interplay of our human-animal nature and our human CONSCIOUSNESS. One of these is, paradoxically, HAPPINESS, a relentless pursuit of which is programmed deep into human nature. Another one is the awareness of DEATH. Despairing of happiness and submitting to death ANXIETY may induce severe psychological distress or psychache;[7] at the same time, intervening on the root causes of these conditions runs the risk of turning the sufferer into someone or something else.

The profitability of the status quo distorts the very conception of personal suffering, as it is being sold to the public that does not know better. The depression of the unemployed, the anger of the disenfranchised, the listlessness of the overworked—all are medicalized and treated as psychiatric disorders. By displacing and suppressing the traditional human takes on suffering—RELIGIOUS, EXISTENTIAL, MORAL, and POLITICAL—medicalization perpetuates ignorance about the true causes of misery, while enriching a few at the expense of the many. Yet even those few may be worse off for it, as they succumb to the lies and the lure of the very system that they exploit.[8]

Mechanisms

Were it possible for everyone to shut out their own suffering at will, there would be not much point to the book you're reading, nor to any other jeremiad or exposé about the "human condition." But it is not possible. Worse, we seem to be the butt of an unkind joke—it is profoundly ironic that there is one and only one aspect of the entire world that PERCEPTION constructs and CONSCIOUSNESS inhabits that can be unconditionally trusted: pain and suffering.

For whatever it is worth, thanks to an alliance of SCIENCE and philosophy, we now have a pretty good idea why this is so. There are four preconditions to suffering: possessing basic phenomenal CONSCIOUSNESS, which consists in having a *felt* model of the world; having a *self*-model included in it; being able to feel *bad* about things; and what Thomas Metzinger called "Mother Nature's most evil trick"—being made to *identify* with feeling bad, which is what makes suffering inexorably personal. The human mind/brain meets all four of these conditions, crowning it with the ability to figure out how it all works. To understand this is to see why there could have been no other way for *us*, as human animals, to be.[9]

Options

Suffering is built into what we are, and it is impossible to do away with some of its varieties without at the same time doing away with the sufferer. Because of this, the amount of suffering accrued by the world keeps growing in proportion to the number of people who have lived. That the amount of HAPPINESS also grows is irrelevant: suffering cannot be compensated for by the same person's being happy at another TIME, let alone by someone else being happy.

What can be done about suffering, then? One recourse is what I called "The Switch" in chapter 8—quoting Metzinger, "The first option, quite obviously, would consist in painlessly and unexpectedly killing all sentient beings."[10] Of course, having one's Switch controlled by someone else would be MORALLY unacceptable; and given how much we value EXISTENCE,[11] having The Switch under one's personal control is in itself an agonizingly heavy burden (remember Hamlet trying to decide whether to be or not to be). Each of the remaining options has to do with one of the necessary conditions for suffering listed earlier: give up the basic phenomenal CONSCIOUSNESS; or dissolve the self; or abolish negative emotions; or stop identifying with them.

Whether or not in the future these options prove to be technically feasible and personally tolerable, there is no excuse not to do what *can* be done right away: attend to those kinds of suffering, social or personal, that can be alleviated. It may not even be necessary to wait for everyone's EMPATHY to kick in, as long as our collective THINKING is on the right track.[12] Witness the forty-third title in *Los Caprichos*, Francisco Goya's graphical litany of human suffering and STUPIDITY: "El sueño de la razón produce monstruos"; it is the sleep of reason that produces monsters.

Of related interest

To watch:

Ki-Duk Kim, *Spring, Summer, Fall, Winter . . . and Spring* (2003)

Costas Ferris, *Rembetiko* (1983)

To listen:

Pink Floyd, "Comfortably Numb" (from *The Wall*, 1979)

To read:

William Shakespeare, Sonnet LXVI

Venedict Erofeev, *Москва-Петушки* (*Moscow to the End of the Line*, [1969] 1992)

Philip K. Dick, *Martian Time-Slip* (1976)

Stanisław Lem, *One Human Minute* (1986)

Thomas Ligotti, *The Conspiracy against the Human Race: A Contrivance of Horror* (2010)

To go:

To the End of the Line (see Erofeev, above, for detailed directions).

33 Technology

Comfortably numb. The fiery sword. Cura te ipsum.

If it should turn out to be true that knowledge (in the modern sense of know-how) and thought have parted company for good, then we would indeed become the helpless slaves, not so much of our machines as of our know-how, thoughtless creatures at the mercy of every gadget which is technically possible, no matter how murderous it is.

—Hannah Arendt, *The Human Condition*[1]

Comfortably numb

Just as Hannah Arendt was afraid they might, our technological know-how and our moral thought have proved to be estranged from each other—not because they parted ways, but because they never really kept each other's company in the first place.

Technology is more than this or that specific product of applied science, such as insulin: it is the know-how that makes it possible, which for insulin includes analytic chemistry, recombinant DNA, and many other fields and methods. From this perspective, there is not a single technology that can claim to be a pure boon for our species and for our planet, which we share with others. Any technology can create more problems than it solves, or it can be misused; and for every new one, things somehow always work out so that it eventually does or is.

Why is this so? The proliferation of unforeseen consequences is the direct result of the COMPLEXITY of the human mind, of human societies, and of the ecology of the physical environment; and the preponderance of such consequences being adverse rather than benign can be blamed, to begin with, on thermodynamics.[2] As to misuse, because technology brings POWER, the traditional coalition of malice and STUPIDITY is ever looking to exploit it.

These factors, however, stop short of explaining the particular and pronounced helplessness of MORAL thinking in the face of unrelenting technological "progress." Something else is at work here: our infinite craving for comfort and convenience.[3] If a relatively affordable gadget or service becomes available that can make my life in the short run marginally easier or more enjoyable, I would be hard-pressed to reject it just because it may have negative broader or longer-range side effects. This is how we get digital devices that turn over our personal lives to corporate profit-seekers,[4] energy consumption habits that have already irreversibly damaged climate on a planetary scale,[5] and an entertainment ecosystem that keeps us comfortably numb while the world burns.

The fiery sword

As with many of the other topics in this book, the less-than-glowing current state of affairs with regard to technology prompts one to ask: will things ever change to the better? If you have been reading the chapters in the alphabetical order, your expectations for positive news this far along into the book should be low and in that you would be right. The immediate reason for this is that the dynamics of technological advances is at present shaped by its setting: the unregulated, no-holds-barred competitive global marketplace.

It is worth remembering that the global economy is and will remain ultra-capitalist even if a large number of individual nation-states come to be governed by less extreme "social democrats." In this POLITICAL setting, any technology that can be exploited by some players for short-term profit, no matter how destructive it may be for others, or even for its wielders in the long run, will be so exploited. Not to mince words, we are screwed—profoundly and repeatedly, by circumstances that are an integral part of what we are.[6] In the words of Horkheimer and Adorno's *Dialectic of Enlightenment*,[7]

> The angel which, with fiery sword, drove humans out of paradise and on to the path of technical progress, is itself the symbol of that progress.

Cura te ipsum

If technology could lift us out of miserable subsistence, scavenging for carrion scraps left by hyenas and digging for grubs in rotten wood,[8] if it can cure disease, and abolish hunger, maybe it can fix other things too. Here is a partial list of things that need fixing: (1) action, (2) ambition, (3) anxiety, (4) beauty, (5) children, the raising of, (6) complexity, (7) consciousness, (8) death, (9) empathy, (10) emptiness, (11) evolution, (12) existence, (13) fear, (14) free will, (15) happiness, (16) home, (17) language, (18) love, (19) mathematics, (20) memory, (21) morality, (22) old age, (23) parents, the liberation from, (24) perception, (25) politics, (26) power, (27) poverty, (28) regret, (29) religion, (30) science, (31) stupidity, (32) suffering, (33) technology, (34) thinking, (35) time, (36) truth, (37) war, (38) youth.

Number 33 would be especially nice to crack. It's a tough one, but this doesn't mean we shouldn't try. We may be in for a pleasant surprise.

Of related interest

To watch:

Charlie Brooker and Annabel Jones, *Black Mirror* (2011–2014)

Sam Esmail, *Mr. Robot* (2015–2019)

To listen:

Pink Floyd, "Welcome to the Machine" (from *Wish You Were Here*, 1975)

To read:

Walter M. Miller Jr., *A Canticle for Leibowitz* (1959)

Harlan Ellison, "I Have No Mouth, and I Must Scream" (1967)

Ursula K. Le Guin, *The Word for World Is Forest* (1972)

To go:

Set the controls for the heart of the sun.

34 Thinking

Transitional. Treacherous. Transgressional.

"There are only two kinds of people."
   "Humans and animals?"
   "No. The kind of people who say, 'There are two kinds of people' and the kind of people who don't."
—Ursula K. Le Guin, *Buffalo Gals*

Enlightenment is totalitarian.
—Max Horkheimer and Theodor W. Adorno, *Dialectic of Enlightenment*

Nothing's sacred for those who think.
—Wisława Szymborska, "An Opinion on the Question of Pornography"

Tantôt je pense, et tantôt je suis.

(Sometimes I think, and sometimes I am)
—Paul Valéry, *Discours aux Chirurgiens*[1]

Transitional

In a more logical ordering of inconvenient truths than the alphabetical one of this book, thinking would occupy a very special place. At the beginning, there would be EXISTENCE: had we not existed, there clearly would *be*, for us, no inconvenience. Next in line is CONSCIOUSNESS: had we existed, but not in a conscious state—no inconvenience. Then, critically, thinking: had we existed, and been conscious, and yet lacking the capacity for reasoning about our absurd condition, we would not have been any worse off than all those other beings that have sentience but no sense, and whose SUFFERING is therefore not compounded by insight into its causes.[2]

Thinking is a transitional attribute, a umbilical that both connects us with other kinds of animals and sets us apart. All animals think. In their natural environment, many nonhuman animals routinely weigh evidence and make rational decisions, discover causal relationships between events, anticipate the future and make plans, solve problems, invent tools and learn how to use them by observing others, and even reason and learn counterfactually about what could have happened, had they undertaken a particular ACTION in the past.[3]

If some of us can do these things better and maybe can also pull off an extra-special trick or two, it is because not too long ago our ancestors have worked out the ultimate trick, LANGUAGE. With its EVOLUTIONARY origins in social activity (toolmaking and tool use pedagogy), language became our most powerful meta-tool. It was language that made possible sustained deliberative imagination and supercharged cumulative culture, TECHNOL-OGY, MATHEMATICS, and SCIENCE.[4]

Language and its cultural dividends allowed our species to construct a rather expansive niche for itself, within which, moreover, we dominate all other species. But that does not mean that as individuals we are infinitely smarter than those others—definitely not when competing on their terms and their home turf. Any human affecting a personal sense of overweening technological superiority should try surviving alone in the wilderness for a few weeks without recourse to tools, dry rations, or any other legacy of the millions who came before. As to intellectual superiority, the solo survivor is always welcome to do some philosophy or math or science on the side, or perhaps write a novel (try blackberry juice on tree bark).

For those who are spared the FEAR for survival and the ANXIETY induced by POVERTY and who can afford to take time out of their daily routine to think, it is easy to believe themselves capable of perfectly sound and dispassion-ate reasoning. There is, however, little ground for this self-flattering belief. Because it evolved alongside emotions as a means of behavioral control, our faculty of reason is mired in motivations, feelings, and "seat-of-the-pants" thinking. In abstract domains such as MATHEMATICS, one may feel safely insu-lated from those base goings-on (at least for as long as food and shelter are provided), but any attempt to make use of the abstractions immedi-ately brings them down to earth. Our routine thinking is never free: our thoughts drag an emotional load behind them like a ball on a chain and are in turn dragged by inchoate and often obscure motives.[5]

Treacherous

In their *Dialectic of Enlightenment,* Horkheimer and Adorno argue that it is not reason's entanglement with emotions that we should be wary of, but rather the opposite. Reason's inherent and non-negotiable claim to absolute supremacy in human affairs, aided by humanity's collective millennia-long effort to make it so, culminates in its becoming an elemental power:

> Thought . . . has always been equal to the task of concretely demonstrating its own equivocal nature. It is the servant which the master cannot control at will.[6]

Lessons from MATHEMATICS, cognitive psychology, the science of COMPLEXITY, and EVOLUTION support this historical and sociological analysis and reveal even more dimensions of dialectical tension. Of all the modes of reasoning, only deduction—the derivation of statements that are logically implied by given axioms or data—is TRUTH-preserving. One does not have to be very smart to carry out deductive reasoning (this is why theorem-proving was the first human activity that artificial intelligence researchers attempted to replicate). Ensuring that the premises are sound (truth maintenance) is, however, a task that can quickly become too complex for a creature with finite resources and lifespan.

Moreover, truths about the world, which is what we need the premises to be, can only be discovered through *inductive* inference (the key tool and the defining characteristic of SCIENCE). Unlike deductive reasoning, induction is fallible: a learner is never logically guaranteed to have attained all and only the correct beliefs about the world. Finally, drawing conclusions about the specific situation at hand in light of the prior beliefs and the data requires "reasoning to the best explanation"—a process that is sometimes referred to as "abduction" and that is also not guaranteed to be logically sound or even statistically optimal.[7]

But wait: all these insights into the nature of reason and its limitations are themselves derived from our best guess—one based on reason—as to what the world is like and how the mind works. Reason thus undermines itself when it claims absolute superiority; and it ceases to be immune to mysticism and skepticism if it admits that some aspects of the lives of the would-be "rational animals" are exempt from being ruled by it.

Avoiding both a totalitarian devotion to reason and the all-consuming skepticism that results from its total rejection is like walking a tightrope: it takes practice to master and is always dangerous, but it is not impossible.[8] As a first step, one may consider Hume's famous pronouncement: "Reason is and ought only to be the slave of the passions."[9] In itself it may be taking things too far, but maintaining mutual respect and a working relationship between reason and "passions" is definitely in line with our EVOLUTIONARY heritage, which for once we would do well to hew to.

This recipe works best when paired with an effort to keep our beliefs and inferences properly sorted, so that logical consistency needs only be maintained locally, within certain domains (assuming that logic even applies there). It is perfectly fine to insist on seeking help from medical science for a fever, while recognizing that exhaustive logical reasoning is unlikely to be of much use in matters of LOVE. And if keeping these things straight feels at times like too heavy a burden, seek respite in Walt Whitman: "Do I contradict myself? / Very well then I contradict myself, / (I am large, I contain multitudes.)"[10]

Transgressional

There is one respect in which putting strictures on reason this late in the game is like closing the doors of the barn after the horses have bolted. The policies of Enlightenment having had less than an impressive success, to say the least, in solving humanity's problems, it is hard to see how reason can be trusted even within the domains that it can reasonably claim for its own, such as governance. Our capacity for reasoning is powerful enough to hold a mirror to ourselves and help us realize our predicament, yet so far it has proved to be powerless at working out a way to fix our condition once and for all, or even just working out an acceptable MORAL basis for doing so.

Our helplessness in this regard is due in part to the objective COMPLEXITY of the problems we face as a society and in part to the fact, noted earlier, that the conclusions that reason can reach can only be as good as the premises from which it works. The first order of business in improving one's situation is to recognize that there is a problem to be solved; and the second one is to correctly identify the problem. Our collective failure to do either in POLITICS may explain why a vast majority of the world's population is stuck with systems of government that are inimical to individual and societal flourishing.

To get unstuck, one must learn to reason creatively, by actively looking for and examining the hidden premises that anchor the prevailing consensus.[11] A generally useful meta-premise, popularly attributed to Rosa Luxemburg, applies here: those who do not move, do not notice their chains.[12] Chains that *have* been noticed will not last for long:[13]

> Revolution begins in the thinking mind.

And if on the morning after the revolution we find ourselves bound by new chains of our own forging—well, at least there would be the satisfaction of knowing that we have tried; and we can always try again.

Of related interest

To watch:

Berthold Bartosch, *L'Idée* (1932)

To listen:

Daniel Kahn & The Painted Bird, "Думай" ("Think," 2009)

To read:

Hermann Hesse, *The Glass Bead Game* (1949)

Stanisław Lem, "Golem XIV" in *Imaginary Magnitude* (1984)

To go:

To Castalia, for a while; then to the farmers' market near where you live.

35 Time

The sandstorm. Faster, slower, true. The tyranny of now. The arrow of time.

Ветер есть время, изображённое средствами пространства.

(Wind is time, rendered by means of space.)
—Marina Vishnevetskaya, Увидеть дерево (*To Behold a Tree*)[1]

Verweile doch! du bist so schön!

(Stay[, moment]! You are so beautiful!)
—Johann Wolfgang von Goethe, *Faust*[2]

The sandstorm

To feel the full force of the passage of time, arrange for yourself to experience a desert sandstorm. Once, on a hiking trip in Death Valley, my son I. and I were caught unawares by such a storm. We had been in the backcountry and off the grid for a while and so had missed the wind advisory posted online. As the sun was about to set behind the Last Chance range, we arrived at the western end of the long Racetrack Valley and pitched our tents. As we were waiting for the dinner to cook, I. drew my attention to a curious haze that had just appeared over the mountain pass on the far side of the valley, fifteen miles east from our camp. I told him not to worry.

The rapidly approaching cloud, illuminated by the dying light, visibly marked off minutes by swallowing up more and more of the valley. When the wall of flying sand finally hit us a short while later, we took shelter in the jeep and found ourselves in an inside-out hourglass of sorts, where most of the sand was outside and seemed to be moving in all directions at once. As I ventured out to retrieve the tent stakes (which I had left behind earlier, when taking down the tents, in the hope that the storm would pass us by after all), the abrasive wind made me feel the passage of every second with my very skin.

As the storm showed no signs of abating, I. and I decided to leave the valley and search for a calmer place. On the long night drive through the mountains, traveling in a bubble of murky light shot through with horizontal streaks of flying sand, we came across several local creatures: a jackrabbit, an owl perched on a mound of gravel, a rattlesnake winding sideways across the track, in a rush to put some distance between itself and the deadly humans. None of them seemed to mind either the storm or the passage of time.

Faster, slower, true

The sense of time is not unique to humans (the lives of many species are organized around an approximate twenty-four hour cycle, driven by a built-in "circadian clock"), but we are the only animals on this planet who can think *about* time. Now, if THINKING in general is a risky business, which may put you at the mercy of thoughts that are not to your liking, thinking about time is virtually guaranteed to do so. It is not only that thinking about time reminds you of what happens when it starts to run short, in OLD AGE, or runs out altogether, as DEATH catches up with you. Taking notice of time is also liable to break a happy spell by reminding you that it is bound to end[3]—a downside that is hardly compensated for by the upside, such as it is, of easing SUFFERING during an unhappy spell by invoking the Sufi time-passage mantra, "This too shall pass."[4]

Subjective time gives us the short end of the stick also in how, when we are happy, it seems to fly, but when we're sad, it slows down to a crawl. What about estimating objective duration? We may correctly judge an awkward conversation as having lasted exactly five minutes, while complaining that it *felt* like the longest five minutes ever. And yet, the precision of our explicit estimates of objective time may also depend on mood and on emotion. In depression—when time feels as if it barely moves—we're at our most precise in mentally counting off seconds and minutes.[5] Conversely, in a stressful situation (think bungee jumping), time seems to slow down and we judge time intervals to be longer than they actually are—presumably, because our internal clock is speeded up by emotional arousal.[6]

There is a certain air of paradox surrounding our sense of time. If we do have a built-in clock, why not just use it to be always precise and avoid illusions?[7] Because EVOLUTION. Evolution is a sloppy, opportunistic tinkerer, not a perfect, minimalistic designer, and so what passes for our "internal clock" is far from being based on a single computational process or a single molecular or neural mechanism: it is a hodge-podge of different biological means of measuring time, each of which may be influenced by many things.[8] Chances are this sensitivity in itself is not a bug, but a feature: as always, evolution knows best what's good for you, in the only sense that it "cares" about (lifetime inclusive fitness). Presumably, the pattern of distortions and precision across tasks and contexts in one's perception of time works better in the long run than marching to the beat of a perfect clock. And, as always, evolution's gift goes underappreciated: in the interplay between our sense of time and our emotions, just like in the ebb and flow of HAPPINESS, we do not *feel* like evolution has done us any favor.

The tyranny of now

However much we may like or dislike thinking about the past or the future (see chapter 20), where we actually are in time is the present—hence Omar Khayyam's rejection of "unborn Tomorrow and dead Yesterday." Could we take refuge in the present moment from the feelings brought about by the passage of time, like travelers in the desert seeking shelter from a sandstorm? In chapter 12, I have noted that such withdrawal, made possible by practicing mindfulness, amounts—in a manner of speaking—to the loss of mind. It turns out that shrinking down one's time horizon to a point, a single moment, is equivalent to a quite literal loss of CONSCIOUSNESS.

It is hard to tell what T. S. Eliot meant when he wrote, "To be conscious is not to be in time,"[9] but on a literal reading, he got it exactly wrong. To be conscious is one of many possible ways of *being*, and being is not a state but a process, a kind of *doing*. What I—a sometimes conscious agent—am depends a lot on what my brain does; stop time, and there is no brain-doing, and without it no mind-being and no consciousness.[10] The instant Goethe's Faust decides to call the cards in his deal with the devil and makes the "beautiful" moment of perfect happiness stop, he ceases to exist as a conscious being (which is perhaps what Mephistopheles had intended all along).

The arrow of time

Seeing that there is, unfortunately,[11] no black magic in this world that we can call on to stop time or to mess with physics in other exciting ways, the impossibility of being conscious when time is frozen remains beside the point. And it is physics, which is an even harsher ruler than evolution, that has the last word on time: the passage of time is not only inexorable but also irreversible. The fundamental lack of symmetry between the past and the future, or the arrow of time,[12] manifests to us as a deeply felt difference between the two. If we don't like a particular future, we can try to avert it,[13] but if we don't like the past, our only hope is to forget. Time's arrow strikes at the heart of what it feels like to be human: it makes us capable of experiencing REGRET.

Of related interest

To watch:

Nicholas Roeg, *Walkabout* (1971)

To listen:

Maurice Ravel, *Boléro* (1928)

To read:

Alan Lightman, *Einstein's Dreams* (1993)

Jorge Luis Borges, "A New Refutation of Time" in *Selected Non-Fictions* (1999b)

Jorge Luis Borges, "The Garden of Forking Paths" in *Labyrinths* ([1941] 1970c)

Martin Amis, *Time's Arrow* (1991)

To go:

Jerusalem; Rome; Death Valley.

36 Truth

A melancholy pearl. Ministries of information. Into the well.

Happiness is desirable for its own sake: truth is desirable only as a mean of producing happiness; for who would not prefer an agreeable delusion to a melancholy truth?
—James Beattie

Bullshit makes the flowers grow & that's beautiful.
—Malaclypse the Younger, *Principia Discordia*

Of truth we know nothing, for truth is in a well.
—Democritus[1]

A melancholy pearl

In at least four respects, truth is like a pearl: possibly precious, hidden from
view in its natural state, difficult to get at, and rarer than originality in
a simile.[2] Even a well-worn cliche, though, can deliver a surprise. Polish
down a pearl, and you will eventually discover the grain of sand that once
upon a time inconvenienced the oyster that made it. Likewise, under a
smooth and shiny sentiment, there may be hiding a hard core of an inconvenient truth. Most truths about the world, which are more numerous than
the grains of sand on a beach, are entirely inconsequential for any living
creature; but not all are. Surely the fact of having just molted does matter
to the blue crab, until its new shell hardens. And some facts about crusta-
ceans are consequential to some people, an example being the possibility
that the soft-shell crab that is trying to slink away into the surf possesses
CONSCIOUSNESS—a potentially inconvenient truth for someone like myself,
who likes both to watch crabs and to eat them.

Those truths that inconvenience us in some way we may try to mask with mother-of-pearl, or to flush out altogether from the oyster shell that is our constructed world. It is hard to predict what truth a particular person might find irritating, but there *is* an unsurprising pattern to it: generally, it is our own insights—especially the MORAL ones—into our condition that we are the least prepared to abide. It is in this regard that self-knowledge, praised by philosophers,[3] can be more of a burden than a boon. I may find it easy to convince others that someone who tells inconvenient truths about me is a liar, but what if I am both the truth-teller and the audience?[4] When looking in the mirror—a traditional implement in allegorical depictions of Truth personified—my only options are to suffer the truth or to suppress it.[5]

Ministries of information

To the extent that in POLITICS those with POWER have a vested interest in preserving the status quo, they also have an interest in suppressing a wide range of truths. Both in totalitarian regimes and in representative democracies, the oligarchs know that their best bet is to keep the masses in the dark about pretty much everything except sports, celebrity gossip, state-sanctioned RELIGION, and other soporifics and mental opiates.

There are two types of approaches to the formidable task of fooling most of the people most of the time. The less sophisticated one aims for complete control over information through censorship and active repression of those who oppose it. A stark example is the ongoing war on the part of the ruling party in a country of over a billion people against political dissidents and random undesirables, as well as thousands of specific news items, phrases, and cartoon characters that are seen by the system as threatening or by the oligarchs as personally insulting.[6]

The other, arguably more sophisticated and no less effective approach is, in a way, an opposite of the first one. The idea is to exert selective instead of total control over the populace,[7] in part by letting truth drown in a deluge of bullshit (a technical term in philosophy and in psychology).[8] The steady flow of the latter has traditionally been provided by the "old" media, which are in principle entirely free from censorship, yet in practice entirely dependent on wealthy backers and businesses. An even larger volume of bullshit and lies now circulates in the "social media," brought into being by new communication TECHNOLOGIES.[9]

The emergence of the original social medium—the LANGUAGE faculty itself—made possible the subsequent accelerating EVOLUTION of human culture. Cumulative cultural evolution depends on cooperation among individuals, which in turn depends on a certain level of trust. In many instances of animal communication, trust is achieved via "honest signaling": the peacock's tail is so costly to its bearer (in terms of increased energy expenditure and vulnerability to predators) that the peahen has a good reason to take it at face value, as a true expression of the male's potential as a mate. Words, in comparison, are extremely cheap. The mechanisms that nevertheless kept language users honest enough to cooperate effectively must have historically worked well in small groups. Unfortunately, they do not work well at all under conditions of mass propaganda, or in the peculiar information environment created by social media; hence our susceptibility to the modern varieties of bullshit.[10]

The alliance between POLITICS and communication TECHNOLOGY has subverted not only the ancestral human social dynamics that used to keep lies and bullshit in check: the key achievements of Enlightenment have by now also been undermined. Flawed and limited in scope as it was,[11] the alliance of education, science, and humanistic intellect against blind belief and submission to tyranny has proved effective, but only for a while. It is now clear that SCIENCE as a means for seeking after truth is powerless on its own, because the general public is incapable of understanding its complexities.[12] If there is any hope of fixing this problem, it is in education—or would be, were those in POWER not working to control mass education. And humanists and skeptics can hardly be effective in furthering the cause of truth against propaganda in an intellectual environment where the masses are made to see them as elitist enemies of the people.[13]

The dismal state of truth in contemporary public discourse is well captured by the newly popular phrase "post-truth society." While many political theorists, scientists, educators, and public intellectuals are doing their best to figure out how to carry on in this unexpected situation, others resign to feeling powerless in the face of a new Dark Age.[14] And some choose to settle for what they perceive as the lesser evil and to defend this choice. In Russian, the insistence on laying bare the truth, no matter the consequences, is referred to as правду-матку резать ("carving Mother Truth"). Too much truth is clearly not good for a theocracy or a dictatorship, but apparently, as some Western liberal intellectuals have explicitly argued, it is not good for a democracy either.[15] There is, however, a solution to this crisis of POLITICS, and it does not involve having to lie to people. If a social order cannot stand too much truth, what must go is not truth, but the social order.

Into the well

Resignation in the face of the interminable and exhausting struggle against STUPIDITY, malice, and bullshit makes one want to escape the fray and climb deep into Truth's well, hoping perhaps to get to the bottom of it all and maybe find there an ultimate truth or two. Go easy on the expectations, though: inconvenience aside, a seeker for the ultimate truth must be prepared for an ultimate letdown. Here, in any case, is the gist of what some philosophers, scientists, and at least one major RELIGIOUS tradition have to say on a foundational question of EXISTENCE—the ultimate nature of reality:

> The ultimate truth is, as we know, EMPTINESS. Emptiness is the emptiness not of existence, but of inherent existence. To be empty of inherent existence is to exist only conventionally, only as the object of conventional truth. The ultimate truth about any phenomenon is hence that it is merely a conventional truth.[16]

Of related interest

To watch:

Akira Kurosawa, *Rashomon* (1950)

Terry Gilliam, *Brazil* (1985)

To listen:

Gustav Mahler, *Symphony No. 2* (1895)

To read:

Jorge Luis Borges, "The Approach to Al-Mu'tasim" ([1935] 1962a) in *Ficciones*

Philip K. Dick, *The Penultimate Truth* (1964)

Ursula K. Le Guin, *City of Illusions* (1967)

Iain M. Banks, *The Hydrogen Sonata* (2012)

To go:

To Es Toch.

37 War

A room with a view. After Babel. Blowing in the wind.

War is a continuation of politics by other means.
—Carl von Clausewitz

Politics is a continuation of war by other means.
—Zhou Enlai[1]

A room with a view

The one opportunity that I had so far in my life to sit on a toilet with an M16 assault rifle across my lap I owe to an attempt on the part of Saddam Hussein to stick it to Hafez Assad. In the early 1980s, the Iraqis, who were losing one battle after another in the bloody war with Iran that they themselves had started, were scheming to weaken and humiliate Syria, an ally of Iran, by having Israel invade Lebanon, where Syria had stationed tens of thousands of troops and several armored divisions. To that end, the Iraqi intelligence service arranged for the Abu Nidal faction, a terrorist group under its control, to assassinate the Israeli ambassador in London. The Israeli government, which had long had in its sights the Palestine Liberation Organization's headquarters and its fighters' positions around Beirut, declared the PLO (Abu Nidal's sworn enemy) responsible and invaded Lebanon, triggering a "limited war" with Syria on the Lebanese soil.[2] The ambassador was shot by the Abu Nidal people on June 3, 1982; a couple of weeks later, I found myself sitting down to my business[3] while enjoying a view of Beirut through a shell-blown hole in the wall of a villa in the foothills of the Jabal ash-Shouf, east of the city, on the road to Damascus.

When the war broke out, I was a young officer on active duty, bored with my desk job and eager for an adventure, and securely plugged into the general public atmosphere of righteous anger at the terrorist act in London. The anti-war demonstrations hadn't begun in earnest until late September that year, when it became clear to those citizens who could still THINK clearly that the Israeli government and military were deceiving the public about the war.[4] In any case, nothing much came out of those except a reshuffling of the cabinet.

How many times can a man turn his head and pretend that he just doesn't see? I guess it depends on the man[5]—but the cards are stacked against anyone seeing. Our species' EVOLUTIONARY history is one of expansion and violent domination; and in our cultures and in the dynamics of most of our societies, both past and present, there are hardly any signs of an openness toward pacifism, or of conditions that would allow it to take root.[6] Most of us have been conditioned to see war as a tool—the continuation of POLITICS by other means—perhaps an easier tool than others to prick one's finger on, but indispensable.

Democracy, hailed as an antidote to war by no less a philosophical luminary than Kant, proved to be nothing of the sort. A majority of the public in many nation-states, in most "national liberation" movements, and in all empires sees war as a legitimate and indispensable means toward a political or economic end. The combined forces of historical momentum, geopolitical situation, and political culture in these societies elevate war to the status of *force majeure*: pointless to question, futile to condemn.

War's immunity to questioning, gained in this manner, hides the absurdity of the preconceptions that it helps perpetuate. These are often revealed in the LANGUAGE that is used to talk—or to avoid talking—about war. Examples abound both in popular media and in academic writing. Here's one: how many of the people who use the phrase "military sacrifice" realize that consecrating the victims of a war in this manner effectively elevates it to the status of a deity whose entitlement to a burnt offering of human lives is taken for granted?[7]

If there is any sanctity to the human death toll exacted by war, it can only be derived from the value we attach to human life. This implies that the use of the language of sacrifice in connection with any war that could have been avoided, or any victim, military or civilian, who had not had a say in it, is a travesty. In the case of the United States, the absence of this consideration from the public discourse is made particularly stark by this country's history, in the decades following the end of World War II, of engaging in what have arguably been wars of choice (in addition to countless instances of fomenting "slow violence," proxy wars, and other types of organized conflict).[8]

Because our POLITICS effectively concentrates POWER in the hands of a small minority, appealing to the "democratic" approval of these wars is an act of bad faith, as are calls for "national unity" and the glorification of "shared sacrifice." The key question that should be asked about any war is: who benefits from it? (This applies to politics in general; see chapter 25.) The answer to this question is inconvenient, but hard to argue with: it is the aggressor's power elites that reap a lion's share of the material gain from war and that avoid most of its human toll; and it is the ordinary people on all sides who foot most of the bill.[9] Perhaps instead of shyly thanking random military personnel at airports for their service, the children whom we encourage to do that should be taught to ask "What made you enlist?" and "Do you realize whose cause you serve?"

After Babel

It would be a foolish refusal to learn from history to deny that, in between fighting in the rich man's wars, ordinary people occasionally find themselves in genuine need of mobilizing to fend off some other, neighboring ordinary people who would physically enslave or exterminate them. As a species, we are thoroughly divided against ourselves: it is always a subset of humans that faces the need to fight in self-defense, against another subset. John Lennon's call to "imagine all the people sharing all the world" is not likely to be heeded by *all* the people in the foreseeable future. Alien invaders from outer space might unite us, but their arrival on the scene is not likely either, given the physical constraints on interstellar travel.

Once we narrow the scope of our EMPATHY and caring to our in-group allies (an act that, alas, is merely human rather than humanist), the difficulty of mastering appreciation for the value of human life in the abstract ceases to be a problem: it is now us against them. But another, practical problem arises in its stead: how can we tell who is with us? Because in war this is a matter of life and death, the telltale better be reliable. Merely wearing the right uniform or waving the right flag will not satisfy those who obsess about their group's "purity" or its susceptibility to invasion by others: they prefer to look for signs that are more difficult to fake.

A reliable source of such signs is LANGUAGE. It is very common for an ethnic group to refer to themselves collectively by a word that in that group's language means simply "people." Because a person's language is central to their identity, it can be used against that person by in-group inquisitors when the occasion arises. Pronunciation too can serve as a shibboleth[10] (as I know well from experience, my personal Odyssey having left me with a foreign accent in each of the three languages in which I am fluent).

To be singled out as "the other" (through language, skin color, tendency to ask inconvenient questions, or any other trait), and thereby to be made into a target, is depressing and infuriating. This experience can, however, be useful in one respect: it can help people resolve the perpetual MORAL question: Whose side are you on? For the bystanders who are still on the fence, this is the chance to come down and stand by the one who is being targeted, keeping in mind that a refusal to act in this manner is also an ACTION—one that aids the wrong side. As to those who choose the wrong side. . . . When people declare themselves to be fascists, they ought to be believed—and resisted by any means, including violence.[11]

Blowing in the wind

The Second Book of Samuel contains a striking (and rare in the Bible) example of a peaceful resolution of a standoff between two mighty warriors. Abner ben Ner, who is being held at bay after a long and bloody pursuit by Joab ben Zeruiah, decides to appeal to his opponent's common sense:

> Then Abner called to Joab, and said, Shall the sword devour for ever? knowest thou not that it will be bitterness in the latter end? how long shall it be then, ere thou bid the people return from following their brethren?

Abner's rhetorical question does have the intended effect: Joab relents and tells his people to fall back. (Neither of these two gets to die of old age, but that's another story.)[12]

After two world wars and countless local ones just in the last century, and with ongoing fighting in dozens of places all around the globe at any given time, Abner's question looms larger than ever. What reasons do we have today to insist that it deserves any other answer than "Yes, for ever"?

Albert Einstein, in a 1939 public letter addressed to Sigmund Freud, shares his deep pessimism about the prospects of peace, closing his remarks with a question: "Is it possible to control man's mental evolution so as to make him proof against the psychoses of hate and destructiveness?" Freud, whose lengthy reply paints him as no less of a pessimist, nevertheless concludes with a sentiment clearly meant to sound positive: "Whatever fosters the growth of civilization works at the same time against war." I wonder. A year after the Einstein-Freud exchange took place, Walter Benjamin wrote in the seventh of his eighteen *Theses on the Philosophy of History*: "There has never been a document of civilization that was not at the same time one of barbarism."[13] What Benjamin meant by that is best understood, I think, in the context of his ninth thesis, which consists of a single paragraph on Paul Klee's painting *Angelus Novus* (italics in original):

> The Angel of History must look just so. His face is turned towards the past. Where *we* see the appearance of a chain of events, *he* sees one single catastrophe, which unceasingly piles rubble on top of rubble and hurls it before his feet. He would like to pause for a moment so fair, to awaken the dead and to piece together what has been smashed. But a storm is blowing from Paradise, it has caught itself up in his wings and is so strong that the Angel can no longer close them. The storm drives him irresistibly into the future, to which his back is turned, while the rubble-heap before him grows sky-high. That, which we call progress, is *this* storm.

Of related interest

To watch:

Luis Buñuel, *España 1936* (1937)

Stanley Kubrick, *Dr. Strangelove* (1964)

Paul Verhoeven, *Starship Troopers* (1997)

Ari Folman, *Vals im Bashir* (*Waltz with Bashir*, 2008)

Denis Villeneuve, *Incendies* (*Fires*, 2010)

To listen:[14]

Valeriano Orobón Fernández, "A las barricadas" (1936)

Giovanna Daffini, "Bella ciao" (1962)

Bob Dylan, "With God on Our Side" (1964)

Bulat Okudjava, "До свидания, мальчики" ("Farewell, Boys," 1973)

To read:

Frank Herbert, *Dune* (1965)

Stanisław Lem, *Fiasco* ([1986] 1987)

Iain M. Banks, *Matter* (2010)

To go

Visit the central war memorials of any two neighboring nations, or any two contemporaneous global empires (past or present).[15]

38 Youth

Another difficult dilemma. Silver spoon or not. Choice and chance. Janus introversus.

Méphistophélès: La puissance?
Faust: Non! Je veux un trésor qui les contient tous! . . . Je veux la jeunesse!

(Méphistophélès: Power?
Faust: No! I want a treasure that contains eveything! . . . I want youth!)
—Charles Gounod, *Faust*

The force that through the green fuse drives the flower
Drives my green age; that blasts the roots of trees
Is my destroyer.
—Dylan Thomas, "The Force That through the Green Fuse Drives the Flower"

"There's a point, around age twenty," Bedap said, "when you have to choose whether to be like everybody else the rest of your life, or to make a virtue of your peculiarities."
—Ursula K. Le Guin, *The Dispossessed*

Another difficult dilemma

An inconvenient truth is not something one expects to hear in a commencement address at a U.S. college. A commencement ceremony, whose name spells "beginning" even though it also marks an end, is an occasion on which the invited speaker is expected to proffer a vision of the graduates' future so rosy that on any other day it would seem a bit much even for Americans, who are typically offended by any celebrity's failure to project incorrigible optimism and can-do spirit. Yet an inconvenient truth was what the class of 1989 at Dartmouth was treated to, by Joseph Brodsky, whose address ended with these words:

So take one last look at it, while it is still its normal size, while it is not yet a photograph. Look at it with all the tenderness you can muster, for you are looking at your past. Exact, as it were, the full look at the best. For I doubt you'll ever have it better than here.[1]

I do not know to what extent Brodsky's assessment, which like Janus looked both backward and forward in TIME, ended up being true of his audience, all of them "young and newfangled," as he called them repeatedly in his remarks. It being Dartmouth, maybe many of them did go on to have splendid time, even better than what they had had in college.[2] It does not really matter. It seems to me there was in any case a core of truth in the prophecy, which is this: at *some* point in life, every person can predict with confidence that in many regards they will never again have it better than they already had. For many people, perhaps most, this realization signals an end of the stage of life that they perceive as their youth.

Those of us to whom the fleetingness of youth has already been revealed—whether through experience or a report by a respected party—are faced with a dilemma. Should we share this truth with people who have clearly not yet reached the cusp of their mental middle age, in the hope of inducing them to make better use of their time? Or should we spare them the inconvenience, "for in much wisdom is much grief: and he that increaseth knowledge increaseth sorrow"?

There seems to be no good choice here. On the one hand, telling people to make the most of their best years encourages an active pursuit of HAPPINESS, which tends to be self-defeating, and may foster REGRET about having been told.[3] On the other hand, there is the case of regret about *not* having been told, which arises because "no one told you when to run" (as the Pink Floyd line goes). Having myself had the eye-opener when it was mostly too late, I came down on Brodsky's side in this matter, which is why you are now reading this. As to which horn of the dilemma *you* have to look out for, it depends on how old you are.

Silver spoon or not

Another thing that depends on how old you are when you first hear "Time's wingéd chariot hurrying near" is the possible practical effects of this rumor on your conduct and fate. Suppose you're a member of the class of 1989 at

Dartmouth, still somewhat shocked by the commencement speech you just heard. You decide to postpone taking on that job at the finance firm and to go instead on a journey of self-discovery around the world. You return a year later having checked the "travel when young" box on your bucket list and go on to work happily on Wall Street. Or you never return—you settle down in Rajasthan, buy a ranch, and raise camels for the Rabari nomads. Or suppose instead that your revelation comes mid-career; you take a leave without pay, kiss your CHILDREN good-bye, and fly to join the Rabari on their annual migration (alone, because your LOVE does not care for camels).[4] A few years later you reappear with a Rabari partner (who is sick and tired of camels and wants change), settle down in Brooklyn, and write travel articles about exotic destinations for in-flight magazines. Or suppose the eye-opener is delivered to you during an ill-conceived conversation at your retirement party; you become distraught, need to be restrained, and spend the rest of your days sedated but well taken care of, at an exclusive residential facility.

The three scenarios just outlined seem quite varied, but they share an element that gets short shrift in our "meritocratic" society: they all depend on privilege and wealth. Under runaway capitalism, which breeds persistent and deepening transgenerational inequality, the lottery of birth ensures that most young people lack the kind of capital, financial and other, required for getting into and putting themselves through a highly ranked college; for leisure travel; for landing a cushy job; for buying property; or for surviving in Brooklyn on the earnings of a freelance writer or artist. If you didn't find the Ivy League anecdote that opened this chapter a bit tone-deaf (if not outright cringe inducing), you have probably been leading a sheltered life so far (or maybe you just don't care).[5]

Thus it is that people's freedom to make the most of their youth depends, first and foremost, on whether or not they have been born with the proverbial silver spoon in their mouth. Those who have not are set back already at birth, and their disadvantage only deepens as they grow up, affecting their basic existential needs such as food, housing, and health security, as well as their prospects for HAPPINESS, their family and social life, and the kind of OLD AGE that awaits them.[6] Here in the United States, like in most other countries, the opposite of being born with a silver spoon is not being born without one: it is being born with a ball and chain.

Choice and chance

For most of the choices that we make in life, the ramifications, like the waves from a pebble dropped into a pond, subside with time. What I decided to have for breakfast this morning is unlikely to have a lasting effect on the rest of my week (let alone year). It's another matter, though, for the pond to be hit by a truckload of rocks intended to prepare it for being paved over.[7] A few of our choices do turn out in the long run to be life-changing. Given the inertia of daily EXISTENCE that gathers momentum as we grow older, young age is when choices—whether ours or those made for us—are more likely to have a lasting impact. (It is particularly deplorable that the lottery of birth is held at the stage of life when the outcome's consequences are necessarily the most significant.)

To the extent that our choices stem from exercising FREE WILL, dispensing advice (however elliptical) about the need to choose carefully makes sense. The element of chance in such matters cannot, however, be ignored—and of course chance is not something that is easy to be careful about, especially if its import is revealed long after the dice roll. Here's an example from my own youth. I grew up in the great Soviet empire, before the USSR suffered a massive spontaneous existence failure. The Soviet censors were quite bad at recognizing the potential for subversion in fiction literature, especially when the author's bona fide seemed ironclad. A typical case was Lion Feuchtwanger, the left-wing Jewish-German playwright and writer, who barely escaped from the Nazis. A twelve-volume complete collection of his works in a Russian translation has been published, in 1963, by Moscow's State Publishing House of Fiction Literature. Volumes 8, 9, and 10 in this collection contained *The Jewish War* trilogy—the most effective piece of Zionist propaganda (perhaps inadvertent; Feuchtwanger ended up in California, not Palestine) ever to spring from a fine historical novel a thousand pages long.[8] I can tell, because reading that book changed my life.

Because of the peculiarities of the Soviet book-buying scene,[9] this took an intervention by a third party. One could not just go to a store and buy a "hot" book—only trusted citizens with special privileges had access to such luxuries. By chance, my grandmother's brother-in-law, a lawyer of impeccable standing with the Party and the town authorities, could and did populate his bookshelves with the coveted complete works of various sought-after authors (he was not known to actually read books, but that turned out to be unimportant). One summer when I was a teenager, visiting my grandparents, I was made to tag along after my grandmother to her sister's apartment and found myself, by chance, thumbing through *The Jewish War* and getting increasingly intrigued by what I was reading: I had never thought of being Jewish and being warlike as things that go together. I borrowed the books for a couple of weeks. Three years later, I was in Israel, starting boot camp.[10]

Chance intervened in my life again a few years later. On my first long leave from the army, I went skiing on Mount Hermon, where in season the snow is usually wet and heavy—what in California they call "the Sierra cement." After several years of being deprived of real winter (snow in Tel Aviv is about as common as in downtown Los Angeles), I was having so much fun that I could not resist the opportunity to put in an extra run, despite being quite tired. The offer of a free ride up the mountain came, I think, from the liftie—I am not entirely sure, because of the amnesia induced by the morphine that they shot me up with when, on that last run through the heavy snow, I tumbled head over heels, the right binding failed to open, and I broke a leg.

A couple of operations and a full-length cast ensured that my break from the army lasted much longer than planned. I was stuck at home and very bored. By chance, the downstairs neighbor had some philosophy books. A normal person whose first exposure to philosophy is through reading Hegel would probably vow to never ever touch the stuff again; my reaction was to try and find a better philosopher.

Long story short, that chain of chance, in which I was able later to identify only a few key links, is why I am here (and, of course, this is also why you are now reading these lines). Had I not chanced to be born in the USSR, or had I come across Le Guin's books (say) instead of Feuchtwanger's during my formative years,[11] *I* would not exist; someone entirely different, bearing my name and looking a bit like me, would be reaching back in MEMORY to the times when he was young in an attempt to make sense of it all.

Janus introversus

Growing up, growing old, and reaching back in time is our best shot at making sense of life for the simple reason, noted by Kierkegaard, that life must be lived forward, yet can only be understood backward.[12] There is a certain symmetry between the young version of the self, peering into the uncertain future, and the old one, looking back at the immutable past that the future has crystallized into. Think of Janus with the two faces turned inward, or of *komainu*, the *a-gyō* and *un-gyō* lion-dogs guarding the entrance to a Shinto temple, were they made to face each other across the gap. Make the gap wide enough—several decades—and this image becomes terrifying to the older self, the one who is looking backward. The other, younger, self has it easier:

> The only thing that makes life possible is permanent, intolerable uncertainty: not knowing what comes next.
>
> —Ursula K. Le Guin, *The Left Hand of Darkness* (1969, 71)

Of related interest

To watch:

Andrei Tarkovsky, *Иваново детство* (*Ivan's Childhood*, 1962)

Richard Linklater, *Boyhood* (2014)

To listen:

Pink Floyd, "Time" (from *The Dark Side of the Moon*, 1973)

Earth, Wind & Fire, "Fantasy" (1978)

To read:

Ernest Hemingway, *A Moveable Feast* (1964)

Joseph Brodsky, "Песня невинности, она же опыта" ("A Song of Innocence, Also of Experience,"[13] Part I, 1972)

Robert Silverberg, *Breckenridge and the Continuum* (1973)

Ursula K. Le Guin, *The Beginning Place* (1980)

Michael Swanwick, *The Iron Dragon's Daughter* (1993)

To go:

Paris, Timbuktu.

Afterword

Quiero dejar escrita una confesión, que a un tiempo será íntima y general, ya que las cosas que le ocurren a un hombre les ocurren a todos.

(I want to leave a written confession, that will be at once intimate and general, since the things that happen to one man happen to all.)
—Jorge Luis Borges, from a letter to his mother, Leonor Acevedo de Borges

Le bon Dieu donne toujours des culottes à ceux qui n'ont pas de derrière.

(The good Lord always gives pants to those who have no behind.)
—French proverb[1]

Just dropped in (to see what condition my condition was in)

Each of the thirty-eight comments on the human condition that got a chapter of its own in this book, along with many more that did not, applies to the life of each and every one of us. In writing on such stuff, it makes little sense to pretend that one is taking the view from nowhere: I am me, not some fictitious average human, and it's both more honest and more fun to get somewhat personal in one's reporting. People also happen to relate better to anecdotes than to abstractions—perhaps because, as Borges was fond of claiming,[2] we all live the same one life anyway:

Whoever embraces a woman is Adam. The woman is Eve.
Everything happens for the first time.

In parting, I will add only this: to the extent that my report has any value, I suspect that it will be better appreciated by those who stand to benefit from it the least, because they have already been to this movie. But that's just how life works:

> Everything happens for the first time, but in a way that is eternal.
> Whoever reads my words is inventing them.

Of related interest

To watch:

Werner Herzog, *Fata Morgana* (1971)

Joel and Ethan Coen, *The Big Lebowski* (1998)

To listen:

Violeta Parra, "Gracias a la vida" (1967)

To read:

Ursula K. Le Guin, "The Day before the Revolution" (1974a)

To go:

To the beginning.

Acknowledgments

An early inspiration for this book came from reading Freya Stark's *Perseus in the Wind*. Emrys Donaldson helped tip the balance in favor of attempting to write it. The students who took my year-long seminar at Cornell in 2018–2019 have my gratitude and admiration for bravely facing a new inconvenient truth every week and teaching me a thing or two about how to do it. My family provided invaluable general encouragement at all times, as well as insightful comments on early drafts. I thank my agent, James Levine, for finding such a nice home for this book. I am very grateful to the outstanding team at the MIT Press, especially my editor, Robert Prior, for gentle advice, Julia Collins for expert copyediting, and Kathleen Caruso for seeing everything through.

Notes

For, as dark texts need notes, some there must be
To usher Virtue, and say, *This is she.*
—John Donne, "To the Countess of Bedford"

Preface

1. The subtitle I myself had had in mind was the punnier and more noncommittal *Cognitive Science for the Trip of Your Life.*

2. My weakness for notes is probably due to an exposure, as an impressionable teenager, to Hermann Hesse's 1949 novel *The Glass Bead Game*. In Hesse's book, the Game involves collaborative construction of intricate multidimensional conceptual edifices, which integrate insights from MATHEMATICS, music, literature, and other arts and SCIENCES, in response to a given thematic challenge.

Chapter 1

1. In the scene from which these two lines are taken (*Faust*, part 1, Study), Goethe's hero is shown working on a translation of the opening phrase of the New Testament into German. He rejects the commonly accepted version ("In the beginning was the Word"), along with a few others, finally settling on the one quoted: "In the beginning was the Deed." The Philip K. Dick quote is from a 1978 speech titled "How to Build a Universe That Doesn't Fall Apart Two Days Later," http://deoxy.org/pkd_how2build.htm. The quote from *The Left Hand of Darkness* appears in Le Guin 1969, ch. 18.

2. A unifying characteristic of the various strands of gnosticism, a Jewish and early Christian "heresy" dating to the first and second centuries AD, is the belief that the world was created by a demiurge, a lesser and not necessarily benevolent deity, distinct from the biblical creator. As such, gnosticism is related to Eastern dualistic

cosmologies such as Zoroastrianism and Manicheaism. Useful leads into the enormous scholarly literature on gnosticism can be found in Burns 2016 and Van Den Broek 1983.

3. These lines are from T. S. Eliot's "The Hollow Men" (*Dial*, March 1925).

4. For an introduction to the concept of whole-world simulation, see Sandberg and Bostrom 2008.

5. *Dao De Jing*, ch. 69 (Lao Tze [Laozi] 1904).

6. Skepticism, a universally useful attitude toward judgments and beliefs, must also be applied by the skeptics to their own plans. Toward the end of his essay on STUPID-ITY, Robert Musil ([1937] 1979, 41) writes: "I believe that the maxim: 'Behave as well as you can and as badly as you must, but always bear in mind the margin of error in your behaviour!' would already take us half-way towards a most promising way of life" (see also chapter 31). Dunning (2019, 349), in discussing what he calls "best option illusion" in decision making, explains why "occasionally the seemingly best option turns out to be anything but—leading to systematic errors and problems."

7. The cat and dryer cameo is from Smith, Shields, and Washburn 2003, 338. The William James passage that they quote appears in his *Principles of Psychology* (James 1890, 93). See also chapter 22.

8. The doctrine of dependent origination, which is foundational to Buddhism, states that all phenomena depend on—that is, are caused by—other phenomena. See Garfield 1994 for an illuminating discussion of this principle and its relation to the doctrine of EMPTINESS. The relevance of the principle of dependent origination to action (in particular, MORAL action) is made clear by this line from the Maha Hat-thipadopama (Great Elephant Footprint) Sutra: "Whoever sees dependent co-arising [the web of cause and effect] sees the Dhamma [the Way]" (translated from Pāli by Thanissaro Bhikkhu).

9. An introduction to the pitfalls of affective forecasting can be found in Wilson and Gilbert 2005.

10. W. Shakespeare, *Hamlet*, act 3, scene 2.

11. "The unexpected is what makes life possible," spoken by Therem Harth rem ir Estraven in *The Left Hand of Darkness* (Le Guin 1969, ch. 8).

Chapter 2

1. Both of these quotes by Adam Smith are from his *The Theory of Moral Sentiments* (I.iii.2.8 and III.6.7, respectively), published in 1759; the much better-known *The Wealth of Nations* came out in 1776. The sixth and last edition of *The Theory of Moral*

Sentiments appeared in 1790, the year of Smith's death. The second passage from Adam Smith qualifies the import of the first one. Here it is in context:

> Those great objects of self-interest, of which the loss or acquisition quite changes the rank of the person, are the objects of the passion properly called ambition; a passion, which when it keeps within the bounds of prudence and justice, is always admired in the world, and has even sometimes a certain irregular greatness, which dazzles the imagination, when it passes the limits of both these virtues, and is not only unjust but extravagant. Hence the general admiration for heroes and conquerors, and even for statesmen, whose projects have been very daring and extensive, though altogether devoid of justice; such as those of the Cardinals of Richlieu and of Retz.

See Pearsall 2016 for a well-informed and well-reasoned discussion of Smith's ambivalence toward ambition.

2. It is at this point only a guess because there seem to have been no analytical studies or agent-based simulations of the dynamics of ambition (Sallach [2000] suggested that Pareto's theory of the elites could be modeled by attractor dynamics, but did not carry out an actual experiment).

3. As an example, consider Easterlin's conclusion (Easterlin et al. 2012, 9779) of a study of income and life satisfaction in China, 1990–2010: "These findings are consistent with the view common in the happiness literature that the growth in aspirations induced by rising income undercuts the increase in life satisfaction related to rising income itself."

4. See Daqing 2010 for a discussion of the classical Greek spirit of public competition, αγον (agon) and its counterparts in other cultures.

5. The exceptions are the societies in which personal ambition is explicitly suppressed by the group; see Boehm et al. 1993 and Clastres 1987 for documented examples. I am grateful to Professor Darrin McMahon for bringing Boehm's work to my attention.

6. "Place" is social-economic standing, a usage that is exemplified by this stanza from *The Red Flag*, written in 1889 by Jim Connell:

> It suits today the weak and base,
> Whose minds are fixed on pelf and place
> To cringe before the rich man's frown,
> And haul the sacred emblem down.

A yearning for place is never seen kindly by those who already have it, as illustrated by this Yom Kippur joke. A rabbi, during a High Holy Days service, cries out loud "Lord, before you I am nothing!" The cantor follows the rabbi's example. The synagogue's janitor, sitting a few rows back, decides to join in: "Oh Lord, before you I am nothing!" Overhearing that, the rabbi nudges the cantor and whispers, "Look who thinks he's nothing!"

7. See chapters 13, 34, 36, and 37 on why the Enlightenment was not actually as great a victory for humanism as it is usually portrayed.

8. Crowder-Meyer (2018) examined political ambition in the United States, focusing on gender and class differences among candidates. She found that in the years since the 2016 elections, women and "ordinary" people have been disproportionately energized to run for office. Amazingly for a political science study, published in a journal called *Political Behavior*, this paper manages to hide the elephant in the room by not once mentioning any actual *political* motives on the part of the candidates.

9. It has been pointed out that in biological terms, the closest conceptual counterpart to unlimited growth is cancer. Smith (2010) discusses the relationship between growth and capitalism. Jackson (2009) outlines a program for "prosperity without growth." It is worth noting that in economics, optimistic scenarios that do not forgo growth tend to be about the production of food, not cars.

10. Ariza-Montes et al. (2018, 91), who analyze the interaction of ambition and life satisfaction in a European sample of chefs, write that the subjects in their survey data accept "their position in life with humility, devotion, moderation, and respect for tradition. The implicit resignation in these values may possibly cause a contractionary effect on the interaction between work and personal lives. This finding perpetuates the status quo and hampers the development of an ambitious and rewarding professional career aspired by most culinary arts professionals." Note that this phrasing elevates ambition and growth (the opposite of "status quo") over HAPPINESS.

11. For instance, Otto et al. 2017 studied how psychologists' career ambition relates to their professional achievements ("extrinsic" success) and to their job satisfaction and goal attainment ("intrinsic" success). They found that "achievement motivation was negatively related to intrinsic success and even diminished it over time." This made the authors question "whether psychologists might be worsening their career development in the long run by showing high achievement motivation" (23). In this connection, see also chapter 15, note 5; instead of pursuing HAPPINESS, let *it* pursue *you*.

12. Here is the continuation of that passage from Arendt (1958, 201–202): "Omnipotence therefore is never an attribute of gods in polytheism, no matter how superior the strength of the gods may be to the forces of men. Conversely, aspiration toward omnipotence always implies—apart from its Utopian hubris—the destruction of plurality."

13. Posted by @iamspacegirl at 3:33 pm on December 15, 2018. Nesse (2004), who writes about HAPPINESS in the context of EVOLUTION, very explicitly identifies unrealistic goal pursuit as a key symptom of hypomania. The quote from Adam Smith is in *The Theory of Moral Sentiments* (I.ii.2.7).

Chapter 3

1. This quote is from Selye 1973, 693.

2. For a detailed account of the composite computational nature of the self, see Edelman 2008.

3. The disruption is visceral in the sense that it is felt as a bodily condition (Craig 2002). In this connection, it is interesting to note that the word "anxiety" is derived from the Latin *angere*, to choke. The corresponding Russian word, тревога, means both "anxiety" and "siren" (as in "air raid siren").

4. An EVOLUTIONARY perspective of anxiety as a response to uncertainty is discussed in Brosschot, Verkuil, and Thayer 2016. Carleton (2016) reduces all anxiety to the fear of the unknown. The existence of death anxiety (Iverach, Menzies, and Menzies 2014) suggests that certainty in some things can be just as distressing as uncertainty about others.

5. For this, see Sinha 1968.

6. Emotional Regulation Therapy (ERT) has proved effective against the generalized anxiety disorder (Fresco et al. 2013; Renna et al. 2018)—more so in the long run than pharmacological treatments (speaking of which, cannabis use is more likely to induce anxiety than to suppress it; Vučković et al. 2018).

7. Keyes et al. (2017) studied a population-representative sample of over ten thousand U.S. adolescents and found that intelligence was not associated with anxiety disorders (except specific phobia, for which the pattern of results was difficult to interpret).

8. Martin et al. (2007, 769), whose longitudinal study involved a sample of 689 individuals, report that "A 15-point (1 SD) advantage in childhood cognitive performance [measured by IQ at age seven] was significantly associated with a 50% reduced risk of lifetime GAD and an 89 and 57% reduction in risk of GAD in childhood and adolescence, respectively, after adjusting for relevant covariates including socio-economic status and parent history of mental health problems." At the high end of the intelligence scale, Karpinski et al. (2018, 12), who surveyed American Mensa members (scoring at or above the 98th percentile of intelligence), report: "Overall, there was 1.83 times the risk of being formally diagnosed with anxiety (an increase of 83%). When including those who suspected that they should be diagnosed, there was a risk of 3.42, an increase of 242% as compared to the national average."

9. Dick suffered from lifelong anxiety. His stories and novels illustrate and comment on pretty much every variety of anxiety in existence.

Chapter 4

1. An English translation of the essay "The Wall and the Books" by Borges appears in the collection *Labyrinths* (1970e, 221–223).

2. This passage is taken from a short story by Ivan Bunin (1908); here it is in the Russian original:

> И опять мне вспоминаются слова Саади, «употребившего жизнь свою на то, чтобы обозреть Красоту Мира»:
>
> «Ты, который некогда пройдешь по могиле поэта, вспомяни поэта добрым словом!
>
> – Он отдал сердце земле, хотя и кружился по свету, как ветер, который, после смерти поэта, разнёс по вселенной благоухание цветника его сердца.
>
> – Ибо он всходил на башни Маана, Созерцания, и слышал Симаа, Музыку Мира, влекшую в халет, веселие.
>
> – Целый мир полон этим веселием, танцем—ужели одни мы не чувствуем его вина?
>
> – Хмельной верблюд легче несёт свой вьюк. Он, при звуках арабской песни, приходит в восторг. Как же назвать человека, не чувствующего этого восторга?
>
> – Он осёл, сухое полено.»

The Sufi story to which Bunin alludes can be found in the *Gulistan* by Sa'di ([1258] 1966, II,27).

3. A classical source of insights into the virtues of not-doing is the *Dao De Jing* (Lao Tze [Laozi] 1904).

4. The quote is from a letter by John Keats to Benjamin Bailey, November 22, 1817.

5. The philosophical and scientific literature on beauty is vast. Recent trends do suggest something of a consensus regarding its nature: "Beauty is . . . the felt prospect of cognitively representing and achieving processing mastery over a challenging object or experience" (Armstrong and Detweiler-Bedell 2008, 305). In psychological terms, it turns out that beauty requires thought, as shown in a series of experiments by Brielmann and Pelli (2017). For algorithmic approaches to explaining beauty, see Schmidhuber 2009 and Kintsch 2012.

6. The experience of mathematical beauty has been studied by Zeki et al. (2014).

7. This passage appears in Burton's ([1855] 1893, I,148) account of his Hajj pilgrimage, completed in 1853. Burton, who was fluent in Arabic, Persian, and many other languages spoken in the deserts of the Middle East, was among the first Europeans to have visited Mecca and Medina.

8. Like Burton, I believe that the appeal of the desert is universal. Here is how he puts it: "Both sexes, and every age, the most material as well as the most imaginative of minds, the tamest citizen, the parson, the old maid, the peaceful student, the spoiled child of civilisation, all feel their hearts dilate, and their pulses beat strong,

as they look down from their dromedaries upon the glorious Desert" (Burton [1855] 1893, I, 151).

9. A biography of Ruess, a "vagabond for beauty" who disappeared in the south Utah desert at the age of twenty-three, has been compiled by Rusho (1983). It includes as an afterword a sonnet by Edward Abbey, dedicated to Ruess.

10. A teapot may be bigger on the inside than it seems: "As everyone knows, our universe is located in the teapot of a certain Lui Dunbin who sells trinkets at the bazaar in Chanyan" (Pelevin 1998).

11. This maxim opens the second chapter of *Dao De Jing* (Lao Tze [Laozi] 1904, II).

Chapter 5

1. Here is the context of the quote from the Book of Malachi (3:23–24 in the original Hebrew; 4:3 in the King James Version): "23. Behold, I will send you Elijah the prophet before the coming of the great and dreadful day of the Lord: 24. And he shall turn the heart of the fathers to the children, and the heart of the children to their fathers, lest I come and smite the earth with a curse." The reference for *The Circular Ruins* is Borges [1940] 1970b.

2. This is a very partial list of God's problems with tenure. The longest one I found, by googling "God" and "tenure," ran to fifty items.

3. What attitude should parents have toward their children's future flourishing? According to Wolbert, de Ruyter, and Schinkel (2018), the answer is one of hope, rather than expectations. For some entry points into the extensive literature that documents the influence of socioeconomic status, class, and race on parenting styles and outcomes, see Cheadle and Amato 2011 and Redford, Johnson, and Honnold 2009.

4. Parents may end up hedging their bets: Humans evolved to maximize their lifetime reproductive success, which can involve parents withholding support from particular children (Trivers 1972).

5. See the Kierkegaard quote in chapter 38, note 12. Alan Lightman's short story "The Center of Time" in *Einstein's Dreams* (1993) cuts to the bone:

> And so, at the place where TIME stands still, one sees parents clutching their children, in a frozen embrace that will never let go. The beautiful young daughter with blue eyes and blonde hair will never stop smiling the smile she smiles now, will never lose this soft pink glow on her cheeks, will never grow wrinkled or tired, will never get injured, will never unlearn what her parents have taught her, will never think thoughts that her parents don't know, will never know evil, will never tell her parents that she does not love them, will never leave her bedroom with the view of the ocean, will never stop touching her parents as she does now.

6. I recall a *New Yorker* cartoon by Carolita Johnson that depicts a young man with a suitcase who says to his parents at the door: "Bye, mom and dad! I promise only to make mistakes that you haven't made!"

7. Consider the subtitle of Branje 2018: "Conflict Interactions as a Mechanism of Change." See also chapter 23.

8. Concerning the concept of dispersal, see Mace 2016 and Wilkins and Godfrey-Smith 2009. Some tools for mitigating raw EVOLUTIONARY pressure that are available uniquely to humans are discussed by Wilson et al. (2014), who remark that "left unmanaged, evolution often takes us where we do not want to go."

9. As an example of a cultural non-universal, consider attachment, a key concept in developmental personality psychology at the present time: "Attachment theory represents the Western middle-class perspective, ignoring the caregiving values and practices in the majority of the world" (Keller 2018).

10. The poem by Ursula K. Le Guin, whose first line is echoed in title of this section, is titled "High Desert." It is included in Le Guin 2016. The value of the desert for human affairs has been concisely argued by William Godfrey-Smith (1979).

Chapter 6

1. Turing's quote on the unpredictability of computers comes from the celebrated paper in which he introduced the eponymous test for machine intelligence (Turing 1950). Computational complexity is still a little-known subject in philosophy and natural sciences; Aaronson (2012) argues in detail why this lacuna better be addressed.

2. The notion of "mere mindless machine," which is rooted in the fallacy noted by Turing, has been explicitly stated and critiqued by Dennett (2008, 2). For some literary-historical background on the condescension of human masters toward various fictional machine slaves, see Sill's (2013) dissertation ("A Survey of Androids and Audiences: 285 BCE to the Present Day").

3. Note that computational complexity theory, which belongs in computer science, is distinct from complex systems theory (Ladyman and Wiesner 2018), a branch of condensed-matter physics. An accessible, informative, and entertaining introduction to the notion of computation, including complexity, can be found in Rucker 2016. Doria's (2018) survey of some fascinating open questions in complexity theory (including the central unresolved one, commonly referred to as $P = NP$), begins with some very intuitive examples, but quickly gets very technical.

4. The reasons for considering the Universe to be a computer are discussed in chapter 14. The idea that minds are what brains compute is central to modern cognitive science (Edelman 2008).

5. This line of reasoning is related to the so-called anthropic principle in cosmology (e.g., Hoyle and Wickramasinghe 1999). Similar arguments are advanced by van Rooij et al. (2019a), under the title "Tractable Embodied Computation Needs Embeddedness" (that is, being embedded into, and constrained by, the real world).

6. Turing played a central role in the World War II British signals intelligence operations at Bletchley Park, Buckinghamshire, code-named Ultra. Information about German U-boat activity in the north Atlantic, intercepted and decoded by the Ultra project, saved from sinking hundreds of Allied ships with vital supplies and may have been critical to winning the Battle of Britain and perhaps the entire war (Kahn 2009).

7. The MATHEMATICAL genius was supplied by Turing and his colleagues such as I. J. Good; the TECHNOLOGY was that of the Bombe and the Colossus computing devices built and deployed at Bletchley Park; the greed was of the German officer who sold Enigma-related information to the Allies; and the STUPIDITY was that of the Enigma users who often deviated from the standing orders meant to ensure proper operational security, and of the German counter-intelligence, which missed the signs of the code having been broken.

8. Of course, antelope's inertia is good for the cheetah, not the antelope, which, however, has a few tricks in store to make up for it, such as injecting randomness into its behavior (e.g., Brembs 2011). Concerning the role of foresight in advanced cognition, see Edelman 2008 and the references therein. Still et al. (2012, 120604-1) showed that "any system constructed to keep memory about its environment and to operate with maximal energetic efficiency has to be predictive." Chaitin (2018) highlights the dependence of the very possibility of SCIENCE on the simplicity of the laws of physics.

9. The term "satisficing"—a blend of "satisfying" (as in constraint satisfaction) and "sufficing" (as in sufficient as opposed to optimal)—has been coined by Simon (1956). Optimal behavior is out of the question because "maximizing utility in the real world involves a hopelessly complex constrained optimization problem" (Schooler, Ariely, and Loewenstein 2003). Bossaerts and Murawski (2017) review evidence showing that human decision-making is affected by computational complexity (surprise!). Bettis and Hu (2018) invoke complexity considerations specifically in the context of management theory and organizational behavior, noting (142): "The temporal limits on computation imposed by speed are much more severe than most people including scholars in business schools and social science realize." The book *Cognition and Intractability* by van Rooij et al. (2019b) is a definitive review of the state of the art.

10. For a computational account of emotions, see Bach and Dayan 2017.

11. Robert Musil's comment is from Musil [1937] 1979, 41.

Chapter 7

1. The "world's a stage" quote is from *As You Like It*, act 2, scene 7. Prospero's monologue is in *The Tempest*, act 4, scene 1. The question of whether or not Shakespeare has modeled Prospero on himself has been discussed by critics for centuries. In this

matter, I side with Coleridge, who in his "Notes on The Tempest" (published in 1836 in vol. 2 of his *Literary Remains*) refers parenthetically to Prospero as "the very Shakspeare himself, as it were, of the tempest."

2. See Ann Treisman (1986): "Just as reading is 'externally guided THINKING' [Neisser 1967, 136], so perception may be a form of controlled hallucination."

3. Because the mind consists of the computations carried out by the brain (Edelman 2008), it is "multiply realizable," that is, it can be realized in any physical substrate that is capable of supporting the necessary computations. This property naturally extends to the dynamic computation of consciousness (Moyal, Fekete, and Edelman 2020).

4. Feldman Barrett (2013) places emotions within the framework of EVOLUTION. For an overview of the role of emotions in cognition and consciousness, see Panksepp 2001 and 2005. A computational account of emotions can be found in Bach and Dayan 2017.

5. See also chapters 10 and 36. A good introduction to the phenomenon of lucid dreaming is LaBerge 1990. The terrifying aspects of EMPTINESS, in the context of both therapy and of Buddhist enlightenment, are discussed by Didonna and Rosillo Gonzalez (2009).

6. A comprehensive philosophical and scientific argument for the EMPTINESS of the self has been made by Metzinger (2003), whose book is tellingly titled *Being No One*.

7. For a detailed account of the idea of mind as computation, see Edelman 2008; a shorter and more accessible treatment can be found in Edelman 2012. Consciousness as a computational process that involves a self-model is explained by Metzinger (2004). Its brain basis is discussed by Merker (2013). For a synthesis of those two accounts, see Edelman 2008. A computational theory of basic consciousness (phenomenal experience) is developed in Moyal, Fekete, and Edelman 2020 and Fekete and Edelman 2011.

8. Empirical support for this computational theory includes the rubber hand illusion (Botvinick and Cohen 1998); experimentally induced out-of-body experiences (Blanke 2012; Ehrsson 2007; Lenggenhager et al. 2007); the experienced duplication of the bodily self (Heydrich et al. 2013); and sensory substitution (Bach-y-Rita and Kercel 2003).

9. I refer here not to Freudian pseudoscience, but rather to the real psychology and neuroscience of the unconscious (Kihlstrom 1995).

10. The "Splendor and Misery of Self-Models" is the title of Metzinger 2018. The absurdity quote is from Nagel 1971. The immortality of animals is remarked upon by the protagonist of "The Immortal" (Borges [1947] 1970d). Unamuno, whom Borges admired, had noted that "man, because he is man, because he possesses

consciousness, is already, in comparison to the jackass or the crab, a sick animal. Consciousness is a disease" (Unamuno 1972, 22; see also chapter 8). Leary (2004, 46; small caps added) has a stronger word for it: "Had the human self been installed with a mute button or off switch, the self would not be the curse to HAPPINESS that it often is."

11. The phrase "liberation from the self" can be found in Parfit 1984, 95; for an academic discussion of this idea in the context of Buddhism, see Chadha 2015. See also chapter 10.

Chapter 8

1. The four lines by Rachel Bluwstein, who wrote in Hebrew and is known in Israel as "Rachel the Poetess," are the first half of her 1927 poem "Are you the end?" (translation mine). For the complete poem, see http://kybele.psych.cornell.edu/~edelman/poetry/Rachel-are-you-the-end.html, where you can also find a link to the Hebrew original. The Borges quote is from the *Biografía Verbal* by Roberto Alifano (Barcelona: P&J, 1988), 23.

2. For a glimpse of my father's circumstances at the time of his suicide attempt, see Edelman 2014, ch. "58/10."

3. Being conscious of one's own protracted dying, even if it's painless, doesn't sound like fun to me. Strangely enough, Unamuno (1972, 47) makes light of such things: "Though at first blush meditation on our mortality is anguishing, in the end it fortifies us. Withdraw, reader, into yourself, and begin to imagine a slow dissolution of yourself: the light growing dim, things becoming dumb and soundless, silence enveloping you; the objects you handle crumbling between your fingers, the ground slipping from under your feet, your very memory vanishing as if in a swoon, everything melting away into nothingness and you yourself disappearing, not even the consciousness of nothingness remaining by way of grotesque handhold." The actual physiology of dying is described in Laureys 2005. For a focus on the dying brain, see Borjigin et al. 2013.

4. The Switch is analogous to the "bail-out" button in Greg Egan's (1994) novel of virtual reality and CONSCIOUSNESS, *Permutation City*. Another analogy is to the "first option" mentioned by Metzinger (2017) as a remedy to EXISTENCE and SUFFERING: "The first option, quite obviously, would consist in painlessly and unexpectedly killing all sentient beings."

5. On some accounts, Lucretius, whom Unamuno (1972, 104) calls "that terrifying Latin poet . . . whose apparent serenity and Epicurean *ataraxia* conceal so much despair," took his own life.

6. Out of the multitude of philosophical treatments of death, I would like to single out one brief paper by Nagel (1970), as well as part 67 of Parfit's book *Reasons and*

Persons (1984; small caps added). Those who need a reminder of just how emotionally distressing the contemplation of death could be should have a look at Payne 2000. For a review of the centrality of death ANXIETY across psychopathology, see Iverach, Menzies, and Menzies 2014. Surprisingly, RELIGION may not be of much help in these matters, as a comparative study of Buddhist monks and lay people, conducted by Nichols et al. (2018), has shown. Low death denial can actually have good consequences for one's subjective well-being (Cozzolino, Blackie, and Meyers 2014). Unfortunately, people who are not actually facing death find it difficult to imagine how it could be accepted (Goranson et al. 2017).

7. This quote is from Unamuno 1972, 51.

8. For some interesting insights into the traditional concept of salvation through RELIGION, see Björn Merker's *Vehicles of Hope* (1993). Öhman and Floridi (2017) dissect the relatively new notion of digital afterlife. The Silicon Valley take on death, which has everything to do with the systemic socioeconomic POWER differential, is well captured by the piece by Emily Dreyfuss, titled "Silicon Valley Would Rather Cure Death than Make Life Worth Living," which appeared in *Wired* on March 23, 2017.

9. The quoted passage from *The Silmarillion* (Tolkien 1977) concludes its first chapter. I have used it elsewhere in a paper that points out the apparent futility for an immortal being to cling both to its personal identity and its HAPPINESS (Edelman 2018).

10. These five lines from the fictional epic *The Creation of Éa* serve as the epigraph to Ursula Le Guin's *Earthsea* cycle, which begins with *A Wizard of Earthsea* (1968).

Chapter 9

1. This reminiscence by Gandalf is from the chapter "The White Rider" in *The Lord of the Rings: The Two Towers* (Tolkien 1954, bk. 3, ch. 5).

2. I was using Google Scholar, which by default searches papers published in English (a formal review of compassion literature [Gilbert 2019] supports this impression). The bigger picture may or may not be different: Heyes (2018, 503) reports "greater Empathic Concern in collectivist than individualist cultures."

3. Bloom (2017) compares empathy to compassion and discusses their role in MORALITY. Gilbert (2019), focusing specifically on compassion, found no consensus among researchers on what compassion is (emotion or motive). Not surprisingly in light of this conceptual confusion, there is hardly any theory behind the debate. Immordino et al. (2009, 8021) summarize their findings on the brain basis of empathy as follows: "The experience of all 4 emotions [admiration for virtue (AV), admiration for skill (AS), compassion for social/psychological pain (CSP), and compassion for

physical pain (CPP)] engaged brain regions involved in interoceptive representation and homeostatic regulation," as well as those involved in the "default mode of brain operation and in self-related/consciousness." For a more recent review of the neural mechanisms, development, and functions of empathy, see Decety 2015. It should be noted that because emotions in others are hard to recognize (Feldman et al. 2019), much of our compassion must be driven by "theory of mind" mechanisms (Heyes 1998; Siegal and Varley 2002), which in humans are at the same time powerful and relatively prone to biases and to being subverted by explicit THINKING.

4. Heyes (2018), whose paper is titled "Empathy Is Not in Our Genes," writes: "Empathy is both agile and fragile. It can be enhanced and redirected by novel experience, and broken by social change."

5. The following passage (with the Russian original text omitted to save space) from the sci-fi novel *Hard to Be a God* (*Трудно быть богом*) by Arkady and Boris Strugatsky ([1964] 1973) illustrates why it is "of related interest" to this chapter on empathy. It describes an after-dinner conversation between Rumata, a "progressor"—Earth agent tasked with advancing exoplanet civilizations—who is embedded under cover as a nobleman in a feudal society on a distant world, and Budah, a persecuted local intellectual and alchemist, whom Rumata had earlier that day broken out of a state prison. Rumata speaks first:

"But still, imagine that you are God . . ."
Budah laughed.
"If I could imagine myself a god, I would become one!"
"Well, what if you could advise God?"
"You have a rich imagination," Budah said contentedly. "That's good. Are you literate? Excellent! I would love to tutor you . . ."
"You flatter me. . . . But still, what would you advise the Almighty? What, in your opinion, should the Omnipotent do so that you would say: Now the world is good and kind?"
Budah, smiling approvingly, leaned back and crossed his hands on his belly. Kira looked at him hungrily.
"Well," he said, "here's what I would do. I would tell the Lord: 'Creator, I do not know your plans, perhaps you have no intention of making people good and happy. Choose to wish this! It is so easily achieved! Give people enough bread, meat and wine, give them shelter and clothing. Let hunger and need disappear, and with them everything that separates people.'"
"And that's it?" asked Rumata.
"You think that is not enough?"
Rumata shook his head. "God would answer: 'This would not benefit people. For the strong of the world will take from the weak what I have given them, and the weak still will be destitute.'"
"I would ask God to protect the weak. 'Admonish the cruel rulers,' I would say."
"Cruelty is power. Without cruelty, the rulers will lose their power, and other cruel ones will take over."
Budah stopped smiling.
"Punish the cruel ones," he said firmly, "so the strong ones would not dare to be cruel to the weak."

"Man is born weak. He becomes strong when there is nobody around stronger than him. When the cruel among the strong are punished, their place will be taken by the stronger among the weak. Also cruel. In this way one would have to punish everybody, and I do not want that."

"You know best, o Lord. Then simply make it so that people have everything and do not take from each other what you have given them."

"This will not benefit people either," sighed Rumata, "for when they get everything for free, without effort, from my hands, they will forget work, will lose the taste of life and will become my domestic animals, whom I will then have to feed and clothe forever."

"Do not give them everything at once!" said Budah hotly. "Give them a little at a time, gradually!"

"Gradually people themselves will take all that they will need."

Budah laughed awkwardly.

"Yes, I see this is not so simple," he said. "Somehow I have never considered these matters. It seems we have run out of ideas. However," he leaned forward, "here is one more possibility. Make it so that all people love work and knowledge the most, so that work and knowledge become the only purpose in their lives!"

Yes, we were planning to do this, too, thought Rumata. Mass hypnoinduction, positive remoralization. Hypnoradiators on the three equatorial satellites . . .

"I could do that," he said. "But is it worth it to deprive the human race of its history? Is it worth it to substitute this humanity by another one? Would it not be the same thing as erasing this humanity from the face of the Earth and creating a new one in its place?" Budah considered this silently. Rumata waited. Outside the window, the carriages were squeaking gloomily. Budah said quietly:

"Then, o Lord, erase us from the face of this Earth and create again, more perfect. Or better still, let us be and choose our own way."

"My heart is full of pity," said Rumata slowly. "I cannot do that."

Chapter 10

1. A penetrating introduction to the doctrine of emptiness, which is central to Mahāyāna Buddhism, can be found in Garfield 1994; for the MATHEMATICS that can be used to formalize it, see Priest 2009. Here, suffice it to say that emptiness is the immediate consequence of *pratītyasamutpāda*—the "dependent origination" or "dependent arising" of all phenomena, which merely states the fact that nothing exists in itself, in complete disconnection from the rest of the universe (see chapter 14, esp. note 13). As Garfield (1994, 227) explains it, "Dependent origination simply is the explicability and coherence of the universe. Its emptiness is the fact that there is no more to it than that."

2. This quote, which appears also in chapter 36, is from Garfield's essay "Taking Conventional Truth Seriously" (2010, 12). The rest of the quote, which touches upon the concept of SUFFERING, can be found in chapter 36, note 16.

3. The Einstein quote is from a letter to Eduard Study, September 25, 1918, in the Einstein Archive, Hebrew University, Jerusalem; translation in D. Howard, *Perspectives on Science* 1, no. 225 (1993). Einstein's views on what "real" might mean may be compared to those of Williams (1962) on philosophical ontology.

4. There is at least one approach to the foundations to physics that seems like a perfect expression of the doctrine of dependent origination (Hamlin 2017, 587–588): "The TSM [Theory of Structural Multiverse] also explains why physical reality itself appears to be purely structural. We cannot single out any particularly physical objects from an analysis of a single state of reality. . . . There is *no-thing* that is the electron, but it is simply a pattern in the structure of our universe. . . . A structural universe is described in terms of a network of relations. This entails that a structural universe is free of any self-subsistent or material objects."

5. Concerning salvation, see chapter 9.

6. This is the central point made by Siderits (2003), who defends "a semantic interpretation of emptiness," which holds "the doctrine to concern not the nature of reality, but the nature of truth." According to Siderits, "The role emptiness plays in liberation from suffering is ancillary in nature; it is the doctrine of non-self that continues to play the chief role in that project, while emptiness serves just to correct for certain common errors in the application of non-self. . . . The doctrine of emptiness is intended to prevent a subtle form of clinging that may grow out of one's appreciation of the doctrine of non-self, and may thus prove an impediment to complete liberation. . . . Desire and attachment are to be overcome, on the Buddhist path, not because their objects are unsatisfactory, but because they tend to re-inscribe false belief in the 'I'" (16).

7. The essay on the nonexistence of self (Borges [1922] 1999c) is the first item in the definitive collection of his nonfiction, edited by Eliot Weinberger.

8. Which did not quite amount to HAPPINESS:

> I have committed the worst sin of all
> That a man can commit. I have not been
> Happy. Let the glaciers of oblivion
> Drag me and mercilessly let me fall.

From "Remorse" by J. L. Borges (in "The Iron Coin," included in *Selected Poems*, ed. Alexander Coleman, New York: Viking, 1999).

9. In Aguilar Mora 1999, 8. Borges's "Fragmentos" (included in Borges 1969) appear in the present book also in chapters 18, 20, 29, and 32. Concerning Pascal's Wager, see chapter 29, esp. note 16.

Chapter 11

1. The first quote is the title of Dobzhansky 1973. The other two are from Gintis 2007, 1; and Godfrey-Smith 2016b, 495.

2. This remark echoes Xenophanes of Colophon, who has written (Fragment 16) that "Ethiopians say that their gods are snub-nosed and black; Thracians that they

are pale and red-haired." For a review of human religious diversity, see Norenzayan, Hansen, and Cady 2008.

3. Equating evolution with *unconstrained* change would be very wrong. As David Sloan Wilson (2015, 4) wrote, "I am often advised to use the word 'change' rather than 'evolution' to avoid triggering negative associations in the various audiences that I address. I take great care to ignore this advice."

4. Laland et al. (2015) describe the current consensus regarding the "Extended Evolutionary Synthesis"—a conceptual explanatory framework that encompasses a broad range of evolutionary processes, including reciprocal causation (organisms serving as active agents in evolution), inclusive inheritance (more than just genes), and developmental bias (including phenotypic accommodation). For a nontechnical book-length treatment of these ideas, see Jablonka and Lamb 2006. A discussion of cultural evolution within this framework can be found in Mesoudi, Whiten, and Laland 2006. For an application to behavioral sciences in general, see Gintis 2007.

5. Water penetrating into a volcanic hot spot may cause major earthquakes, bringing about rapid and drastic changes in the landscape. These would be analogous to the so-called major evolutionary transitions (Szathmáry and Maynard Smith 1995). Godfrey-Smith (2016a), looking for "pivotal transitions," singles out the emergence of networks of neurons: "A nervous system is a control system that, given its role, must be partly 'decoupled' from metabolic goings-on."

6. The key concept in this connection is *inclusive fitness*; see, for instance, Laland et al. 2015.

7. Gintis (2007, 10) makes this point explicitly: "Fitness cannot be equated with well-being in any creature. Humans, in particular, live in an environment so dramatically different from that in which our preferences evolved that it seems to be miraculous that we are as capable as we are of achieving high levels of individual well-being" (see also Nesse 2004). More generally, "many products of evolution are not adaptive in any sense. Even traits that count as adaptive in the evolutionary sense of the word can be maladaptive from the standpoint of human welfare" (Wilson et al. 2014, 3.1).

8. The concept of territorial dispersal is defined and discussed in Farine, Montiglio, and Spiegel 2015 and Mace 2016. See also chapter 5, note 8.

9. Regarding the economic origins of ultrasociality, see Gowdy and Krall 2016. In humans one consequence of ultrasociality may have been the emergence of experienced pain, as contrasted to mere discomfort brought about by a physiological distress (Finlay and Syal 2014).

10. See note 7 for this chapter. Gintis (2007, 10) writes that "our preference predispositions have not 'caught up' with our current environment and, given especially

the demographic transition and our excessive present-orientation, they may never catch up."

11. My family receives periodic reassurances from me to the effect that I do not do crazy things while hiking solo.

12. In the original, "Дело помощи утопающим—дело рук самих утопающих," in chapter 34 of *The Twelve Chairs* (1928) by I. Ilf and E. Petrov. This appears to be a parody on a slogan that was well-known in the USSR at the time: "The emancipation of the working class must be the work of the working class itself." It is a quote from an 1879 essay by Karl Marx and Friedrich Engels, "Strategy and Tactics of the Class Struggle," sent in a letter to some of Germany's leading Social Democrats—Bebel, Liebknecht, and others. https://www.marxists.org/archive/marx/works/1879/09/17 .htm.

13. For an overview of the CRISPR technology, see Ledford 2015.

14. See the discussion and references in Williams 2007, 310.

15. See *Evolving the Future: Toward a Science of Intentional Change* (Wilson et al. 2014). Wright (2013) discusses the possibilities for positive change in POLITICS.

Chapter 12

1. The Sophocles quote (from *Oedipus at Colonus*, 1224) and the "old Jewish reply" appear in an essay titled "The Makropulos Case: Reflections on the Tedium of Immortality" (Williams 1973, 87).

2. In philosophy, a present-day stance that echoes Shammai's in normatively preferring nonexistence over existence is referred to as anti-natalism; see, for instance, Parfit 1984, part 4 or, more recently, Benatar's book *Better Never to Have Been: The Harm of Coming into Existence* (2006). Harman (2009) offers a critique of Benatar's arguments. Metzinger (2017) discusses the positive implications of anti-natalism for the reduction of SUFFERING in the world.

3. Existentialist philosopher Jean-Paul SARTRE, the author of *Being and Nothingness* (*L'être et le néant*, [1943] 1956), also published a series of novels *Les chemins de la liberté* (*The Roads to Freedom*). The first three books (Sartre 1963a, b, c) were titled *L'âge de raison*, *Le sursis*, and *La mort dans l'âme*; the fourth manuscript, left unfinished, was *La dernière chance*. The Last Chance mountain range in Death Valley, California, which makes an appearance in chapter 35, has been named independently.

4. In a study of mind-wandering, Killingsworth and Gilbert (2010) reported that "mind wandering occurred in 46.9% of the samples and in at least 30% of the samples taken during every activity except making love." For some more recent findings, see Seli et al. 2018.

5. Killingsworth and Gilbert (2010) found that mind-wandering negatively affects momentary subjective well-being (happiness). For reviews of the negative effects of rumination on emotions in general, see Mor and Winquist 2002, Rogers and Joiner 2017, and Thomsen 2006.

6. "Man has been created . . ." (Человек создан для счастья, как птица для полёта; from the essay "Paradox," published in 1894 by V. G. Korolenko).

7. On the relationship between EVOLUTION and HAPPINESS, see Nesse 2004.

8. Learning and practicing mindfulness may or may not help; see Gu et al. 2015.

9. Rumination and prospection are two sides of the same cognitive process that implements MEMORY in the brain (Buckner 2010; Eichenbaum, MacDonald, and Kraus 2014; Gilbert and Wilson 2007).

Chapter 13

1. The mask incident is from act 1, scene 2 of *The King in Yellow*, a fictional play that is mentioned and quoted from in the eponymous series of short stories by Robert W. Chambers, published in 1895. The Bene Gesserit Litany against Fear, which serves as the second epigraph, appears in several places in Frank Herbert's 1965 novel *Dune*. The terror/civilization quote is from Horkheimer and Adorno [1944] 2002, 180: "One cannot abolish terror and retain civilization. Even to relax the former means the beginning of disintegration. The most diverse conclusions can be drawn from this: from the worship of fascist barbarism to a flight into the circles of Hell."

2. The black ghost knifefish (*Apteronotus albifrons*) is a "weakly electric" fish endogenous to the Amazon basin, which generates a weak electrical field allowing it to sense its immediate environment in complete darkness. See MacIver 2009 for an instructive discussion of EVOLUTIONARY and behavioral aspects of visual and other modes of sensing.

3. Audiences everywhere enjoy the thrills of watching a made-up WAR on one's screen, but shun reports from real wars, of which any number are under way at any time out there in the wide world. Watching a made-up war is not only safer: people are generally good and they want the good guys to win, which cannot be guaranteed in a real war.

4. Snow and Taylor (2006) offer an early survey of the U.S. war propaganda following the 9/11 terrorist attacks. Since then, meticulous and extensive document-based research into government propaganda has been carried out. For instance, Norton (2017, 543), who specializes in U.S. constitutional law, concludes in her analysis of the "war on terror" that "the government has also engaged in wartime fearmongering and lies, with at times devastating effects not only on its intended targets but also on the American public." Likewise, Robinson (2017, 47), who studied the U.K.

involvement in the Iraq war, reports evidence that it had been driven by "a broader and covert geo-strategic policy, including action against Syria and Iran, . . . which was underpinned by a 'close knit propaganda campaign.'"

5. The terrible toll of having to live for decades under the rule of terror comes across starkly in the *Narratives of Fear in Syria* by Pearlman (2016), who studied civil WAR and conflict with political Islam in Syria through the lens of interviews with 200 refugees from that country. Here is a typical passage from one of the interviews: "'My three-year-old can tell the difference between different missiles and rockets,' a mother from Aleppo said" (28). While the civil war inflicted extreme SUFFERING on millions of people, participating in the uprising also helped some of the citizens assert their individual and collective existence in spite of the regime's murderous oppression: "Fear no longer seems as automatic as breathing" (32).

6. The first chapter of *Dune* recounts how Paul Atreides, the young heir of Duke Leto, managed to master extreme pain by reciting the Litany against Fear. The science of fear and pain suggests that it would be a mistake to do so in real life: pain is actually inhibited by fear, which thereby serves a useful purpose of facilitating escape behavior (Bolles and Fanselow 1980). Concerning the roots of feigned fearlessness in privilege, DiTommaso (1992) offers some very useful insights (as well as conceptual tools for understanding the *Dune* universe in general): "Paul represents the zenith of this training. He has been taught by a Bene Gesserit (Prana/Bindu and the Way), a mentat (hyper-computation and the use of mnemonics), warmasters (personal combat and battle tactics), and a Duke (politics and leadership). He is at the apex of the pyramidal faufreluches, even down to his superior genetic history."

7. It should be noted that fear of death has been found to amplify retributive justice motivations and to encourage political violence (Hirschberger et al. 2016).

8. Instilling fear at home as well as abroad is common practice in the governance of states, especially ones with imperial aspirations. For examples and discussion in the context of the United States, see Skoll 2016; for parallel findings from Russian politics, see Dutkievicz and Kazarinova 2017 and Gel'man 2015.

9. The "noonday panic" quote is from Horkheimer and Adorno [1944] 2002, 22.

Chapter 14

1. Einstein's response to the question of "free will" appears in "What Life Means to Einstein: An Interview by George Sylvester Viereck," *Saturday Evening Post*, October 26, 1929, 17. The snippet of dialogue of Borges with a time-displaced version of himself is from Borges 1999a.

2. Khodja Nasreddin (Nasir ud-Din Mahmood al-Khoyi) was a contemporary and compatriot of Mawlana Jalal ud-Din Rumi, who lived in the thirteenth century CE

in the Seljuk sultanate of Rum, in present-day Turkey. The "khodja" honorific signifies that Nasreddin had completed the Hajj pilgrimage to Mecca. Several hundred stories about Nasreddin have been collected by Idries Shah (1966) in two volumes, *The Exploits of the Incomparable Mulla Nasrudin* and *The Subtleties of the Inimitable Mulla Nasrudin* (London: Octagon).

3. The principles of the Special Relativity Theory have been laid out in Einstein 1905. The concept of light cone is based on a particular way of plotting SRT's constraint on causality. When plotted in four-dimensional spacetime coordinates, with time measured in seconds and distances in light-seconds, all possible causes and effects of a given event are confined to a region shaped like a 45° double cone, whose apex is at that event. It must be noted that the understanding of the ultimate nature of space and TIME in physics is far from complete; for a peek into the complications arising out of these concepts, see Callender 2017.

4. I am aware that appeals to physical theories—even the most empirically successful and universally accepted ones, such as Special Relativity—are generally unpopular with philosophers working on free will. Here is a case against invoking physics in this context, as advanced by J. M. Fischer (2012, 118): "It is implausible that our status as agents, who do things and are responsible for their effects, should hinge on subtle ruminations of theoretical physicists" ("Semicompatibilism and Its Rivals," *Journal of Ethics* 16:117–143). I'll leave it to you to decide whether or not this argument has intrinsic merit. Note: I came across the Fischer quote in Usher 2018, which offers a useful snapshot of contemporary philosophical thinking about free will.

5. For a useful introduction to the psychological aspects of the experience of free will, see Wegner 2004. I have offered elsewhere a somewhat detailed discussion of these matters (Edelman 2008, 10.1.3).

6. The conceptual vacuity of "free will" has been argued by Voltaire (Philosophical Dictionary, 224; quoted in Dennett 1984, 143): "Now you receive all your ideas; therefore you receive your wish, you wish therefore necessarily. . . . The will, therefore, is not a faculty that one can call free. The free will is an expression absolutely devoid of sense, and what the scholastics have called will of indifference, that is to say willing without cause, is a chimera unworthy of being combated."

7. The phrase "Chance and Necessity," which serves as the title of a famous book on EVOLUTION by Jacques Monod, is part of a quote attributed by him to Democritus: "Everything existing in the Universe is the fruit of chance and necessity." It has been noted that chance is not a concept that is native to Greek philosophy and that the above quote is not actually found among any of the surviving texts by Democritus; A. Danchin, "Order and Necessity," in *From Enzyme Adaptation to Natural Philosophy: Heritage from J Monod*, ed. E. Quagliariello, G. Bernardi, and A. Ullmann (Amsterdam: Elsevier 1987), 187–196.

8. Thus, what the widely accepted Copenhagen interpretation of quantum mechanics sees as irreducible "ontological" or being-related randomness, Einstein considered to be merely "epistemic," that is, having to do with knowledge (or rather, ignorance). The God and dice quote is from a letter to Max Born (December 4, 1926): "Quantum mechanics is certainly imposing. But an inner voice tells me that it is not yet the real thing. The theory says a lot, but does not really bring us any closer to the secret of the 'old one.' I, at any rate, am convinced that *He* does not throw dice."

9. The theoretical debate and the experimental work concerning the nature and role of randomness in quantum mechanics has been focusing on the interpretation and the testing of Bell's inequality (The BIG Bell Test Collaboration 2018). It involves seemingly simple and intuitive but in fact highly technical concepts such as measurement, hidden variables, and "local realism," which cannot be discussed here without some major digressions into contemporary physical thinking. One general observation that can be made, though, is that Bell's inequality and related results (such as the "Free Will Theorem" of Conway and Kochen 2006) relate to randomness, not freedom. In addition, as The BIG Bell Test Collaboration 2018 authors acknowledge, Bell's approach is conditional: "Assuming no faster-than-light communication, such experiments can prove the conditional premise that *if human will is free*, there are physical events (the measurement outcomes in the Bell tests) that are intrinsically random, that is, impossible to predict" (my italics; compare 't Hooft 2016, 47: "Bell's theorem requires more hidden assumptions than usually thought: *The quantum theory only contradicts the classical one if we assume that the 'counterfactual modification' does not violate the laws of thermodynamics.*"). Elsewhere in that paper, the authors note: "The theory that the entire experiment, including choices and outcomes, is pre-determined by initial conditions is known as superdeterminism. Superdeterminism cannot be tested" (47).

10. See the previous note. In stating that "superdeterminism cannot be tested," The BIG Bell Test Collaboration (2018, 217) cites Belle et al., "An Exchange on Local Beables," *Dialectica* 39 (1985): 85–110.

11. The view of the Universe as a deterministic computer that computes its fate over TIME brings to mind the opening lines of T. S. Eliot's "Burnt Norton" (1943):

Time present and time past
Are both perhaps present in time future
And time future contained in time past.

For another passage from that poem, see chapter 35, note 9.

12. A notable proponent of superdeterminism is theoretical physicist and Nobel laureate Gerard 't Hooft. In 't Hooft 2019, he writes:

Today's attempts at formulating "theories of everything" must look extremely clumsy in the eyes of beings whose brains have had more time, say another few million years, to evolve further. The present author is convinced that many of the starting points researchers have investigated up to now are totally inappropriate, but that cannot be helped. We are just baboons who have only barely arrived on the scene of science. Using my own limited brain power, I am proposing a somewhat different starting point.

't Hooft acknowledges that his views are in the minority: "I am aware of the large numbers of baboons around me whose brains have arrived at different conclusions."

13. To be spared the chore of reading Hegel, consider instead this passage from Engels 1878, I, xi:

> Hegel was the first to state correctly the relation between freedom and necessity. To him, freedom is the insight into necessity (die Einsicht in die Notwendigheit).
>   "Necessity is blind only in so far as it is not understood [begriffen]."

Or, have a look at some of the recent discussions of Hegel's conception of freedom, such as Dyde 1894 or James 2012. The notion of necessity in the context of causation is of course much older than Hegel. It can be discerned in the metaphor of Indra's net, invoked in Hinduism (e.g., in Atharva Veda) and in Buddhism, where it is used to motivate the key doctrine of *pratītyasamutpāda*—"dependent origination" or "dependent arising" (Garfield 1994) (see chapter 1, note 8, and chapter 10, note 1, as well as the rest of chapter 10). Interestingly, while superdeterminism gives a new meaning to the doctrine of dependent origination, and therefore to the Buddhist idea of emptiness, an epitome of philosophical idealism, it is fundamentally a realist stance.

14. See 't Hooft 2016, 4: "Neither determinism nor 'superdeterminism' imply 'pre-determinism,' since no human and no machine can ever calculate faster than Nature itself." The same point has been made in Edelman 2008 and, more recently, in Lloyd 2012. On a related note, in the second film of the *Matrix* trilogy, the tension between determination and indeterminacy is embodied, on the one hand, in the Merovingian's restaurant-scene monologue about cause and effect ("Why are you here?") and, on the other hand, in the Oracle's pronouncement that "We can never see past the choices we don't understand."

15. In the philosophical literature on free will and morality, there is much nuance that I gloss over here. A good introduction to the philosophical deliberations on these matters can be found in Pereboom 1995, who concludes his paper as follows:

> Given that free will of some sort is required for moral responsibility, then libertarianism, soft determinism, and hard determinism, as typically conceived, are jointly exhaustive positions (if we allow the "deterministic" positions the view that events may result from indeterministic processes of the sort described by quantum mechanics). Yet each has a consequence that is difficult to accept. If libertarianism were true, then we would expect events to occur that are incompatible with what our physical theories predict to be overwhelmingly likely. If soft determinism were true, then agents would deserve blame for their wrongdoing even though their actions were produced by processes beyond their control. If hard determinism were true, agents would not be morally responsible—agents would never deserve blame for even the most cold-blooded and calmly executed evil actions. I have argued that hard determinism could be the easiest view to accept. Hard determinism need not be of the hardest sort. It

need not subvert the commitment to doing what is right, and although it does undermine some of our reactive attitudes, secure analogues of these attitudes are all one requires for good interpersonal relationships. Consequently, of the three positions, hard determinism might well be the most attractive, and it is surely worthy of more serious consideration than it has been accorded.

16. The relevant notion of the self is due to Dennett 2003, 136:

> [The boundaries of the mind are] far enough back to give my *self* enough spread in space and time so that there is a *me* for my decisions to be up to!

This may be compared with the tradition passed down from one of the most prominent Buddhist philosophers, Nāgārjuna (ca. 150–250 AD), as recounted by Gier and Kjellberg (2004, 136):

> Thus while we would assume that there has to be a self in order for there to be freedom, Nagarjuna would say that there is freedom only to the extent that there is not a self. . . . If we cannot call the karmic web free since it lacks a self, by the same token we cannot call it determined, since nothing outside of it is causing it. To the extent that people identify a self, that self is determined by causes outside of it. The more cultivated they become on the Buddhist model, the less they think this way. The less who thinks this way? A question that the European philosopher might ask. Nagarjuna's answer is *no one*, really. The non-personal web of causes and conditions sheds the delusion, or, rather, ceases to give rise to it. (italics in original)

See Edelman 2008, ch. 9, 10, for a computational take on these ideas.

17. Concerning the doctrine of dependent arising, see note 13 above.

18. The quote is from Virgil's *Georgica* (II, v. 490): "Felix qui potuit rerum cognoscere causas."

Chapter 15

1. Abdel-Jaouad (1993) describes Isabelle Eberhardt (1877–1904) as "a legend. This Rimbaud-type woman repudiated Europe and its civilization, converted to Islam, dressed as a man, assumed a male identity, and roamed the Sahara, untrammeled by the constraints of her youth and sex." The quote in the epigraph of chapter 15 is from an article about her, titled "Isabelle Eberhardt—Portrait of a Legend" by Leslie Blanch, *Cornhill Magazine* 166, no. 991 (Spring 1952): 5.

2. This joke dates back to the 1970s "energy crisis," precipitated by an oil embargo that was imposed on the United States by the Organization of Oil Exporting Countries (OPEC) in response to U.S. support of Israel in the 1973 Arab-Israeli War.

3. For a critical look at the positive psychology movement, see Held 2004 and Lazarus 2003a, b.

4. Dozens more examples can be found in Robert Burton's *The Anatomy of Melancholy* (1638).

5. The evolutionary roots of happiness are discussed in Nesse 2004. Schooler, Ariely, and Loewenstein (2003), among others, have documented the ways in which active pursuit of happiness is self-defeating (see also chapter 34, note 2). Edelman (2012) phrased the well-known advice against clinging to happiness as follows: "When fishing for happiness, catch and release."

6. The Keats quote is from his 1819 *Ode to a Nightingale*. An account of Solon's remark ("count no man happy"), made to Croesus, king of Lydia, can be found in both Herodotus (*The Histories*, 1.30) and Plutarch (*Lives, Solon*, 26).

7. For a brief catalog of the types of ecstasy, see Beer 2000. An overview of twentieth-century research up to the 1980s appears in Holm 1982, where many pointers to primary literature can also be found. The concept of ideal affect and its variation across cultures are reviewed in Joshanloo and Weijers 2014; Tsai 2017.

8. These examples, along with some others, are discussed in a paper titled "A Dark Side of Happiness? How, When, and Why Happiness Is Not Always Good" by Gruber, Mauss, and Tamir (2011). It also briefly reviews the relevant literature, including works on clinical conditions, such as hypomania and related disorders of affect.

9. Metzinger (2017) points out the ubiquity of suffering in the world, calling people's refusal to acknowledge it a "cognitive scotoma." The views of Epicurus on pleasure and happiness are analyzed by Annas (1987).

Chapter 16

1. The quote by Novalis (a pseudonym of Friedrich von Hardenberg) is from Part Second of *Henry of Ofterdingen*. The novel, in John Owen's English translation, is freely available online from Project Gutenberg. Le Guin's twist on the "going home" sentiment is from the opening page of *The Dispossessed* (1974b).

2. The concept of a housing "project" is familiar to city dwellers everywhere; and virtually everywhere such projects have created enormous social problems while trying to make housing affordable in the face of endemic POVERTY. Cupers (2016) discusses the possible roots of those problems in human territoriality. The Russian name for the projects we lived in, Хрущобы, is a pun that combines the Secretary-General Khrushchev's name with the Russian word for "slums," трущобы. These were all built in the early 1960s, when the government decided to do something about the decades-old "housing question," which had developed as millions of former peasants and displaced persons flooded the big cities after the 1917 revolution.

3. An often-cited passage containing this phrase is: "WAR is implacable; it poses a mercilessly sharp dilemma: either die, or catch up with the leading countries and overtake them also economically" (V. I. Lenin, *Collected Works*, 5th ed., vol. 34 [Moscow: State Publishing House of Political Literature, 1962], 198).

4. For some statistics and analysis of homelessness in the United States, see Tsai 2018); for data on бомжи (the homeless) in the USSR and post-Soviet Russia, see Stephenson 2000.

5. Edward Said, in his essay "Reflections on Exile" ([1984] 2000, 182), has noted this penchant for complaining: "No matter how well they may do, exiles are always eccentrics who feel their difference (even as they frequently exploit it) as a kind of orphanhood. Anyone who is really homeless regards the habit of seeing estrangement in everything modern as an affectation, a display of modish attitudes. Clutching difference like a weapon to be used with stiffened will, the exile jealously insists on his or her right to refuse to belong."

6. Erdős's extensive collaboration network—he coauthored papers with over five hundred people—inspired a measure of "distance" from its hub: the Erdős number. It is defined as 0 for the members of the set of people who coauthored a paper with Erdős himself, 1 for those who published with the members of that set, and so on. My Erdős number is 3.

7. Instead of Robert Ardrey's *The Territorial Imperative*, give Bruce Chatwin's *Songlines* a read. Here's a germane quote from Chatwin 1987, 178:

> Psychiatrists, politicians, tyrants are forever assuring us that the wandering life is an aberrant form of behavior; a neurosis; a form of unfulfilled sexual longing; a sickness which, in the interests of civilization, must be suppressed.
>
> Nazi propagandists claimed that gipsies and Jews—peoples with wandering in their genes—could find no place in a stable Reich.
>
> Yet, in the East, they still preserve the once universal concept: that wandering reestablishes the original harmony which once existed between man and the universe.

Robyn Davidson's (1996) book *Desert Places* documents her travels with the Rabari, a nomadic people of Rajasthan. The Israeli policy of "sedentarization" toward the Bedouin population of the Negev desert is discussed, for instance, in Falah 1989 and in Yahel and Kark 2016.

8. The medieval European invention of the immortal "Wandering Jew" (*le Juif errant*) is a classical expression of the mix of romanticization, mistrust, fear, and disdain of Jews as an "eternal" people without a homeland. Slezkine (2004) offers a brilliant analysis of the Jewish history in the twentieth century in terms of the concept of "service nomads." The founding of the State of Israel, which gained independence following a UN resolution in 1948, did not quite resolve all the problems arising from the Jewish historical background and intellectual tradition. Gordon (2017, 157) points out that the conflict between Zionist and universal humanist strands of political thinking in pre–World War II Jewish diaspora is not unique to Jewish politics: it reflects "a broader tension manifested in some shape or form in other national movements: many of the concepts of what nationhood is are adopted from alien cultures and often from the very culture from which the national movement seeks to dissociate." The emotional tools whereby the humanism of Jewish

settlers in the occupied West Bank is being perverted are analyzed by Hagemann (2015).

9. This proverb corresponds roughly to the biblical saying that a leopard can't change its spots; my usage is nonstandard. Note that with dogs, it's a different matter: a dog whom you feed will *not* leave you for the woods. In EVOLUTION theory, the changes in human traits that parallel the transition from wolf to dog are captured by the concept of self-domestication (Bunge 2017; Theofanopoulou et al. 2017).

10. The concept of existential migration is due to Madison (2016), who had published his analysis of collected interviews with "existential migrants" in *The End of Belonging*. In fantasy literature, two works that come to mind in this connection are Roger Zelazny's *Roadmarks* (in which Walt Whitman's book *Leaves of Grass* appears as a character) and Philip Jose Farmer's *Riverworld* series.

11. The Walt Whitman quote is from the "Song of the Open Road" (*Leaves of Grass* 82:11).

12. The existential restlessness of Tennyson's "Ulysses' is based on a few lines from Dante's *Inferno*, canto XXVI (Ulysses is in Dante's Hell for the treachery of the Trojan Horse). It is hard to believe that Tennyson wrote "Ulysses" in 1833 when he was only twenty-four; the depth of his insight into OLD AGE is a testament to his genius. The final line in that poem—"To strive, to seek, to find, and not to yield"—has always had a special meaning for me. I first came across it as a boy, reading Veniamin Kaverin's novel *The Two Captains*, where it bookends the protagonist's youth and his adult achievement. I have made much of this line in my 2012 book *The Happiness of Pursuit*. Only now, as I reread Kaverin while researching this chapter, it struck me that in *The Two Captains*, this line appears last, just like in Tennyson; and, moreover, that in Kaverin's novel, it serves as the inspirational hero's epitaph.

Chapter 17

1. For a handy (sorry, could not resist) visual reference, see the 1993 version of the film *Body Snatchers*.

2. The possible role of toolmaking pedagogy in language evolution has been discussed by several researchers (Kolodny and Edelman 2018; Laland 2017; Stout 2018).

3. Jakobson (1960) famously lists six functions of language: conative, referential, emotive, poetic, phatic, and metalingual; see his essay for the definitions of these terms. Mercier and Sperber (2011) defend the idea that language serves argumentation, not communication.

4. Related alternative takes on the standard notion of what language is for (communication) are available (e.g., Edelman 2019; Harris 1981; Love 2004; Ramscar and Baayen 2013).

5. The conversation between Frodo and Gandalf appears in *The Lord of the Rings: The Fellowship of the Ring* in the chapter "The Shadow of the Past" (Tolkien 1954, bk. 1, ch. 2). The occasion on which Círdan the Shipwright gave Narya to Gandalf is described in appendix B, section "The Third Age": "For this is the Ring of Fire, and with it you may rekindle hearts in a world that grows chill." Tolkien, who was a philologist by profession, may have been influenced here by Pushkin's famous poem "The Prophet": И, обходя моря и земли, / Глаголом жги сердца людей. (Through lands that dim and seas that darken, / Burn thou men's hearts with this, my Word), translated by Avraham Yarmolinsky.

6. It is worth noting that bullshit has become a technical concept in the philosophy of language (Frankfurt 2005). Likewise, the psychology of getting people to do what you want them to do is now studied as "Machiavellian intelligence" (Lucas et al. 2018).

7. The conception of language as a Game is due to Wittgenstein (1958); see also Edelman 2008, ch. 7.

8. See Edelman 2017.

9. Rabbits, rabbit parts, and events involving rabbits have figured rather prominently in the philosophy of language ever since the publication of Willard Van Orman Quine's *Word and Object* (1960).

10. For how the acquisition of the infant's first language is assisted by parents' actions, see Moerk 1996 and, more recently, Waterfall et al. 2010. Syal and Finlay (2010) identify social motivation as a key factor in the evolution and development of language. In linguistics too, the essentially social character of language is now increasingly recognized (Du Bois 2014; Linell 2013), except by the formalists, as discussed in Edelman 2019.

11. Hart and Risley (1995) were among the first to document the contribution of low socioeconomic status (SES) to a lasting disadvantage in language development. A more recent notable study is Romeo et al. 2018. For insight into the nature of the common profound individual differences in language proficiency, see, for example, Dąbrowska 2018 and Dąbrowska and Street 2006.

12. Le Guin's paradox of ineffability in fiction can be found in her introduction to a 1976 edition of *The Left Hand of Darkness*. Ineffability is a vast and infinitely entertaining topic, which, ironically, is best dealt with by getting it entangled in a web of fine language, as, for instance, Scharfstein (1993) has done. Liang (2011) develops a conceptual analysis of ineffability starting with the observation that language is digital and its grain is finite, as dictated by the need for it to be learnable. Polyglot readers need no reminding that ineffability is intimately related to the fundamental problems arising in translation, especially when wordplay is involved. A great example of the latter, which only Russian-English bilinguals will appreciate,

is *непостижимолость*, for which I can only offer the not nearly as punny translation "phoneysuckle." Some of the best commentaries on the vagaries of translation invoke the work of the Grand Master of language, Borges; two examples are Scholes 1977 and Hurley 1999.

13. According to Mieder 2004, the trope "a picture is worth a thousand words" (86) first appeared in an ad, created by Fred Barnard in 1921; its reversal can be traced back to the 1980s. For an argument against the possibility of forming a perfect visual counterpart to a text, see "Against Representation: A Note on Jorge Luis Borges' Aleph," by Stavans 2017.

Chapter 18

1. The two quoted lines by Rachel (see chapter 8, note 1) close her 1927 poem "A Song" (the translation is mine). For the complete poem, see http://kybele.psych.cornell .edu/~edelman/poetry/Rachel-zemer.html, where there is also a link to the Hebrew original. The Borges line is #50 (the penultimate one) in his "Fragmentos de un Evangelio apócrifo," in *Elogio de la sombra* (Borges 1969).

2. The tale of "Julnar the Sea-Born and Her Son King Badr Basim of Persia" is included in Richard Francis Burton's translation of *The Book of Thousand Nights and a Night* (Burton 1885). It is spread over Nights 738 through 756, all appearing in vol. 7 (https://www.wollamshram.ca/1001/Vol_7/tale153.htm).

3. The "Funniest Joke in the World" sketch first appeared in *Monty Python's Flying Circus*, series 1, episode 1 (1969).

4. Romantic love "suppresses mate-search mechanisms" (Fletcher et al. 2015).

5. The much-retold story of Layla and Majnun is based on a real seventh-century Bedouin couple, Qays ibn al-Mulawwah and his cousin Layla bint Mahdi, also called al-Aamiriya. One of the most famous versions is the twelfth-century Persian poem, "Laylī u Majnūn," by Niẓāmī Ganjavī (see Anvar 2011).

6. Braithwaite and Holt-Lunstad (2017) discuss the relationship between romantic love and mental health. Mirsu-Paun and Oliver (2017) reported a meta-analysis of twenty-one studies of the association between romantic relationships and mental health, in a total of more than nineteen thousand young adults. They found statistically significant but modest effects of both RRQ (romantic relationship quality) and RRB (romantic relationship breakups) on mental health outcomes (including depression, suicide ideation, deliberate self-harm, and suicide attempt). Fisher et al. (2016, 2) state that "regardless of its official diagnostic classification, we propose that romantic love should be considered as an addiction . . . : a positive addiction when one's love is reciprocated, non-toxic and appropriate, and a negative addiction when one's feelings of romantic love are socially inappropriate, toxic, not

reciprocated and/or formally rejected." Therapeutic interventions that contribute to self-expansion (the "inclusion of the other in the self" or IOS) have been proposed as means for alleviating romantic addiction. This makes me think of these lines from a poem by Guillaume Apollinaire, "Il me revient quelquefois . . .": "Si ton cœur cherche un cœur / Ton cœur seul est ce cœur" (If your heart seeks another heart / Your heart alone is that heart). See Apollinaire's *Early Poems* (1896–1910). For a link to the complete poem and my translation into English, see http://kybele.psych.cornell.edu/~edelman/poetry/Apollinaire-the-future.html.

7. Clearly, Badr-Basim, who was seventeen, was in love with his idea of the Princess, rather than with the Princess herself. In the story, when he meets her for the first time—after a shipwreck and not knowing it is her—he says to himself: "If this be not the Princess herself, 'tis one yet goodlier than she." This may not be an uncommon occurrence with impressionable teenagers; interestingly, Frankie Lymon, who wrote the 1956 hit "Why Do Fools Fall in Love," called his band The Teenagers.

8. Concerning human pair-bonding, see Fieder and Huber 2012; Fletcher et al. 2015. With regard specifically to love, Berscheid (2010) distinguishes four types: companionate, romantic, compassionate, and adult attachment.

9. Cf. Joan Baez: "Speaking strictly for me we both could've died then and there" (from her 1975 song "Diamonds and Rust"; see chapter 20). See also chapter 15.

Chapter 19

1. The Einstein quote is from a conversation between him and Princeton University mathematics professor Oscar Veblen, May 1921. *The Lord of the Rings* quote is from *The Return of the King* (Tolkien 1954, bk. 5, ch. 10). The talking math that wants you to go places is from M. John Harrison's novel *Light* (2002, 16).

2. The book was the Pulitzer-winning *Gödel, Escher, Bach: An Eternal Golden Braid* by Hofstadter (1979).

3. Einstein's complaint about his math difficulties is from his letter to high school student Barbara Lee Wilson (January 7, 1943), Einstein Archives 42-606, Hebrew University, Jerusalem, http://www.alberteinstein.info/.

4. The word "egghead" has often been used by right-wing politicians to refer to the academics and intellectuals whose independent THINKING they found so hard to tolerate. Here is part of U.S. Senator Milton Young's (R-ND) remarks on the death (of "acute hepatitis") of the great anti-Communist crusader, Senator McCarthy, as it appears in Congressional record:

> Mr. YOUNG. Mr. President, with the passing of Senator Joseph R. McCARTHY, the Senate of the United States and the Nation have sustained a tremendous loss. . . . At the moment, it is small comfort for the many supporters of Senator McCarthy's upright and fearless brand of Americanism that he was able to clean out many of the enemies of our Government despite

the hindrance of *eggheads*, leftwingers, New Dealers, and Communists. But history will record that Senator McCarthy was a relentless fighter for the right as he saw it, and those who were on his side are legion. (14763; my italics)

For an overview of the recent political history of the Know Nothing movement and its exploitation by the hegemony, see the essay on agnotology, or the science of ignorance, by Kadir (2017).

5. "As far as Ulrich was concerned, however, it could at least definitely be said that he loved mathematics because of the people who could not endure it. He was not so much scientifically as humanly in love with science" (Musil [1978] 1995, vol. 1, 35). Dipert (2003) analyzes Musil's stance on mathematics, as expressed in his essays and in *Man without Qualities*. The book *Infinite Resignation* by Thacker (2018) has some interesting observations on the power and pleasures of spite.

6. See Wigner 1960. A more recent treatment is Hamlin 2017, in which many additional useful references can be found.

7. "It is indeed quite surprising that mathematics, being non-empirical and characterized by deductive inferences should find such indispensable utility in our best description of empirically-studied physical reality" (Hamlin 2017, 572).

8. The preceding quote is from Hamlin 2017, 586–587; note the curious conceit of placing mathematicians somehow outside the physical universe. For a detailed step-by-step explanation (which quickly gets quite formal) of the concept of "structure" in this context, see Marquis 2018. The classical introduction to the discipline of metamathematics is Kleene 1952.

9. One version of Euclid's Fifth Postulate is as follows: "If a line segment intersects two straight lines forming two interior angles on the same side that sum to less than two right angles, then the two lines, if extended indefinitely, meet on that side on which the angles sum to less than two right angles." The problematic axiom in set theory, the Axiom of Choice, states that "given any collection of bins, each containing at least one object, it is possible to make a selection of exactly one object from each bin, even if the collection is infinite."

10. The title of Whitehead and Russell's three-volume work echoed Isaac Newton's (1687) magnum opus, *Philosophiæ Naturalis Principia Mathematica*. The ideas in Gödel's original paper (Gödel 1931) are discussed enthusiastically and at length by Hofstadter (1979).

11. My closest professional brush with Gödel's First Incompleteness Theorem came when as a first-year MSc student I chanced to read a technical report (Barricelli 1983) whose author claimed to have found a flaw in Gödel's original proof. An exchange of letters that ensued convinced me that, unlike myself, Barricelli subscribed to the so-called Intuitionist (Brouwer 1952) interpretation of set theory, so that in effect we were talking past each other. This experience made me want to write a thesis

comparing the many published proofs of Gödel's Theorem, but I could not find a faculty member willing to supervise such a project and so I ended up working on computer vision instead.

12. For the record, I do have an informed opinion on the implications of the incompleteness results for cognitive science and AI, but any attempt to spell it out would take me far outside the scope of this book. Readers interested in a modern and accessibly written article on these topics are advised to have a look instead at Chaitin 2018.

13. A version of rationality rooted in Bayesian statistics is discussed by Chater et al. 2018.

14. Hamlin (2017) notes that "random or stochastic processes have no place in structural universes" but also mentions some structural frameworks, such as Everett's many-worlds interpretation of quantum mechanics (Deutsch 1997) that can accommodate randomness.

15. This phrase is from McCulloch 1956, 152. It is best thought of in the context of the Le Guin quote on uncertainty, which appears in chapter 38.

16. The Mishna reference is Pirkei Avot 4:1.

Chapter 20

1. Any essay on memory must begin by acknowledging that most of what is worth writing about it has already been written by Borges. The first quote in the epigraph, on memory, is from *Dreamtigers* (*El Hacedor*, Borges 1964). The second quote, on oblivion, is #27 in "Fragmentos de un Evangelio apócrifo," published in Borges 1969. It should be considered alongside another line by Borges (from a poem bearing the English title "Everness"): "Sólo una cosa no hay. Es el olvido" (One thing does not exist. It is oblivion).

2. This chapter focuses on *episodic* memory (Tulving 2002). For an overview of the role of memory in behavior and its brain basis, see Glenberg 1997 and Squire 2004. Fivush and Haden (2003) survey the involvement of memory in constructing the narrative self. The *Waters of Lethe* painting (1879–1880) is by John Roddam Spencer Stanhope. The Naihe bridge is mentioned in Yang 1993 and is invoked, in the context of historical memory and POLITICS in China, by Schwarcz (1991).

3. No, holding onto memory's diamonds would do us no good. "We are all nostalgic for a time when we were not nostalgic. But there seems to be no way back" (Boym 2001, 355).

4. Consider these lines from Dante's *Inferno* (canto 5, lines 121–123), which refer to the Christian hell: "Nessun maggior dolore / Che ricordarsi del tempo felice / Nella

miseria (There is no greater sorrow / Than to be mindful of the happy time / In misery). Immersive virtual reality TECHNOLOGY can in principle support the construction of virtual hells, as in Iain M. Banks's novel *Surface Detail* (2010).

5. The quote is from Tennyson's "Ulysses," lines 51–52.

6. Regarding the importance of forgetting, Richards and Frankland (2017) write: "The goal of memory is not the transmission of information through time, per se. Rather, the goal of memory is to optimize decision-making. As such, transience is as important as persistence in mnemonic systems" (1071). For a review of adaptive forgetting, see Wimber et al. 2015.

7. The correlation in mammals between the volume of cerebral cortex and longevity has been documented by Merker (2004), who explains it by positing that long-term memory retention takes up cortical volume in proportion to the amount of information.

8. The name of Borges is usually associated with writing about memory, but forgetting also figures prominently in his works. In particular, Weinrich ([1997] 2004, 211) noted that "for Borges forgetting makes the passage of TIME concrete—in an anguishing, disturbing way" (quoted in Karageorgou-Bastea 2017; small caps added).

9. Mind-wandering in TIME includes both retrospection and prospection (Gilbert and Wilson 2007). For an account that integrates these ideas with the virtual-reality function of PERCEPTION and CONSCIOUSNESS, see Edelman 2012, ch. 4.

10. The quoted lines ("the baseless fabric of this vision") are from Shakespeare's *The Tempest*, act 4, scene 1. The centrality of memory to imagination is well established (Buckner 2010; Schacter and Addis 2007). Of course, Borges had known that all along: "La imaginación está hecha de convenciones de la memoria. Si yo no tuviera memoria no podría imaginar" (Imagination is made of the conventions of memory. Without memory, one cannot imagine; from an interview given to *El Pais*, 1985). For a theoretical account of creativity as the pursuit of variations on a theme, see Hofstadter 1985.

11. That people usually fail to notice when their minds are wandering actually stands to reason, given that it takes meta-awareness, a faculty that is not often deployed in everyday life.

12. For the emotional dimensions of memory, see LaBar and Cabeza 2006. The impact of ruminative introspection on hedonic experience is typically negative (Thomsen 2006) and can lead to suicidal ideation (Rogers and Joiner 2017). Schooler, Ariely, and Loewenstein (2003, 52) offer the following relevant intuition: "It is possible that engaging in hedonic appraisal might cause individuals to attend to elements of the experience that might have, could have, or should have been, and such comparisons may lead to disappointment and regret."

13. Here is the epilogue to *Dreamtigers* (*El Hacedor*, 1964) by Borges: "Un hombre se propone la tarea de dibujar el mundo. A lo largo de los años puebla un espacio con imágenes de provincias, de reinos, de montañas, de bahías, de naves, de islas, de peces, de habitaciones, de instrumentos, de astros, de caballos y de personas. Poco antes de morir, descubre que ese paciente laberinto de líneas traza la imagen de su cara" (A man sets out to draw the world. As the years go by, he peoples a space with images of provinces, kingdoms, mountains, bays, ships, islands, fishes, rooms, instruments, stars, horses, and individuals. A short time before he dies, he discovers that the patient labyrinth of lines traces the lineaments of his own face).

14. The wish to "forget about today until tomorrow" is Bob Dylan's, from his song "Mr. Tambourine Man" (1964). I have grappled elsewhere (Edelman 2014) with the opposite desire that sometimes gets hold of me, a desire for total recall. For a formal analysis of the trade-offs among memory, immortality, and happiness, see Edelman 2018.

Chapter 21

1. José Saramago's words are from *Cadernos de Lanzarote*, bk. II, 56–57, entry for February 23, 1994 (Lisbon: Editorial Caminho, 1998). For an overview of Saramago's magnum opus, *O Evangelho Segundo Jesus Cristo*, see Frier 2005. The Le Guin quote is from *The Telling* (2001, 95).

2. In *Infinite Resignation*, Thacker (2018, 117) labels this as pessimism: "Whereas the philosopher says 'the world is morally neutral,' the pessimist says 'the world is morally indifferent.'" I see it rather as realism.

3. In moralizing RELIGIONS, the problem of theodicy is to explain the silence of God in the face of evil. Betenson (2016) begins his extended anti-theodicy argument with a quote from *The End of Philosophy of Religion* by N. Trakakis (London: Continuum, 2008): "Theodicies mediate a praxis that sanctions evil." Mavelli (2016) decries a secular variety of theodicy, which invokes the "war on terror" to justify torture and other atrocities (see also note 20 below). Hamilton (2015) documents the TECHNOLOGICAL theodicy built on the concept of the "Good Anthropocene."

4. *On What Matters* is the title of Parfit 2011—a sweeping, rigorous, and moving philosophical treatment of ethics, in the spirit of Sidgwick and Kant.

5. The textbook that I mention here is *Computing the Mind: How the Mind Really Works* (Edelman 2008). Danielson (2007) argues that ethics must be part of any attempt to unify behavioral science.

6. Concerning the role of reason in ethics, see, for instance, Dewey 1903, Parfit 1984, Putnam 2004, and Wittgenstein 1961.

7. Putnam (2012, 48–49), writes: "[In] science, and particularly in the social sciences, we are unavoidably dealing with an entanglement of facts, theories, and values. It is

like a three-legged stool all three legs are needed, or it falls over. The all-too popular idea that if something is a 'value judgment,' then it must be wholly 'subjective' rests not just on shaky foundations, but on foundations that have completely collapsed."

8. See Arnswald (2009, 22) on Wittgenstein: "The individual world-view determines ethics and every individual must answer the question of the right conduct, without concrete reference to philosophical theories, in accordance with his own life situation; and that questioning is not an exception, but rather the continual activity that endures throughout his lifetime." In his *Notebooks*, Wittgenstein writes that "ethics must be a condition of the world, like logic," and that "good and evil only enter through the subject. And the subject is not a part of the world, but a boundary of the world" (*Notebooks* 1914–1916, ed. G. H. von Wright and G. E. M. Anscombe, trans. G. E. M. Anscombe [Chicago: University of Chicago Press, 1979], 77, 79). Good entry points into this literature, should you be interested, are Shafer-Landau 2013 for the philosophy of ethics and Churchland 1998, Dewey 1903, and Mascaro et al. 2010 for the science.

9. How infants learn to fear snakes has been studied by DeLoache and LoBue (2009). For a case against moral nativism, see Sterelny 2010. It should be noted that the very concept of nativism or innateness is problematic (Mameli and Bateson 2006).

10. The question "Whose side are you on?" appears also in chapter 37. The Edward Abbey quote is from his *Desert Solitaire* (1968, 20).

11. The Moral Machine experiment (Awad et al. 2018), designed to explore the moral dilemmas faced by autonomous vehicles, has revealed cross-cultural variation in moral intuitions and has shown that it "correlate[s] with modern institutions and deep cultural traits."

12. Even studying actual driving behavior (as opposed to abstract choice behavior in driving-related dilemmas) would be more to the point. The few studies that have been undertaken showed that drivers of expensive cars tend to be deferred to (Doob and Gross 1968; Piff et al. 2012).

13. The sixty-society study of the morally sanctioned components of cooperation is Curry, Mullins, and Whitehouse 2019. A unifying theory of morality as an evolutionary tool for cooperation had been stated and motivated earlier in Curry 2016.

14. Interestingly, the development of fairness standards in childhood differs across countries (Blake et al. 2015).

15. A key concept here is multilevel selection, an idea that has long been dismissed as a red herring, but is becoming mainstream (Aktipis et al. 2018; Boyd et al. 2003; Gintis 2003; Trivers 1971; Wilson and Wilson 2007). A recently proposed general principle that can make the evolution of altruism possible is assortment of cooperators and defectors (Fletcher and Doebeli 2009).

16. The phrase "ordinariness of goodness" is due to Rochat and Modigliani (1995), who offer it as a counterpoint to Hannah Arendt's thesis of the "banality of evil." Their case study—the story of how the inhabitants of the French village of Le Chambon resisted the Vichy regime's policy of collaboration with the Nazis—has been elaborated upon by Scott (2012).

17. The Willie Stark quote (which is part of his conversation with Adam Stanton) is from Robert Penn Warren's *All the King's Men* (1946), 386–387.

18. Woergoetter and Porr (2007) offer a brief introduction to reinforcement learning.

19. The hypocrisy quote is from Shklar 1979. An important distinction between interpersonal and intrapersonal hypocrisy is made by Graham et al. (2015). Moberg (1987) discusses hypocrisy in RELIGION. In philosophy, a curious case is that of Arthur Schopenhauer, the author of *On the Foundation of Morals*, in which he endorses the following general precept: *Neminem laede, immo omnes, quantum potes, juve* (Hurt no one, instead help everyone, as much as you can). This has been roundly criticized by Nietzsche in rather personal terms (in *Beyond Good and Evil*, part 5, aphorism 186). More to the point, Schopenhauer (who in 1851 published a profoundly misogynistic essay "On Women") once pushed a woman down a flight of stairs for talking too loudly outside his door.

20. In an interview, Le Guin pointed out that the conceit of HAPPINESS predicated on cruelty toward a SUFFERING "scapegoat," which underlies the plot of her short story "The Ones Who Walk Away from Omelas" (1973) is well known and can be found, for instance, in Dostoevsky. Cruelty is surprisingly rarely singled out as a sin by various RELIGIONS (see also chapter 29). Shklar (1982) points this out in the context of a detailed discussion of the cruelty of Spanish priests and soldiers in the New World, citing it as an instance of a broader pattern: "Hypocrisy and cruelty go together, and are, as it were, unified in zeal."

21. A key tenet of socialization theory is that a society's values are passed from generation to generation through the internalization of norms (Gintis 2007). This is possible because "human preferences are programmable" (8). A case for moral progress as a feasible goal and aspiration is made by Moody-Adams (2017).

22. Compare this with Wittgenstein's claim of the ineffability of ethics: "It is clear that ethics cannot be put into words. Ethics is transcendental. (Ethics and aesthetics are one and the same)" (Wittgenstein 1961, 6.42, 6.421). For once, it appears that Wittgenstein's intuition was wrong. Le Guin's side in this debate is supported by the work of Tappan and Brown (1989), who describe a "narrative approach to moral development and moral education." Zagzebski (2010) advances "a radical kind of virtue theory" that she calls exemplarism, "which is foundational in structure but which is grounded in exemplars of moral goodness, direct reference to which anchors all the moral concepts in the theory."

23. From a pragmatic standpoint, Aragorn's little speech in *The Lord of the Rings: The Two Towers*, delivered at spearpoint in front of a Rohirrim posse, is understandable (see Tolkien 1954, bk. 2, ch. 2). The downside of using compassion or EMPATHY as the basis of morality is discussed by Bloom (2017). For some data regarding compassion and RELIGION, see Saslow et al. 2013.

24. What Voltaire actually wrote was: "Certainly anyone who has the power to make you believe absurdities has the power to make you commit injustices" (*Questions sur les miracles*, 1765). The connection between bad reasoning and morality (pointed out for instance by Mercier and Sperber 2011, 4.1.4) is what you may expect. Interestingly, flexible, creative thinking might also be detrimental to moral behavior (Gino and Ariely 2012).

25. See "The Mirror of Galadriel" in *The Lord of the Rings: The Fellowship of the Ring* (Tolkien 1954, bk. 2, ch. 7).

Chapter 22

1. The quoted passage is number 2.2 in the Mahâpadāna Sutta: The Great Discourse on the Lineage (DN14 in the Sutta Pitaka or the Buddha's discourses, the Pali Canon). Tradition has it that it was told by the historic Buddha, the Prince Siddhārtha Gautama, whose own story (which did not make it into the canon) was similar: he first ventured outside his father's palace at the age of twenty-nine, encountered an old man, and so on.

2. For studies of EMPATHY across an age gap, see Richter and Kunzmann 2011 and Wieck and Kunzmann 2015. An account of some of the common findings in terms of the "terror management theory" is offered by Chonody and Teater (2016).

3. Rereading recently Gertrude Bell's *Arabian Diaries*, I took note of this passage, which came up in her conversation with an elderly sheikh who hosted her on one of her journeys:

> I quoted Labid: "And if he live to 70 years and even more, what remains but the stick and the fingers closed over it."

(Short, hooked sticks have traditionally been used by camel riders in Arabia to control their mounts.) Labid is the renowned author of one of the Mu'allakāt, the seven pre-Islamic Hanged Poems, so called because they were hung on the walls of the Kaaba at Mecca. I am grateful to Professor Suzanne Pinckney Stetkevych for providing me with the actual wording of the relevant two lines from that other poem by Labid:

> Is there anything left for me once my desire flags
> but clinging to a stick with my fingers wrapped around it.

Labid's poem is included in Ibn Qutaybah's compendium, *Kitab al-Shi'r wa al-Shu'ara'*, ed. M. J. de Goege (Leiden: E. J. Brill [1902] 1904), 151–152.

4. There seems to be a built-in limit to the human lifespan (Dong, Milholland, and Vijg 2016).

5. Were human physiology better designed, our mood in old age would not be what it is. For some perspective, consider this: the standard measures of depression, which have been developed for adults, do not work well with the elderly (Margrett et al. 2010). All in all, it should not be surprising that feeling sad makes us feel older (Dutt and Wah 2017).

6. An early and notable example of this genre is Cicero's essay "De Senectute" (Of the Old Age); see https://en.wikipedia.org/wiki/Cato_Maior_de_Senectute. A scientific approach of sorts to rehabilitating the conception of old age is being offered within the framework of "positive psychology"; see, for instance, Carstensen and Michels 2005 and Ramírez et al. 2014.

7. After the fall of Troy, when she was raped by Ajax the Lesser, Cassandra was taken into captivity by Agamemnon, who made her his concubine. She was murdered at Mycenae by Agamemnon's wife Clytemnestra and her lover Aegisthus.

8. Contrary to a common belief, there is no cognitive decline in old age (Ramscar et al. 2014). Ardelt (1997, 2004) discusses wisdom and old age, noting its emotional aspects. Indeed, older adults show better cognitive performance for emotional relative to non-emotional information (Carstensen 2006).

9. Иных уж нет, а те далече, / Как Сади некогда сказал (Some gone forever, others far away / As Sadi once has said)—a couplet from Alexander Pushkin's novel in verse, *Eugene Onegin* (1833). The "Sadi" here is the poet Sa'di ([1258] 1966), mentioned also in chapter 38.

10. The summit is the steep and rugged Corkscrew Peak, which rises 5,800 feet above the surrounding plain and commands a wide view of central Death Valley.

11. This is the refrain of a 1966 song "Прощание с горами" (A Farewell to Mountains) by the Russian folk singer Vladimir Vyssotsky. Here it is in the original: "Лучше гор могут быть только горы, на которых ещё не бывал."

12. Going back is not an option for most refugees, though.

13. For the fans of David Lynch's *Twin Peaks* only: One of the most terrifying phrases in the English language is what Laura Palmer says to Dale Cooper in the closing scene of the original series: "I'll see you in 25 years." It sounds harmless enough to the younger self; to the older self, in retrospective, it is devastating.

14. My translation of Brodsky's poem can be found here: http://kybele.psych.cornell.edu/~edelman/poetry/soi.html.

Chapter 23

1. For the context of the quoted passage from the Book of Malachi, see chapter 5, note 1. The Le Guin "going home" quote is from *The Dispossessed* (1974b, 1).

2. The "war" between parents and children, which is driven by EVOLUTIONARY pressure, can turn deadly (Daly and Wilson 1988). However, it also has a positive side: "Parent-adolescent conflicts are adaptive for relational development when parents and adolescents can switch flexibly between a range of positive and negative emotions" (Branje 2018).

3. Wilson et al. (2014), who discuss possible remedies for the intergenerational conflict, refer to it as "parents locked in a negative coevolutionary spiral with their children." Interestingly, in the Israeli kibbutzim, where child rearing was traditionally (Peled 2017) a collective undertaking, similar issues have been identified (Lieblich 2010). For a broader look at what it means to be a child in a range of cultures, see Lancy 2015.

4. See Edelman 2014, the chapter titled "58/10."

5. It has been pointed out that the display of filial piety on part of Aeneas in Virgil's version of the story is not quite what it seems on the face of it (Fajardo-Acosta 1990).

6. As part of my due diligence, I tried unsuccessfully to find a similar piece, but written for daughters instead of sons. Linda Sunshine's "A Defense Manual for Daughters," included in her 2006 book *How Not to Turn into Your Mother*, turned out to belong to an altogether different genre.

Chapter 24

1. The Thelonious Monk quote is from a feature, "Jazz: The Loneliest Monk," which appeared in *TIME* magazine, February 28, 1964. The two passages from the Laṅkāvatāra Sūtra are #37 in section LXV and #154 in the Sagathakam appendix.

2. The hole-in-the-face eye-opening exercise appears in Merker 2013 in the context of his theory of the brain basis of CONSCIOUSNESS. If you try it at home, make sure to protect your corneas.

3. The Umwelt quote is from von Uexküll [1934] 2010, 117.

4. The inseparability of species-specific or rather Umwelt-specific perception and ACTION has been stressed by ecological psychologists such as Warren (2006). It is important to note that action control is ongoing and does not wait for perception to finish (whatever that could mean in a dynamically changing world). On the level of brain circuitry, this is reflected in the structure of thalamic collaterals, which entirely bypass the cortex, in quick steering of ongoing action (Sherman and Guillery 2006, ch. 10).

5. The notion of "seeing as," originally due to Wittgenstein (1958, 194), has also been discussed by Hofstadter (1995). It is a key component of theories of visual perception (Edelman 2009) and CONSCIOUSNESS (Fekete and Edelman 2011).

6. Most of the scientific studies of perception to date have been performed under highly artificial conditions; Malcolm, Groen, and Baker (2016) describe a recent shift of the focus to real-world scenes and tasks. For some examples of the dependence of perception on the perceiver's state and goals, see Proffitt 2006. The effects of culture on perception are discussed in Miyamoto, Nisbett, and Masuda 2006; Nisbett and Masuda 2003; Nisbett and Miyamoto 2005.

7. The claim that perception cannot be objective is central to the Interface Theory, advanced by Hoffman, Singh, and Prakash 2015. I have discussed some EVOLUTION-related qualifications to this theory elsewhere (Edelman 2015). This theory and the debate that surrounds it are very relevant to THINKING (Felin, Koenderink, and Krueger 2017).

8. The concept of EMPTINESS or śūnyatā is central to Mahayana Buddhism (Siderits 2007, 142). The T. S. Eliot quote is from "Burnt Norton" (Eliot 1943). Le Guin's character George Orr, from *The Lathe of Heaven*, turns it on its head in Le Guin 1971, ch. 11.

Chapter 25

1. Apollinaire's "Un son de cor . . ." is from his *Early Poems* (1896–1910). My English translation is here: http://kybele.psych.cornell.edu/~edelman/poetry/Apollinaire-all -black.html. The Le Guin quote is from *The Dispossessed* (1974b, 225).

2. "Die Politik ist die Lehre vom Möglichen" (Politics is the art of the possible), a remark that Otto von Bismarck, the unifier of Germany and its first Reichskanzler, made in an interview given to the St. Petersburgische Zeitung on August 11, 1867.

3. Here is a liberal scholar commenting on the role of hypocrisy in government: "One cannot, however, govern with overt antihypocrisy as one's only rule of conduct. Antihypocrisy is a splendid weapon of psychic warfare, but not of government" (Shklar 1979, 14). Tillyris (2015, 1), referencing Machiavelli and Shklar, claims that "democratic societies are implicated in creating the impetus to hypocritical behavior," calling hypocrisy "a necessary political virtue and one of the strings that hold together a virtuous political life."

4. Some useful entry points into the huge literature of inequality studies are Alvaredo et al. 2017, Bonica et al. 2013, Oishi, Kesebir, and Diener 2011, and Royce 2009.

5. Shklar mentions her concept of "bare bones liberalism" on page 5 of her *Legalism. An Essay on Morals, Law, and Politics* (Cambridge, MA: Harvard University Press, 1964). Benhabib (1994) called Shklar's views on liberalism "dystopic."

6. The Popper quote is from *The Open Society and Its Enemies* (1945, 265).

7. Marxists were the first to see fascism as an extreme form of capitalism: "Fascism is the unconcealed, terroristic dictatorship of the most reactionary, chauvinistic, and imperialist elements of finance capital" (from a 1933 statement by the Executive Committee of the Third International, quoted in Sinclair 1976, 88). Many liberal scholars concur, albeit in less strong terms. For instance, Sinclair concludes his assessment of the political economy of Italy and Germany between the wars by essentially accepting the Marxist thesis, to the effect that big capital supported fascism in both cases: "It is reasonable to assert that, as in Italy, there was a complementarity of interests between much of German big business and the Nazi state" (93). In twenty-first-century United States, the synergy between capitalism and fascism is still very much a decisive political factor: fascism is still a *"response to capitalist crisis* that seeks to contain any challenge to crisis that may come from subordinate groups" (Robinson and Barrera 2012, 8; italics in original).

8. Inequality (see chapter 24, note 4) is in part to blame here: "Attitudes to democracy in the longstanding democracies of Europe and North America correlate surprisingly well with inequality in pretax income" (Foa and Mounk 2016, 15). This holds even for Sweden and Germany (Foa and Mounk 2017). The concern about the state of democracy in the West is shared by Norris (2017), whose commentary on Foa and Mounk ends on a somber note: "In conclusion, the popular zeitgeist about the state of Western democracies—and the postwar international order—has swung from a mood of complacency to a pervasive sense of unease and even strident alarm."

9. "According to the EIU [Economist Intelligence Unit], countries like France, the United States, and Belgium, which had once been rated as 'full' democracies, have since deteriorated to being rated as 'flawed' democracies" (Foa and Mounk 2017, 12–13).

10. Foa and Mounk (2016, 11) comment: "Democracy has usually been associated with redistributive demands by the poor and therefore regarded with skepticism by elites. The newfound aversion to democratic institutions among rich citizens in the West may be no more than a return to the historical norm."

11. For the signs of rising fascism, see Umberto Eco's "Ur-Fascism," *New York Review of Books*, June 22, 1995, 12–15. Number 17 on Timothy Snyder's list "20 signs of tyranny," posted on Facebook on November 16, 2016, is also useful: "Watch out for the paramilitaries. When the men with guns who have always claimed to be against the system start wearing uniforms and marching around with torches and pictures of a Leader, the end is nigh. When the pro-Leader paramilitary and the official police and military intermingle, the game is over."

12. I placed "communist" in scare quotes because the Soviet regime was in fact oligarchically controlled, totalitarian state capitalism. As to the USSR's founders' declared intentions of building an earthly paradise, they motivated Karl Popper

(1992, 147) to remark that "the attempt to create the Kingdom of Heaven on earth may easily succeed in turning our earth into a hell for our fellow men."

13. Reading Slezkine 2004 may help one understand better where this joke comes from.

14. We arrived just in time to witness the beginning of the transformation of the country of our destination, Israel, into an ultra-nationalist theocracy (Krylov 2016; Leon 2018).

15. For a personal account of inner emigration in the U.S. academia, see Barrow 2018.

16. Compare Horkheimer and Adorno [1944] 2002, 185: "Genuine thought, which detaches itself from that function, reason in its pure form, takes on the trait of madness which down-to-earth people have never failed to observe."

17. Held (2004) offers a great analysis of the negative side of positive psychology (see also Lazarus 2003b).

18. Incarcerating dissidents in psychiatric hospitals was standard practice in the USSR from the 1960s until the collapse of the Soviet regime. This should be compared to the remarks of B. F. Skinner (1971, 165): "A literature of freedom may inspire a sufficiently fanatical opposition to controlling practices to generate a neurotic if not psychotic response. There are signs of emotional instability in those who have been deeply affected by the literature." Brinkmann (2014, 642) summarized such ideas and their political consequences as follows: "Viewing people's lives through a diagnostic lens de-politicizes their problems and turns them into a matter of personal health and illness." See also chapter 32, note 8.

19. Regarding the general usefulness of asking *cui bono?*, see Dennett 2006.

20. The author of the article in question, which appeared in the *New York Times* on November 23, 2018, was the AEI president Arthur C. Brooks. Another anodyne op-ed of his, published on March 11, 2019, in the *Washington Post* under the title "The Path Away from Internet-Driven Hate," was coauthored by no less a spiritual authority than Tenzin Gyatso, the fourteenth Dalai Lama (see chapters 21 and 29).

21. The passage quoted in this paragraph is from Wolff 1970, 12. As to why direct democracy is infeasible, Wolff writes: "The paradox of man's condition in the modern world is that the more fully he recognizes his right and duty to be his own master, the more completely he becomes the passive object of a TECHNOLOGY and bureaucracy whose COMPLEXITIES he cannot hope to understand" (10). And further: "If democracy is to make good its title as the only morally legitimate form of politics, then it must solve the problem of the heteronomous minority" (28).

22. This classical Marxist thesis ("It is not the consciousness of men that determines their existence, but their social existence that determines their consciousness" [Marx

(1859) 1977, preface]) should be compared to Bill Clinton's 1992 U.S. presidential campaign slogan "It's the economy, stupid," which proved extremely effective.

23. In this connection, consider Anderson's (1999) philosophy of oppression and inequality: "The proper negative aim of egalitarian justice is not to eliminate the impact of brute luck from human affairs, but to end oppression, which by definition is socially imposed. Its proper positive aim is not to ensure that everyone gets what they morally deserve, but to create a community in which people stand in relations of equality to others."

24. This quote is from Williams 2007, 310.

25. Two very different expressions of this sentiment are Conlon's (1986) concise and forceful *The Spanish Civil War: Anarchism in Action* and *Two Cheers for Anarchism* by Scott (2012).

26. The phrase "real utopias" is from Wright 2013.

27. Vilanova (1992) shows how important literacy was for political participation in revolutionary Spain. Peters (2017a) links Bookchin's works on anarchism with Dewey's philosophy of education.

28. Anarcho-syndicalism is explained by Seidman (1982) in his social-economic history of Spanish anarchism. See also Casanova 2005.

29. Thus: "We cannot replace the determinate prediction of *no cooperation* with a determinate prediction of *always cooperate*" (Ostrom, Walker, and Gardner 1992, 414).

30. Seidman (1982, 424) quotes union officials complaining that "production necessities would contradict 'our ideas of equality and liberty.'" This problem was addressed by "La Pasionaria [Dolores Ibárruri] herself," who published an article under the title "Our Cry: WORKER, WORK" (427).

31. The following quote is from Banks 2007, 137.

32. Why socialism? Read Einstein [1949] 2009.

33. In Iain M. Banks's Culture novels (such as Banks 2010), which describe a galaxy-spanning society of plenty, there is socialism within individual space habitats (each housing billions of people) and anarchism between.

34. The quote that closes this chapter is from *The Dispossessed* (Le Guin 1974b, 283).

Chapter 26

1. This gem is from Malaclypse the Younger 1965, 48.

2. Concerning the omnipresence of power, see Sidanius et al. (2016, 149): "Within any given society, group-based social inequality appears to be a human universal

present in all kinds of societies." Ennis (1967) writes about the relationship between power, RELIGION, and SUFFERING in everyday life.

3. These quotes are from Skinner 1971, 169. It is amusing how Skinner's attempts to condemn what he calls "the literature of freedom" backfire by singling out the society's power players to whose interests freedom runs counter:

> What we may call "the literature of freedom" . . . often emphasizes the aversive conditions under which people live, perhaps by contrasting them with conditions in a freer world. It thus makes the conditions more aversive, "increasing the misery" of those it is trying to rescue. It also identifies those from whom one is to escape or those whose power is to be weakened through attack. Characteristic villains of the literature are tyrants, priests, generals, capitalists, martinet teachers, and domineering parents. (30)

4. The three power hierarchies are discussed in Sidanius et al. 2016, 145. For an introduction to the concept of intersectionality, see Choo and Ferree 2010. Being subjected to power has repercussions for health: "depression is best understood in terms of systems of power, including gender, and where a given individual is situated within such social relations" (Neitzke 2016, 59; see also chapter 32, note 8).

5. Smith and Hofmann (2016, 10043), who used experience sampling to study power in everyday life, conclude: "Subjective feelings of power resulted more from within-participant situational fluctuation, such as the social roles participants held at different times, than from stable differences between people." It must be noted, though, that their subjects were "proficient in English, and having a smartphone with touchscreen, texting, and data plan"—not necessarily a representative population for a study of power and powerlessness.

6. Rucker and Galinsky (2017) studied interactions between power and social class. Evans (2016) reports that CHILDHOOD experience of powerlessness is associated with more externalizing symptoms such as aggression in adults.

7. As Horkheimer and Adorno ([1944] 2002, 16) remark, "the oppression of society always bears the features of oppression by a collective." The web-like structure of social power (which pertains to a person's relationships with others) complements the intersectional nature of power (which is an expression of a person's multiple identities). Neal and Neal (2011, 163) see power as a structural-relational phenomenon: "'power over'—that is, the ability of an individual or group to control another individual or group—derives from occupying an advantageous position within the pattern of *relationships* through which resources are exchanged" (my italics). Roscigno (2011) argues that power is *dynamical*-relational. Sidanius et al. (2016) point out numerous aspects of the dynamics of power that makes it self-perpetrating.

8. In Western philosophy, the idea of legitimizing power by attaching it to secular reason is commonly associated with Plato's *Republic*. In China, a comparable philosophical tradition is Confucianism (see "The Utopian Vision, East and West" by

Longxi 2002). In recent science, a remarkable, theoretically explicit and empirically supported program for improving society has been outlined by Wilson et al. (2014). Another recent example is Wright 2013, whose title, curiously, also refers to utopia: "Transforming Capitalism through Real Utopias."

9. *Beyond Freedom and Dignity* is the title of Skinner 1971. Here is Skinner getting the concept of human dignity utterly and completely wrong: "We recognize a person's dignity or worth when we give him credit for what he has done" (58). And here is a passage that is difficult to argue with: "Control is clearly the opposite of freedom, and if freedom is good, control must be bad. What is overlooked is control which does not have aversive consequences at any time. Many social practices essential to the welfare of the species involve the control of one person by another, and no one can suppress them who has any concern for human achievements" (41). Robert Paul Wolff, writing on the anarchist ideal and the failings of democracy in a book published just a year before Skinner's, concedes that "in some situations, it may be wiser to swear allegiance to a benevolent and efficient dictatorship than to a democracy which imposes a tyrannical majority on a defenseless minority" (Wolff 1970, 35). A "benevolent and efficient dictatorship" is what Singapore (which had attained independence in 1965) turned out to be.

Chapter 27

1. The Gogol quote is from act 4, scene 15 of *The Inspector General* (1836). The excerpt from James Joyce's *Ulysses* (1922) is part of a monologue uttered by Leopold Bloom in episode 16 (*Eumæus*).

2. For some evidence of the rich blaming the poor for poverty, see Cozzarelli, Wilkinson, and Tagler 2001 and Dorey 2010. In the United States, pathologizing poverty has effectively been an official policy since the 1996 "welfare reform" (Hansen, Bourgois and Drucker 2014).

3. Statistics concerning work hours by income can be found in Bick, Fuchs-Schündeln, and Lagakos 2018. Heisig (2011) discusses specifically household work. For both general and household work, the less well-off work longer hours. With regard to these statistics, it is important to keep in mind that under conditions of rampant unemployment, many people who would like to work just cannot find any. Moreover, the so-called "gig economy" likely causes work hours to be undercounted.

4. For experimental evidence for system justification, see Friesen et al. 2018.

5. Wegemer and Hinze (2013) document the "race to the bottom" in wages and its effects on job security.

6. The title of Mills and Zavaleta 2015 says it all: "Shame, Humiliation and Social Isolation: Missing Dimensions of Poverty and Suffering Analysis."

7. See the article "Millions of Americans Are One Pay Check Away from the Street" by Quentin Fottrell, *Market Watch*, January 20, 2018. Brown et al. (2016) document the relationship between poverty-related stress and learned helplessness, a condition with long-term repercussions.

8. The rich and healthy vs. the poor and sick quip is a flipped version of a maxim included in the *Book of Ben-Sira*, written by Shimon ben Yeshua ben Eliezer ben Sira around 200BCE: "Better to be poor and healthy than rich and sick" (30:14). Amazingly, part of the social services safety net designed to keep the sick and the elderly out of poverty has a side effect of transferring wealth from the poor to the rich (Hupfeld 2009; Sánchez-Romero and Prskawetz 2017).

9. The Pamuk quote is from page 282 of his 2004 novel *Snow* (London: Faber & Faber).

10. Mani et al. (2013) and Haushofer and Fehr (2014), among others, report controlled quantitative studies of the detrimental cognitive effects of poverty. On the systemic rather than the personal level, the dynamics of poverty is no less malignant. Brady and Bostic (2015, 291) conclude their quantitative study of poverty and welfare by formulating two "paradoxes of social policy": first, that "what is salient to poverty is not related to redistribution preferences, and what is salient to redistribution preferences is not robustly related to poverty"; and, second, that "a social policy effective at reducing poverty (i.e., resulting in a high transfer share) is also likely to be a social policy that undermines public support for redistribution (i.e., resulting in low-income targeting)."

11. Evans (2016) has described lingering effects of childhood poverty on adult functioning.

12. For statistics on adult poverty, see Benjaminsen 2016 and Verbunt and Guio 2019. A comparison of child poverty in the United States and in Europe is offered by Smeeding and Thévenot (2016). Galloway et al. (2015) look into the possible reasons for child poverty in Scandinavian countries being higher among immigrant children. In this connection, it is worth asking: should poverty only matter to us if the poor are in the same country as we are? See also chapter 25.

13. Marked inequality also characterizes the distribution of resources in natural systems other than economies. For instance, a study of the Amazon rainforest revealed that roughly 1 percent of the tree species account for 50 percent of the total stored carbon (see Scheffer et al. 2017 for data and a discussion of the common mechanisms behind this startling finding).

14. Bloom's tirade, which appears in Episode 16 (*Eumæus*), concludes as follows: "Ubi patria, as we learned a small smattering of in our classical day in Alma Mater, vita beni. Where you can live well, the sense is, if you work." The Latin quote is, of course, a mangled version of *Ubi bene, ibi patria*: where things are good, that's where

the homeland is. Concerning Bloom's morals in general, Raleigh (1977, 596) has concluded that "in effect a history of Western ethics is woven into the character." A similar sentiment is held by Boysen (2008), who attributes to Bloom (and Joyce) a kind of "cosmopolitan *caritas*"—a wholly secular and human-universal version of the Christian virtue of compassion.

15. The idea of Universal Basic Income (UBI) was being considered for a while in the 1960s and 1970s in the United States and in Canada. Forget (2011) describes how in the United States, it was sidelined through a series of political decisions, some made by Democrats and others by Republicans, and eventually killed by the Nixon administration; and how in Canada Guaranteed Annual Income was tested in a "field experiment" in Manitoba in 1974–1979. After that project ran out of funding, its encouraging findings were buried in bureaucracy and never followed up on.

Chapter 28

1. This tanka, titled "Cowardice," is from the collection *Tangled Hair* (1901) by Akiko Yosano (Yosano Shiyo). In this English version, I have combined several translations found online.

2. The notion that an unexamined life is not worth living has been put forward by Socrates at his trial, which ended with the people of Athens sentencing him to death (see Plato's *Apology*, 38a5). While it is often taken to be a key reason for practicing philosophy, not all philosophers agree that it applies to all people (Famakinwa 2012). The text of *Apology* suggests that Socrates did mean for his dictum to apply to everyone, not the least to those of his jurors who voted to condemn him to death: "For if you think that by killing men you can avoid the accuser censuring your lives, you are mistaken; that is not a way of escape which is either possible or honorable; the easiest and noblest way is not to be crushing others, but to be improving yourselves." For a Talmudic take on the idea of an examined life, see chapter 12. For some comparisons between classical Greek and Confucian perspectives, see Chandler 2003 and Morton 1971.

3. The universality of regret across cultures and populations is well documented (Breugelmans et al. 2014).

4. In this connection, see Davidai and Gilovich 2018, 439: "People are quicker to take steps to cope with failures to live up to their duties and responsibilities (ought-related regrets) than their failures to live up to their goals and aspirations (ideal-related regrets). As a consequence, ideal-related regrets are more likely to remain unresolved, leaving people more likely to regret not being all they could have been more than all they should have been."

5. The recording in question was made by Piaf in 1960. It was adopted by the 1er Régiment Etranger de Parachutistes (1st Foreign Paratroopers Regiment), which soon afterward (in 1961) attempted a putsch against President Charles De Gaulle,

whose Algiers policy they saw as too moderate. In 2012, President François Hollande acknowledged the "unjust" and "brutal" nature of France's occupation of Algiers, but stopped short of an apology (Pecastaing 2013).

The atrocious wartime conduct of the French soldiers in Algiers, over which they expressly had no regrets, was perfectly legal in France, where they were seen as patriots. It is instructive to compare this case to another one in which there were no regrets over wartime behavior, even though it involved treason: the Hotsumi Ozaki affair. Ozaki, a journalist and an advisor to Japan's prime minister, had been recruited in the early years of World War II by the Soviet spy Richard Sorge (Andrew and Gordievsky 1990, ch. 8). He was executed in 1944, after disclosing to the Soviets Japan's plan to direct its expansion toward South-East Asia and away from Siberia, which allowed Stalin to move troops and tanks to the Western front in the nick of time, as the fate of the war was hanging in balance. The Ozaki affair served as the inspiration behind Akira Kurosawa's film *No Regrets for Our Youth* (1946). Its title reprises a favorite saying of its protagonist, an antifascist who dreamed of a better Japan.

6. Concerning regret about inaction, see Zeelenberg et al. 2002.

7. In a paper titled "Cassandra's Regret," Gigerenzer and Garcia-Retamero (2017, 179) write, "We show that deliberate ignorance exists, is related to risk aversion, and can be explained as avoiding anticipatory regret." They also discuss the Minimax regret criterion (182). For a snapshot of the state of the art in using the computational construct of regret in machine learning, see Brown et al. 2019.

8. Irons and Hepburn (2007) discuss regret, decision-making, and the tyranny of choice in behavioral economics.

9. Hoerl and McCormack (2016) present a detailed case for the EVOLUTIONARY role of episodic MEMORY, and specifically of regret, in planning future behavior. Frith and Metzinger (2016) consider regret to be the core evolutionary-functional role of CONSCIOUSNESS: "Regret is a powerful, negative emotion that is suggested to integrate group norms and preferences with those of the individual. The transparent and embodied nature of the experience of regret ensures that cultural norms become an inescapable part of the self-narrative" (197); in other words, self-consciousness serves as "a functional platform for the representation of group preferences in the brain of individual organisms" (212).

10. Here's the context for that quote from Empson 1960, 33: "Milton regularly (every time for Satan, Eve, Adam, and Delilah) presents a Fall as due to an intellectually interesting temptation, such that a cool judge may feel actual doubt whether the fall was not the best thing to do in the circumstances."

Chapter 29

1. The Borges quote is #7 in his *Fragmentos de un Evangelio apócrifo*, published in Borges 1969. The passage that I quoted from Marx ([1843] 1970) includes the

original context in which the familiar "opium for the masses" phrase appears. The dialogue between Levy Matthew, the sole disciple of Jesus in *The Master and Margarita*, and Woland, alias Lucifer, is from Bulgakov 1967, ch. 29.

2. From *A Contribution to the Critique of Political Economy* (Marx [1859] 1977).

3. The English translation of the Dante lines, in the meter of the original, is by Geoffrey L. Bickersteth, from a bilingual edition published by Shakespeare Head Press, 1965.

4. Serra (1713–1784) was a Franciscan friar and the chief Inquisitor for the provinces of New Spain, including Baja and Alta California.

5. Sandos (1997, 222) exculpates the Spanish missionaries as follows: "Some have even directly and wrongly accused the Franciscans of genocide, comparing Serra to Adolf Hitler and the missions to Nazi death camps, thereby confusing results with intent." In connection with Serra's canonization by the "liberal" Pope Francis in 2015, see "California Mission Gulags: Putting Junípero Serra's Canonization in Perspective" (Welizarowicz 2016).

6. The proverb about the way to Hell and good intentions is quoted in Marx [1867] 1887, I, bk.1, 134.

7. Consider, for instance, the "paradox of religious fertility"—the seeming contradiction between observant parents having more offspring *and* their offspring doing better economically than those of secular controls. Shaver et al. (2019) offer an empirical resolution of this paradox, based on the concept of alloparenting.

8. From *To His Coy Mistress* by Andrew Marvell, published posthumously in 1681.

9. The Sabbath comment is from an opinion piece published in *Shiloach* (Ahad-Ha'am 1898). Recent research suggests that Ahad-Ha'am's intuition was correct: historically, the Sabbath did help preserve the Jewish people's identity (Livni 2017).

10. For an overview of the increasingly dominant role of religion in the Israeli politics, see Krylov 2016. The turning point appears to have been the shift of political power from Labor to the nationalists in 1977 (Leon 2018). Similar processes are under way elsewhere as well: "Generally, the opinion shared by most researchers of religion's role in the modern era is that while religion is weakening in certain locales, such as Western Europe, in others, such as the United States, Eastern Europe, Latin America, and the Muslim world, religion has not only maintained its hold, but has grown even stronger, attracting new followers. It therefore appears that religion's revival and growing influence are not unique to Israel" (Yuchtman-Yaar, Alkalay, and Aival 2018, 14).

11. Moberg (1987) discusses the ubiquity of hypocrisy in religion. In the United States, for instance, one may single out the regressive POLITICS of the self-styled "Moral Majority" and the megachurch leaders (see, e.g., Powell and Neiva 2006;

the lip service paid to religion by all candidates for public office; and the frequency with which some of the most sanctimonious politicians are caught at acts that are criminal by their own laws.

12. "Buddhism, . . . though strong on ethics, lacks a coherent understanding of societal suffering" (Flores 2015, 65). See also King 2016.

13. This has been documented by Levine (1988, 253): "Typical activities include sewing, visiting the sick, or 'social action,' which usually means collecting money, clothing or food for those in extreme need." The elevation of theology, or what sounds like theology, over action by the liberation theology theorists is exemplified by this statement by McLaren: "In a world of dehumanised, alienated social relationships, we can only symbolise love through its absence, and so we can say that love, and generosity, and goodness, and Christ are present in this world but *present only in the form of their absence*" (McLaren and Jandrić 2018, 603; italics in original).

14. See the discussion of "theodiversity" by Norenzayan (2016).

15. Also, some of the best practical jokes; witness the serious debate as to whether or not the Church of the SubGenius is a real religion (Bekkering 2016).

16. Devastating philosophical criticism of Pascal's Wager can be found, for instance, in Hájek 2003 and Mougin and Sober 1994. A concise, entirely nontechnical takedown of the Wager has been offered by Empson (1960, 39): "The answer is political not mathematical; this argument makes Pascal the slave of any person, professing any doctrine, who has the impudence to tell him a sufficiently extravagant lie."

Chapter 30

1. This passage (Bacon [1620] 1854, 371) concludes the text of the *Novum Organum*.

2. For a while now it has been clear that science is inherently subject to "standards adapted to the purpose of domination"; this quote from Horkheimer's notebooks (Notizen 1950–1969, Frankfurt am Main 1974, 12) appears in Horkheimer and Adorno [1944] 2002, 243). There seems, however, to be no clear solution in sight to this problem. Modern sociologists of science merely kick this can down the road; thus, for instance, Agazzi (2014, 436) writes: "In the last analysis the problem of regulating a free science can find its real solution in the diffusion of *a sense of responsibility* and of *a sense of duty* in science, a diffusion which (sustained by the participation of all citizens in the decision-making process) would make this regulation at the same time acceptable and reasonable. But this is a problem of *public education* that we cannot tackle here" (italics in original).

3. The Leibniz quote can be found in Merchant 2006, fn. 33; Durant's version is from his doctoral dissertation (Durant 1917, 75). There is an obvious parallel between this attitude toward nature and the biblical doctrine of human dominion

over it (see Schultz, Zelezny, and Dalrymple 2000 for an overview and for empirical data linking Judeo-Christian beliefs to environmental attitudes). From there, the road is short to the human-induced eco-catastrophe that we are living now (Rees 2019).

4. Of course, RELIGIONS too deal in TRUTHS, which are numerous and contradictory. Some of those are based exclusively on revelation, to which this well-known phrase from John 8:32 refers: "And ye shall know the truth, and the truth shall make you free." Others originate in insight and are buttressed by reasoned THINKING, as in Buddhist philosophy: "Buddhism is about solving a problem—the problem of the omnipresence of suffering—and the central intuition of Buddhism is that the solution to that problem is the extirpation of ignorance" (Garfield 2010, 11). It should (but will not here) go without saying that, unlike science-generated truths, divinely revealed or merely reasoned ones are not expected to help cure cancer or feed the hungry.

5. For a case study of the imperfection of science as a mode of inquiry, see Ioannidis 2012. Brewer and Chinn (1994) document across disciplines scientists' response to anomalous experimental data, which nominally should trigger a revision of the theory that motivated the experiment.

6. Hence the "war on science" on the part of politicians, especially of the populist and the "conservative" right-wing bent (Hardy et al. 2019).

7. A classic example is the inconvenience that the Copernican heliocentrism propounded by Galileo inflicted on the Catholic Church. Modern examples include Big Pharma's apparent preference for marketing and management over eradication of diseases (Connors 2010) and the fossil fuel industry's complicity in covering up global warming (Smith 2017).

8. The Latin quote is from Horace (*Epistles*, bk. I, ep. I, l.14). The phrase "nullius in verba" has served as the motto of the Royal Society since its founding in 1660.

9. Two great fictional takes on how power sees campus free thinking are Edward Abbey's (1980) fugitive professor in *Good News* and, in Philip K. Dick's *Flow My Tears, the Policeman Said* (1974), radical students finding refuge from the government in their "warrens" under Berkeley, California. In real life, meanwhile, one witnesses mostly a transition "from radical resistance to quiet subversion" (Barrow 2018).

10. A rather extreme example of the growing body of work criticizing the academia is *The Toxic University* (Smyth 2017).

11. University coats of arms often invoke truth, justice, and freedom. The "founding principle" of my employer, in comparison, is the rather more practical sentiment on the part of its founder, Ezra Cornell, a self-made man: "I would found an institution where any person can find instruction in any study" (see Bishop 1962 for the relevant history). In terms of the degree of academic freedom, it should be noted that faculty at state universities in the United States are generally worse off than at

private ones, because of their inherent dependence on state POLITICS. Finally, one must realize that tenure has always been a rare privilege, which is not as strongly linked to academic merit as one would wish it to be, and is in any case rapidly becoming even rarer. Tenure-track faculty have not nearly as much freedom as their senior colleagues; and in many institutions most of the teaching is carried out by the much cheaper labor force consisting of adjunct faculty and graduate students.

12. Interdisciplinary research has been shown to have lower funding success than traditional disciplinary work (Bromham, Dinnage, and Hua 2016). Moreover, funding agencies in the United States seem to be guided by the slogan "conform and be funded" (Nicholson and Ioannidis 2012); this may be compared to the cult of "disruption" in the high TECHNOLOGY sector.

13. If you find this ending plausible, I have a used car to sell you.

Chapter 31

1. The Faulkner quote is from an interview with Jean Stein, which appeared in *The Paris Review*, no. 12, *The Art of Fiction*, Spring 1956.

2. Consider the epigraph to Vila Matas 2000: "The glory or merit of certain men consists in writing well; that of others consists in not writing" (Jean de la Bruyère). On a related note, when the subject matter of the would-be opus is folly, one might just as well put the words in Folly's mouth, as Erasmus ([1511] 1876) has done to great effect.

3. Compared to intelligence, stupidity has not received nearly as much scholarly attention (Bernstein 2009). I single out here a discussion of stupidity as an epistemological question by Engel (2016), a little book by Livraghi (2009), and another, famous one by Cipolla (1987), who offers an economic analysis of stupid behavior. Cipolla's one regrettable mistake is his claim that stupidity is a matter of "genetic traits," which he immediately qualifies by adding that "stupidity is an indiscriminate privilege of all human groups and is uniformly distributed according to a constant proportion," so that "the probability that a certain person be stupid is independent of any other characteristic of that person."

4. The Dunning-Kruger effect (see Dunning 2011 for a thorough overview) is typically at play when people disparage others as stupid—a common manifestation of the practice of downward comparison (Wills 1981).

5. See especially Cipolla 1987, ch. 7.

6. Peters and Jandri (2017) take up the important question of how situations arise in which the opposite effect of what has been termed "wisdom of crowds" obtains.

7. Engel (2016) considers, a propos the personage of Don Quixote, the idea that "the contrary of fool is not intelligent or clever; it is wise." Ultimately, however, he

sides with a different notion: "But the proper opposite of the fool may not be wise. It may well be, as Musil ([1937] 1979) suggests, the person who is modest, sober, or who exemplifies the virtue of intellectual humility."

Chapter 32

1. The German phrase *Durch Leiden Licht* had been used by Romain Rolland in his essay on Shakespeare (1920, 116). In Erofeev [1969] 1992 it appears (verbatim, but transliterated into Russian) in chapter Электроугли—43й километр. The Borges quote is #5 in his *Fragmentos de un Evangelio apócrifo*, published in Borges 1969.

2. Borges dedicated his essay "A New Refutation of Time" to Juan Crisóstomo Lafinur. The quoted passage concludes the prologue to this piece, which can be found in *Labyrinths* (Borges 1970e), as well as in other collections.

3. Mucius Scaevola was sent to assassinate the king of the Clusians, who were waging war on Rome in 508 BCE. The story of the Spartan boy and the fox is mentioned in passing by Plutarch in *Lives* (Lycurgus XVIII): "The boys make such a serious matter of their stealing, that one of them, as the story goes, who was carrying concealed under his cloak a young fox which he had stolen, suffered the animal to tear out his bowels with its teeth and claws, and died rather than have his theft detected. And even this story gains credence from what their youths now endure, many of whom I have seen expiring under the lash at the altar of Artemis Orthia."

4. The quoted passage from Le Guin's *The Dispossessed* (1974b) appears in chapter 2.

5. Although in this chapter, as in this book in general, I have deliberately avoided discussing "mere" physical pain, one remark is in order: humans may be uniquely sensitive to it. On a theory advanced by Finlay and Syal (2014), pain, accompanied by an overt response such as screaming, is part and parcel of our ultrasociality and predisposition to altruism. Rather than being a "pointless" automatic reaction to tissue damage, pain thus has a specific role, namely, to recruit others who may help the physically suffering (e.g., injured) individual.

6. Robert Burton's (1638) *The Anatomy of Melancholy* is an interminable and fascinating jumble of anecdotes, parables, comments, quotations, and quips about people making themselves and others miserable. The distinction between "unnecessary" and other suffering is argued for by Roy (2015), a physician, who defines "existential" suffering as that for which there can be no palliative care in principle. Anderson 2015 is a collection of chapters on the topic of "world suffering and quality of life."

7. Shneidman (2005, 8) defines "psychache" as "an unbearable flow of painful consciousness"; the context is a call for "anodyne psychotherapy for suicide."

8. Brinkmann (2014) lists "four other languages of suffering—religious, existential, moral, and political ones—that are today often delegitimatized by the dominant psychiatric language." Summerfield (2004) offers "cross-cultural perspectives on

the medicalization of human suffering." A transdiagnostic perspective on suffering, which pushes back against wholesale medicalization of psychopathology, can be found in Garland and Howard 2013.

9. The detailed and highly technical theoretical investigation by Metzinger (2018) states "the four central necessary conditions for suffering . . . : The C-condition (having a phenomenal model of reality), the PSM-condition (a self-model), the NV-condition (the ability to represent negative valences—for example via homeostatic cost functions folded into the self-model, representations of decreasing functional coherence or low levels of self-control), and the T-condition (transparency, Mother Nature's most evil trick: forcing organisms to identify with negatively valenced states)." Ligotti (2010, 75), whose book *The Conspiracy against the Human Race* often refers to Metzinger, makes his stance on this issue very clear: "The pessimist's credo, or one of them, is that nonexistence never hurt anyone and existence hurts every-one. Although our selves may be illusory creations of consciousness, our pain is nonetheless real."

10. For sentiments similar to that of the quoted passage from Metzinger 2017, see Contestabile 2014 as well as the references for anti-natalism in the notes to chapter 12.

11. The positive value placed by people on EXISTENCE is called "existence bias" by Metzinger (2017); see also Eidelman, Crandall, and Pattershall 2009.

12. Bloom (2017) and Heyes (2018) call for a reevaluation of the nature of EMPATHY and its role in MORAL behavior.

Chapter 33

1. This is from Arendt 1958, 3.

2. Cf. chapter 3. In this connection, the so-called thermodynamic arrow of TIME is based on the assertion that, in the long run, things become messier.

3. Consider Snyder's (2019) observation that "total faith in reason without the truth of others becomes unbridled concern with the one absolutely sure thing: one's own bodily desires." A character in Elliott Downing's 2019 novel *Airplane Mode* makes a similar comment about humans: "They'll trade anything for an incremental increase in convenience. Anything."

4. Privacy is possible (Ekert and Renner 2014), or would be, if we didn't give it up (Fuchs and Trottier 2015) in exchange for convenience. The implications of "data capitalism" (Myers West 2019) for POLITICS in a "democracy" are widely discussed (e.g., Couldry 2017; Deibert 2019). Anton (2018) shows how the "new media" work to undermine public-space MORALITY by promoting hypocrisy. An example of a ubiquitous surveillance society, that of China, is described in Liang et al. 2018.

5. Ellis et al. (2018) offer a useful introduction to the concept of the Anthropocene. Hamilton (2015) and Marzec (2018) document attempts on the part of the economic elites to neutralize or subvert it. Whyte (2018) provides a literary perspective.

6. If Watts (2018) is right, it's too late to do something about it. A radical change might still happen, if the "technological singularity" prophesied by Vinge (1993) comes to pass.

7. The quote is from Horkheimer and Adorno [1944] 2002, 148.

8. See Sandeford 2019 on the energetics of ancient agriculture.

Chapter 34

1. The joke about kinds of people is from Le Guin 1988, 32. Here it is in context—a dialogue between Coyote and a lost human child whom she has adopted:

> "There are only two kinds of people."
> "Humans and animals?"
> "No. The kind of people who say, 'There are two kinds of people' and the kind of people who don't." Coyote cracked up, pounding her thigh and yelling with delight at her joke. The child didn't get it, and waited.
> "OK," Coyote said. "There's the first people, and then the others. That's the two kinds."
> "The first people are—?"
> "Us, the animals . . . and things. All the old ones. You know. And you pups, kids, fledglings. All first people."
> "And the—others?"
> "Them," Coyote said. "You know. The others. The new people. The ones who came." Her fine, hard face had gone serious, rather formidable. She glanced directly, as she seldom did, at the child, a brief gold sharpness. "We were here," she said. "We were always here. We are always here. Where we are is here. But it's their country now. They're running it . . . Shit, even I did better!"
> The child pondered and offered a word she had used to hear a good deal: "They're illegal immigrants."
> "Illegal!" Coyote said, mocking, sneering. "Illegal is a sick bird. What the fuck's illegal mean? You want a code of justice from a coyote? Grow up, kid!"
> "I don't want to."
> "You don't want to grow up?"
> "I'll be the other kind if I do."

The second epigraph is from Horkheimer and Adorno (1944) 2002, 4. The third epigraph is a line from Wisława Szymborska's *View with a Grain of Sand* (New York: Harcourt, Brace & Co., 1993, trans. Stanisław Baranczak and Clare Cavanagh). Finally, Paul Valéry's twist on Descartes's Cogito appears in "Discours aux Chirurgiens," *Variété V, Œuvres complètes* (Paris, Gallimard, La Pléiade, 1957), I, 916.

2. Compare this with Thomas Nagel's (1971, 725) argument intended to show why only a self-consciously examined life can be absurd:

Why is the life of a mouse not absurd? The orbit of the moon is not absurd either, but that involves no strivings or aims at all. A mouse, however, has to work to stay alive. Yet he is not absurd, because he lacks the capacities for self-consciousness and self-transcendence that would enable him to see that he is only a mouse. If that did happen, his life would become absurd, since self-awareness would not make him cease to be a mouse and would not enable him to rise above his mousely strivings. Bringing his new-found self-consciousness with him, he would have to return to his meagre yet frantic life, full of doubts that he was unable to answer, but also full of purposes that he was unable to abandon.

This philosophical point is quite in line with psychological findings on the dialectics of self-reflection. For instance, Schooler, Ariely, and Loewenstein (2003) write:

Our analysis suggests that there are several serious paradoxes surrounding the relationship between introspection, the pursuit of happiness and actual hedonic experience. On the one hand, an explicit focus on the value of one's hedonic experience may both misrepresent and undermine its quality. On the other hand, a general lack of reflection may cause individuals to fail to recognize those experiences that provide them with maximum utilities. A similar dilemma occurs with the pursuit of HAPPINESS, as the goal of maximizing utilities appears to be undermined by this very goal.

3. Griffin (1978) was one of the first ethologists in the twentieth century to take up the notion that animals think. Dennett (1983) defends the methodological value of the assumption that they do. The concept of minimal rationality, due to Cherniak (1986), helps frame this question. More recently, there has been an accumulation of evidence that nonhuman animals are capable of some quite sophisticated modes of thinking; for instance, counterfactual thinking (Byrne 2002) has been demonstrated in rats (Laurent and Balleine 2015), while honeybees proved capable of doing basic arithmetic (Howard et al. 2019).

4. Concerning the possible evolutionary origin of language in toolmaking pedagogy, see chapter 17, note 2.

5. Because an artificial intelligence would presumably either lack emotions entirely or feel differently from us, its thinking patterns are likely to appear to us extremely alien. In this connection, it is interesting to recall that the eminent science fiction editor, John W. Campbell Jr., used to ask the would-be contributors to his magazine to describe "something that thinks as well as a human, but not like a human" (Campbell 1959). The peculiarly human way in which we think, which is tied to the way our PERCEPTION works, has been discussed by Felin, Koenderink, and Krueger (2017, 1054): "We see both perception and rationality as a function of organisms' and agents' active engagement with their environments, through the probing, expectations, questions, conjectures and theories that humans impose on the world." Then, there is the social aspect of thinking: "According to the argumentative theory, however, the function of reasoning is primarily social" (Mercier and Sperber 2011, 71).

6. That quote from Horkheimer and Adorno [1944] 2002, 29, may be compared to this one: "The not merely theoretical but practical tendency toward self-destruction

has been inherent in rationality from the first, not only in the present phase when it is emerging nakedly" (xix). Nagel (1971, 722), whose essay on the absurdity of the human condition focuses on its personal rather than societal determinants, concurs: "The absurdity of our situation derives not from a collision between our expectations and the world, but from a collision within ourselves."

7. The three modes of reasoning—deduction, induction, and abduction—are explained, for instance, in Edelman 2008, section 8.3. It should be noted that much of MATHEMATICS consists of truth-preserving deductive reasoning from premises (axioms or previously deduced theorems) to a conclusion (a new theorem). In contrast, SCIENCE relies heavily on induction of general rules or laws from data, along with intervention-based deductive validation of hypotheses. Both involve creativity (as in coming up with new conjectures in mathematics or new laws in science) and on cumulative cultural efforts.

8. The "Tightrope of Reason" simile is the title of Fogelin 2003, where the challenge is stated and discussed of not succumbing either to absolute dogma or to absolute skepticism. Alternative (from the Western standpoint) logics such as the Buddhist varieties make for quite strange (again, to the Western mind) and often nonbinary conundrums (e.g. Garfield and Priest 2009).

9. The reason vs. passions quote is from Hume 1740, bk. 2, pt, 3, sec. 2.

10. The Walt Whitman quote is from section 51 of "Song of Myself" (which is part of *Leaves of Grass*).

11. Doubting the consensus requires that our predisposition to so-called system justification be overcome (see chapters 27 and 29, as well as chapter 27, note 4). A related phenomenon is the naturalistic fallacy: the false belief that whatever is natural (that is, occurs in the world) is necessarily good (Moore 1903). So is our psychological bias for the status quo; as Kay et al. (2009) write, "Several purely cognitive factors, ranging from mere exposure to primacy effects, may also contribute to a psychological preference for the status quo (e.g., Eidelman and Crandall 2009). However, the results of these studies make clear that, at least in situations in which crucial aspects of one's sociopolitical system are at stake, motivational concerns also drive people's preference for the status quo."

12. The earliest definite reference to this pseudo-quote seems to be a banner on an opposition demonstration in East Germany (the GDR) on January 17, 1989, that is, on the seventieth anniversary of Rosa Luxemburg's murder by Nazi thugs. One authentic Luxemburg quote on thinking is "Freiheit ist immer der Freiheit des anders Denkenden" (Freedom is always the freedom for those who think differently) in *Die Russische Revolution*, Paul Levi (Berlin: Verlag Gesellschaft und Erziehung G.m.b.H., 1922), S. 109.

13. The following quote is from *The Dispossessed* (Le Guin 1974b, 333).

Chapter 35

1. "Wind is time, rendered by means of space" is from the book Увидеть дерево (*To Behold a Tree*) by Marina Vishnevetskaya (Moscow: Vagrius, 2000).

2. Here are lines 1698–1706 from Goethe's *Faust* (English translation follows):

Und Schlag auf Schlag! Werd ich zum Augenblicke sagen:
Verweile doch! du bist so schön!
Dann magst du mich in Fesseln schlagen,
Dann will ich gern zugrunde gehn!
Dann mag die Totenglocke schallen,
Dann bist du deines Dienstes frei,
Die Uhr mag stehn, der Zeiger fallen,
Es sei die Zeit für mich vorbei!

If ever I to the moment shall say:
Beautiful moment, do not pass away!
Then you may forge your chains to bind me,
Then I will put my life behind me,
Then let them hear my death-knell toll,
Then from your labours you'll be free,
The clock may stop, the clock-hands fall,
And time come to an end for me!

3. On TIME and HAPPINESS: "Счастливые часов не наблюдают" (The happy are oblivious to time), notes Sophia in Aleksandr Griboyedov's 1831 play Горе от ума (*Woe from Wit*).

4. The Sufi version of the origin of this phrase is found in a story by Farid ud-Din al-Attar, the author of the *Parliament of the Birds* (Attar [1177] 1984). According to al-Attar, a king once ordered his servants to create for him a ring that would make him happy when he was sad. Upon consultation with the king's sages, the silver-smith made him a ring with the inscription "This too will pass." Although the ring did make the king happy when he was sad, it also made him sad whenever he was happy. In a related story, King Solomon's ring inscribed with this phrase gave him many powers of magic, including dominion over the Jinn.

5. For a review of time perception and emotion, see Droit-Volet et al. 2013. The slowing down of the subjective speed of time passage in depression is described in Gil and Droit-Volet 2009. Wearden (2015) distinguishes between judgments of the passage of time and judgments of interval duration, the former being more relevant to the "feel" of time and to how we experience life. The notion of "depressive realism" in time perception (Kornbrot, Msetfi, and Grimwood 2013) brings to mind the perennial debate between optimists and pessimists as to whose view of the world is closer to the TRUTH.

6. To find out whether or not subjective time really slows down during a stressful event, read Stetson, Fiesta, and Eagleman 2007.

7. The paradoxical nature of our perception of time is noted by Droit-Volet and Gil 2009.

8. Biological/perceptual time is complicated: "One person trained in a single discipline (e.g., psychology) without significant computational, engineering, genomic, and neurobiological knowledge is unlikely to grasp enough of the elephant to make a difference no matter how hard they try" (Allman, Penney, and Meck 2016, 307). Somewhat surprisingly, the physics of time is not well-understood or agreed upon either (Callender 2017).

9. This phrase is from Eliot's "Burnt Norton" (II), written in 1935, which is one of the *Four Quartets* (Eliot 1943). Here is the immediate context:

> Time past and time future
> Allow but a little consciousness.
> To be conscious is not to be in time
> But only in time can the moment in the rose-garden,
> The moment in the arbour where the rain beat,
> The moment in the draughty church at smokefall
> Be remembered; involved with past and future.
> Only through time time is conquered.

10. A key insight into the time course of CONSCIOUSNESS is due to William James, who used in this connection the expression "the specious present" (James 1890, 608). For a modern philosophical treatment, see the discussion of "Extensional Presentism" in Dainton 2016, 96. Psychological, neurobiological, and computational arguments for the time-extended nature of consciousness are advanced in Fekete and Edelman 2011; see also Edelman, Fekete, and Zach 2012.

11. [Margarita] "Ведь не каждый же день встречаешься с нечистой силой! Еще бы,— подтверждал Азазелло, если б каждый день, это было бы приятно!" Margarita, the heroine of Mikhail Bulgakov's *The Master and Margarita* (1967), tells Azazello, one of the Devil's attendants, that she wouldn't miss any opportunity to run into black magic, given how rare such opportunities are. Azazello agrees, noting that if such meetings were common, it would be very nice indeed.

12. There are actually multiple independent physical formulations of the arrow of time (Dolev and Roubach 2016).

13. See chapter 14; also Edelman 2008, 464ff.

Chapter 36

1. The "melancholy truth" remark was made by James Beattie in a letter to William Forbes. It is included on page 77 of *Life and Writings of James Beattie, LL.D., Late Professor of Moral Philosophy and Logic in The Marischal College and University of Aberdeen*, published by Forbes in 1824. The *Principia Discordia* quote is from Malaclypse the

Younger (1965, 42). The "truth in a well" [literally, "in an abyss"] quote by Democritus is included in Diogenes Laertius's *Lives of Eminent Philosophers* IX, 72, published online by the Perseus Project, Tufts University. (Burton's *Anatomy of Melancholy* [1638], whose pretend author is called "Democritus Junior," has index entries for "TROPHONIUS' Den" and for "TUSCANS, attended by naked women," but not for "TRUTH.") Democritus's saying has inspired a 1896 painting by Jean-Léon Gérôme, *La Vérité sortant du puits armée de son martinet pour châtier l'humanité* (Truth Coming Out of the Well Armed with Her Whip to Chastise Mankind).

2. Pearl imagery is a perennial favorite with poets. Threading pearls was a "traditional" (Anvar 2011, 65) simile for poetry itself already in the time of the author of *Laylī u Majnūn*, Nizamī:

> Laylī who had such sweetness / Was also eloquent in poetry.
> An unpierced pearl who pearls would pierce / Her verses were as precious as she was.

(LM19, verses 56–57; I thank Reza Shahbazi for translation advice. The LOVE story of Layla and Majnun is mentioned in chapter 18; see also note 5 for that chapter.) The rhetorical move likening truth to a pearl is exemplified by the following quote from Édouard René de Laboulaye (the man who came up with the idea of the Statue of Liberty): "Truth is like a pearl: he alone possesses it who has plunged into the depths of life and torn his hands on the rocks of Time." This maxim, along with 259 others on truth, is included in C. N. Douglas's compendium *Forty Thousand Quotations: Prose and Poetical* (1917), available online at bartleby.com.

3. Compare the Delphic slogan "know thyself" with the Buddha's definition of mindfulness as "complete self-mastery by means of self-knowledge" (Eliot 1921, X) and Laozi's (Lao Tze [Laozi]1904, 33) assertion that "knowing others is wisdom; knowing the self is enlightenment."

4. The conundrum here boils down to the Epimenides paradox; see Hofstadter 1979 for a thorough treatment.

5. "It is, however, not concealed from enlightened men, who are able to discern the tendency of words, that pearls of curative admonition are strung upon the thread of explanation, and that the bitter medicine of advice is commingled with the honey of wit, in order that the reader's mind should not be fatigued, and thereby excluded from the benefit of acceptance; and praise be to the Lord of both worlds." From the *Gulistan* (Sa'di [1258] 1966, conclusion).

6. The offending items of information range from any mention of the massacre of peaceful demonstrators by the army in the capital's main square to pictures of Peppa Pig.

7. As per Robinson and Barrera 2012, 4: "the sophistication of such a project [fascist revival], made possible by the ideological domination of media together with new

surveillance and social control technologies that allow it to rely *more on selective than generalised* repression" (my italics).

8. For a philosophical overview, see the little book titled *On Bullshit* by Frankfurt (2005). A social-psychological study of the reception of "pseudoprofound bullshit" has been published by Pennycook et al. (2015).

9. A small sample of recent studies of the impact of social media on truth is Bradshaw and Howard 2018, Farrell and Schneier 2018, and Kavanagh and Rich 2018.

10. The Handicap Principle, formulated by Amotz Zahavi, is explained in Zahavi and Zahavi 1997. A representative application of this principle to theories of animal signaling and human language is Lachmann, Számadó, and Bergstrom 2001. Levine (2014, 378) reviews the arguments for the idea that "people tend to believe others," to which he adds the hypothesis that this "truth-default" is adaptive. A key claim of this Truth Default Theory is "the view that the tradeoff between efficient communication and vulnerability to occasional deceit is more than worth it" (385). This may have been the case in ancestral environments, but not when TECHNOLOGY makes the spread of lies as easy as it is at present. Friedkin and Bullo (2017, 11384), who show that in a discourse situation truth may win over lies by virtue of its uniqueness, conclude their discussion with the following qualification: "one-true versus many-false calculative logics condition of truth wins is not satisfied when social movements or social media elevate the adoption of a particular set of false facts and logic."

11. For some representative discussions of the historical context of Enlightenment (notably, colonialism), see Carey and Trakulhun 2007 and Conrad 2012. Kwame Antony Appiah's (2019) review of *Irrationality: A History of the Dark Side of Reason* by Justin E. H. Smith offers a particularly penetrating commentary on THINKING, reason, and the concept of Enlightenment. Appiah mentions, among others, the work of Berlin and Sternhell, along with classics such as Horkheimer and Adorno's *Dialectic of Enlightenment* ([1944] 2002).

12. Thus, Wolff (1970, 10) writes: "The paradox of man's condition in the modern world is that the more fully he recognizes his right and duty to be his own master, the more completely he becomes the passive object of a technology and bureaucracy whose complexities he cannot hope to understand." On the technical side of THINK-ING, a degree of liberation from the tyranny of the majority opinion may be found in Bayesian methods (Prelec 2004).

13. Polanyi (1936, 118) concluded his review of the effectiveness of Soviet propaganda in the 1930s with a call to arms: "Unless intellectuals make a new departure, inspired by unflinching veracity, truth will remain powerless against propaganda."

14. Peters (2017b) takes up the challenges for education in a post-truth world. Rogerson (2003) revisits Polanyi's ideas for the "information age." Iyengar and Massey (2018) focus specifically on scientific communication in post-truth social settings.

Thacker's (2018) book *Infinite Resignation* is a study in pessimism in the face of the nature of human personal and social EXISTENCE.

15. Shklar (1979) and Tillyris (2015) both consider hypocrisy desirable in some situations, including democratic governance. See chapter 25 and especially note 3.

16. This quote, which appears also in chapter 10, is from Buddhist philosopher Jay Garfield (2010, 12). On a related note, see Bostrom 2003 for a now classical early attempt to address the question of whether or not we live in a simulation. Edelman (2011) shows that the nature of reality may be impossible to decide by computational means, which need not, however, have any practical consequences concerning how one should live one's life. Garfield (2010, 12) makes a somewhat similar point, from an entirely different set of premises:

> The conventional truth is merely deceptive and conventional because, upon ultimate analysis, it fails to exist as it appears—that is, because it is ultimately empty. It is the nature of the conventional to deceive. Ultimately, conventional truth is all the truth there is, and that is an ultimate, and therefore, a conventional, truth. To fail to take conventional truth seriously as truth is therefore not only to deprecate the conventional in *favour* of the ultimate, but to deprecate *truth*, per se. That way lies SUFFERING. (small caps added)

Chapter 37

1. The Clausewitz quote—*Der Krieg ist eine bloße Fortsetzung der Politik mit anderen Mitteln*—is from his book *On War* (1832), ch. 1, sec. 24, in the Princeton University Press translation (1976). Zhou Enlai's quip appears in an interview given to E. Snow and published in *Saturday Evening Post* 226, no. 39 (March 27, 1954) under the title "Red China's Gentleman Hatchet Man."

2. The strategic regional background to these events, as well as the local power dynamics in the three countries directly involved in the 1982 war—Israel, Syria, and Lebanon—are hopelessly complicated and cannot even be sketched here. It may, however, be useful to note that Lebanon's traditionally intractable POLITICS can be blamed to a large extent on its neglect of nonfactional and RELIGION-independent education (Baytiyeh 2018). For the specific historical facts concerning the Syria-Iran axis and the Iraq involvement, see Goodarzi 2009. As to the Israeli angle, an analysis of the 1982 Lebanon War within the context of the broader Israeli military doctrine describes it as "an ambitious attempt [on the part of Israel] to solve the Palestinian problem by violent means, and to bring about a radical change in regional order by weakening Syria and reconstructing Israel's strategic dominance" (Bar-Joseph 2004, 150).

3. I cannot now think of that bizarre occasion without being reminded of a scene from Hemingway's *Across the River and into the Trees*:

> The river was slow and a muddy blue here, with reeds along the edges, and the Colonel, no one being in sight, squatted low, and looking across the river from the bank where you could never show your head in daylight, relieved himself in the exact place where he had

determined, by triangulation, that he had been badly wounded thirty years before. "A poor effort," he said aloud to the river and the river bank that were heavy with autumn quiet and wet from the fall rains. "But my own."

He stood up and looked around. There was no one in sight and he had left the car down the sunken road in front of the last and saddest rebuilt house in Fossalta.

"Now I'll complete the monument," he said to no one but the dead, and he took an old Solingen clasp knife, such as German poachers carry, from his pocket. It locked on opening and, twirling it, he dug a neat hole in the moist earth. He cleaned the knife on his right combat boot and then inserted a brown ten thousand lira note in the hole and tamped it down and put the grass that he had cored out over it.

"That is twenty years at five hundred lira a year for the Medaglia d'Argento al Valore Militare. The V.C. carries ten guineas, I believe. The D.S.C. is non-productive. The Silver Star is free. I'll keep the change," he said.

It's fine now, he thought. It has merde, money, blood; look how that grass grows; and the iron's in the earth along with Gino's leg, both of Randolfo's legs and my right knee-cap. It's a wonderful monument. It has everything. Fertility, money, blood and iron. Sounds like a nation. Where fertility, money, blood and iron is; there is the fatherland. We need coal though. We ought to get some coal.

4. A turning point in (some of) the Israeli public's perception of the 1982 war was the Sabra and Shatila massacre (see Falk 1984).

5. See the chapter titled "The Left Turn" in Edelman 2014.

6. Kissel and Kim (2019, 141) see war and peace as two sides of the same cognitive-capacity coin:

We propose that socially cooperative violence, or "emergent warfare," became possible with the onset of symbolic thought and complex cognition. Viewing emergent warfare as a byproduct of the human capacity for symbolic thought explains how the same capacities for communication and sociality allowed for elaborate peacemaking, conflict resolution, and avoidance. Cultural institutions around war and peace are both made possible by these changes.

They conclude: "We suggest that the story of warfare is necessarily part of the larger story of being, and processes of becoming, human" (143).

7. Consider, for instance, the paper titled "Invisible Inequality: The Two Americas of Military Sacrifice" by Kriner and Shen (2016). I by no means wish to single out these authors for their use of the word "sacrifice": it merely reflects the strikingly broad tacit acceptance of war on the part of our society. Orwellian Newspeak has not, however, become universal yet: the title of Anderson, Getmansky, and Hirsch-Hoefler 2018—"Burden Sharing: Income, Inequality and Willingness to Fight"—does avoid the language of sacrifice.

8. Four out of the five wars for which Kriner and Shen (2016), mentioned earlier, examined the casualty statistics (World War II, Korea, Vietnam, Iraq, and Afghanistan) were, for the United States, "wars of choice." Difficult as that concept has been (see, e.g., Katz 2017 and Kelsay 2015), a modern taxonomy of warfare (Ssorin-Chaikov 2018) makes it even more complicated.

9. Some examples of analysis of historical and present-day elites' role in the POLITICS of war can be found in Bouchat et al. 2019; Inbar 1990; Reyna, 2016; Saunders 2015; and Torres-Sánchez, Brandon, and 't Hart 2018. The privatization of war (which of course facilitates profiteering by the moneyed classes) is mentioned by Robinson and Barrera (2012, 6), who briefly discuss the dynamics of the "military-prison-industrial-security-financial complex." Levy (1998) offers a conceptual analysis of the "militarization of inequality"; the U.S. data of Kriner and Shen (2016, 560) indicate specifically that "while sacrifice was shared equally in World War II, beginning with the war in Korea, significant income gaps emerged."

10. See the Book of Judges 12:5–6.

11. The question "Whose side are you on?" is discussed also in chapter 21. As to antifascist action: making the right choice about it is (or ought to be) easy, but, as in any war, even a just one, following through the right course of action to a conclusion without complications is never easy. Paul Mason, in his essay "Reading Arendt Is Not Enough" (*New York Review of Books Daily*, May 2, 2019), discusses the cases of four writers, each of whom had participated in armed struggle against fascism:

> [George] Orwell and [Arthur] Koestler fought fascism in Spain—Koestler as a card-carrying communist, Orwell as a member of the far-left POUM militia. [Primo] Levi fought as a partisan in 1943, in a group allied to the liberal-socialist Partito d'Azione. [Vassily] Grossman, the first Soviet journalist to enter the remains of the Treblinka concentration camp, had served throughout the war as a Red Army journalist. Every one of them understood they were morally compromised by the antifascist war they had taken part in.
>
> Levi's partisan unit disintegrated after they were forced to shoot two volunteers for indiscipline. Koestler's portrait of a ruthless Soviet commissar was based in part on his own actions as a Comintern spy. Grossman had denounced other writers and managed to report the Red Army's advance across Europe without public mention of its mass rapes and massacres. Orwell's poem, "The Italian Soldier," about an anarchist volunteer in the Spanish Civil War dramatized the problem of fighting fascism in alliance with Stalinism. "The lie that slew you is buried," Orwell wrote, in a bitter eulogy to his presumed-dead comrade, "under a deeper lie."
>
> Each of these writers committed violence in the name of antifascism. In their work, antifascist violence is seen as inevitable, if tragic—and leads ultimately to the strengthening of Stalinism, bureaucracy, or inhuman attitudes.

Whether or not "ultimately" is the right word here, the tragedy is undisputed; but had it not been for World War II antifascists, the Thousand-Year Reich would likely still be going strong. On the upside, I would have been spared the pains of EXISTENCE, and thus also the effort (in which I have failed) to sound coolly detached and logical while arguing that fascists need to be resisted by any means available.

12. The events documented in Samuel 2:2, happened during the brief period when David was King in Judah and Saul was King over Israel. Abner was Saul's general; Joab was David's nephew and captain. The following chapters recount how Joab later killed Abner to avenge the death of his brother Asahel at Abner's hand and was in turn killed on King David's orders.

13. The two letters were published as a booklet under the title *Why War?* (Einstein and Freud 1939). The original language of Walter Benjamin's ([1950] 1968) civilization/barbarism quote is: "Es ist niemals ein Dokument der Kultur, ohne zugleich ein solches der Barbarei zu sein." This sentence was made into the epitaph for Benjamin's grave in Portbou, Catalonia. The spirit of Benjamin's theses on history may be compared to that of Horkheimer and Adorno's *Dialectic of Enlightenment* ([1944] 2002), quoted in chapter 34. Note: the numbering of Benjamin's theses used here follows that of the 1974 German edition (*Gesammelten Schriften* [Collected Writings] I:2, Frankfurt am Main: Suhrkamp Verlag), as translated by Dennis Redmond (2005). I thank Professor Samantha Rose Hill for providing me with a facsimile of the relevant page from Benjamin's manuscript.

14. Each of the four songs listed here requires some notes. The first one, "A las barricadas" (1936), is based on original Polish lyrics by Wacław Święcicki; music by Józef Pławiński. The second one, the much-covered *"Bella ciao,"* which dates to World War II, is based on a much older song of Italian peasants working in rice paddies. The third song, "With God on Our Side," has also been extensively covered, including by Joan Baez. The fourth one, "До свидания, мальчики" (Farewell, boys), bears the name of a very popular film (itself based on a novel) about World War II in the USSR.

15. This chapter has been completed on the Holocaust Commemoration Day, Nisan 27, 5779 (May 2, 2019). It is humbly and respectfully dedicated to the memory of the members of the Jewish Resistance who fought in the doomed Warsaw Ghetto uprising in April–May 1943.

Chapter 38

1. The Dartmouth commencement speech by Brodsky, a Nobel laureate for literature and one of the sharpest wits and best wordsmiths of the twentieth century, appears as an essay, titled "In Praise of Boredom," in the collection *On Grief and Reason* (Brodsky 1995).

2. The class notes for 1989 graduates of Dartmouth can be found online here: https://dartmouthalumnimagazine.com/class-notes/1989/all.

3. Regarding the pursuit of happiness, see Edelman 2012. Gigerenzer and Garcia-Retamero (2017) discuss "Cassandra's regret"—the kind that arises from wanting to not have known.

4. Here's how it may start:

> Had it been such a bad life? He had been healthy, prosperous, and beloved. His father was managing partner of Falkner, Breckenridge & Co., one of the most stable of the Wall Street houses, and Breckenridge, after coming up through the ranks in the family tradition, putting in his time as a customer's man and his time in the bond department and as a floor

trader, was a partner too, only ten years out of Dartmouth. What was wrong with that? (from *Breckenridge and the Continuum* by Robert Silverberg [1973], a suggested reading for this chapter)

5. Regarding the lottery of birth, see Fischer at al. 1996. The myth of meritocracy is exposed by Frank (2016); Mijs (2016) discusses its implications specifically for education. The concept of the veil of ignorance in theory of justice has been introduced by Rawls (1971).

6. Evans (2016), among many others, documents the lasting effects of childhood poverty on adult well-being. Stephan et al. (2018) found that higher IQ in adolescence is related to a younger subjective age in later life.

7. I tried very hard to refrain from dragging the Chicxulub Impactor, which finished off the dinosaurs, into the pond metaphor.

8. The story of Feuchwanger's Josephus Trilogy, about Flavius Josephus, begins in the year 60 in Rome. The three books that comprise it are *Der jüdische Krieg* (*Josephus*, 1932); *Die Söhne* (*The Jew of Rome*, 1935); and *Der Tag wird kommen* (*The Day Will Come*, 1942).

9. Anything-buying scene, really: in the USSR, nothing of any value was easy to obtain at all times. This included even the most basic and indispensable commodities such as bread. Following the drought of 1963 (which happens to be the year when the hard-to-get Feuchtwanger books came out), there was a shortage of wheat, which caused white bread to disappear from bakeries. There was a surplus of meat, though, as the cattle could not be fed and had to be slaughtered. The following year, the shortage of beef was much more severe than the Soviet normal.

10. See also chapter 37. Some of the personal anecdotes that I mention here made their way into Edelman 2014.

11. Regarding the concept of formative years, a brief overview of cognitive development can be found in Steinberg 2005.

12. In Kierkegaard's own words: "It is perfectly true, as the philosophers say, that life must be understood backwards. But they forget the other proposition, that it must be lived forwards." In Journals IV A 164 (1843).

13. My translation of Brodsky's poem can be found here: http://kybele.psych.cornell .edu/~edelman/poetry/soi.html.

Afterword

1. The Borges confession is in *Dedicatoria de Jorge Luis Borges en sus Obras Completas* (Buenos Aires: Emecé, 1974). The title of the first and only section in this chapter is from the eponymous 1967 song written by Mickey Newbury. It has been performed,

among many others, by Jerry Lee Lewis and by Kenny Rogers. My favorite version is by the First Edition, as included in the Coen brothers' 1998 film *The Big Lebowski*.

2. This and the next quote are from Borges's "Happiness" in *The Limit*, reprinted in *Selected Poems*, ed. Alexander Coleman (New York: Viking, 1999). The recurrence motif is echoed also in other works by Borges, for instance, the closing sentences of both "The Immortal" (Borges [1947] 1970d): "I have been Homer; shortly, I shall be No One, like Ulysses; shortly, I shall be all men; I shall be dead."; and of "Tlön, Uqbar, Orbis Tertius" (Borges [1941] 1962b): "All men, in the vertiginous moment of coitus, are the same man. All men who repeat a line from Shakespeare are William Shakespeare."

References

Aaronson, S. 2012. "Why Philosophers Should Care about Computational Complexity." In *Computability: Gödel, Turing, Church, and Beyond*, ed. B. J. Copeland, C. J. Posy, and O. Shagrir, 261–328. Cambridge, MA: MIT Press.

Abbey, E. 1968. *Desert Solitaire: A Season in the Wilderness*. New York: McGraw-Hill.

Abbey, E. 1980. *Good News*. New York: E. P. Dutton.

Abdel-Jaouad, H. 1993. "Isabelle Eberhardt: Portrait of the Artist as a Young Nomad." Special issue: Post/Colonial Conditions: Exiles, Migrations, and Nomadisms. *Yale French Studies* 83 (2): 93–117.

Agazzi, E. 2014. "The Context of Making Science." Chapter 9 in *Scientific Objectivity and Its Contexts*, 413–436. Cham, Switzerland: Springer.

Aguilar Mora, J. 1999. "Felices los felices (homenaje a Borges)." *Kipus: Revista Andina de Letras* 10:3–10.

Ahad-Ha'am. 1898. "Sabbath and Zionism." *Shiloach* 3 (6). In Hebrew.

Aktipis, A., L. Cronk, J. Alcock, J. D. Ayers, C. Baciu, D. Balliet, A. M. Boddy, O. S. Curry, J. A. Krems, A. Munoz, D. Sullivan, D. Sznycer, G. S. Wilkinson, and P. Winfrey. 2018. "Understanding Cooperation through Fitness Interdependence." *Nature Human Behaviour* 2:429–431.

Allman, M. J., T. B. Penney, and W. H. Meck. 2016. "A Brief History of 'The Psychology of Time Perception.'" *Timing & Time Perception* 4:299–314.

Alvaredo, F., L. Chancel, T. Piketty, E. Saez, and G. Zucman. 2017. "Global Inequality Dynamics: New Findings from WID.world." Technical report, National Bureau of Economic Research.

Amis, M. 1991. *Time's Arrow*. New York: Penguin.

Anderson, C. J., A. Getmansky, and S. Hirsch-Hoefler. 2018. "Burden Sharing: Income, Inequality and Willingness to Fight." *British Journal of Political Science* 50 (1): 1–17.

Anderson, E. S. 1999. "What Is the Point of Equality? *Ethics* 109:287–337.

Anderson, R. E., ed. 2015. *World Suffering and Quality of Life.* Vol. 56, *Social Indicators Research Series.* New York: Springer.

Andrew, C. M., and O. Gordievsky. 1990. *KGB: The Inside Story of Its Foreign Operations from Lenin to Gorbachev.* New York: HarperCollins.

Annas, J. 1987. "Epicurus on Pleasure and Happiness." *Philosophical Topics* 15:5–21.

Anton, C. 2018. "Technology, Hypocrisy and Morality: Where, Oh Where, Has All the Hypocrisy Gone?" *Explorations in Media Ecology* 17:119–135.

Anvar, L. 2011. "The Hidden Pearls of Wisdom: Desire and Initiation in *Laylī u Majnūn.*" In *A Key to the Treasure of the Hakīm: Artistic and Humanistic Aspects of Nizāmī Ganjavī's Khamsa,* ed. J.-C. Bürgel and C. van Ruymbeke, 53–75. Leiden: Leiden University Press.

Appiah, K. A. 2019. "Dialectics of Enlightenment." *The New York Review of Books* 66 (8), May 9. Review of *Irrationality: A History of the Dark Side of Reason* by Justin E. H. Smith.

Ardelt, M. 1997. "Wisdom and Life Satisfaction in Old Age." *Journal of Gerontology: Psychological Sciences* 52B:P15–P27.

Ardelt, M. 2004. "Wisdom as Expert Knowledge System: A Critical Review of a Contemporary Operationalization of an Ancient Concept." *Human Development* 47:257–285.

Arendt, H. 1958. *The Human Condition.* Chicago: University of Chicago Press.

Ariza-Montes, A., J. M. Arjona-Fuentes, H. Han, and R. Law. 2018. "The Price of Success: A Study on Chefs' Subjective Well-Being, Job Satisfaction, and Human Values." *International Journal of Hospitality Management* 69:84–93.

Armstrong, T., and B. Detweiler-Bedell. 2008. "Beauty as an Emotion: The Exhilarating Prospect of Mastering a Challenging World." *Review of General Psychology* 12:305–329.

Arnswald, U. 2009. "The Paradox of Ethics—'It Leaves Everything as It Is.'" In *In Search of Meaning: Ludwig Wittgenstein on Ethics, Mysticism and Religion,* ed. U. Arnswald, 1–24. Karlsruhe: KIT Scientific Publishing.

Attar, F. [1177] 1984. *The Conference of the Birds.* New York: Penguin.

Awad, E., S. Dsouza, R. Kim, J. Schulz, J. Henrich, A. Shariff, J.-F. Bonnefon, and I. Rahwan. 2018. "The Moral Machine Experiment." *Nature* 563:59–64.

Bach, D. R., and P. Dayan. 2017. "Algorithms for Survival: A Comparative Perspective on Emotions." *Nature Reviews Neuroscience* 18:311–319.

Bach-y-Rita, P., and S. W. Kercel. 2003. "Sensory Substitution and the Human–Machine Interface." *Trends in Cognitive Sciences* 7:541–546.

Bacon, F. [1620] 1854. *The New Organon, or True Directions Concerning the Interpretation of Nature*, ed. and trans. Basil Montague. Philadelphia: Parry & MacMillan.

Banks, I. M. 2007. *The State of the Art*. San Francisco: Night Shade Books.

Banks, I. M. 2010. *Surface Detail*. London: Orbit.

Bar-Joseph, U. 2004. "The Paradox of Israeli Power." *Survival* 46 (4): 137–155.

Barricelli, N. A. 1983. "Challenge to Gödel's Proof." Theoretic papers. Blindern, Norway: Blindern Theoretic Research Team.

Barrow, C. W. 2018. "From Radical Resistance to Quiet Subversion." In *The Entrepreneurial Intellectual in the Corporate University*, 31–38. London: Palgrave Macmillan.

Barthelme, D. 1975. "A Manual for Sons." *New Yorker*, May 12, 40–50.

Bashevis Singer, I. 1964. "A Wedding in Brownsville." *Commentary*, March.

Baytiyeh, H. 2018. "Education to Reduce Recurring Conflicts." *Peace Review* 30 (1): 95–102.

Beer, M. D. 2000. "The Nature, Causes and Types of Ecstasy." *Philosophy, Psychiatry, & Psychology* 7:311–315.

Bekkering, D. J. 2016. "Fake Religions, Politics and Ironic Fandom: The Church of the SubGenius, Zontar and American Televangelism." *Culture and Religion* 17:129–147.

Benatar, D. 2006. *Better Never to Have Been: The Harm of Coming into Existence*. Oxford: Oxford University Press.

Benhabib, S. 1994. "Judith Shklar's Dystopic Liberalism." *Social Research* 61:477–488.

Benjamin, W. [1950] 1968. "Theses on the Philosophy of History." In *Illuminations: Essays and Reflections*, ed. H. Arendt, trans. Harry Zohn. New York: Schocken. First published in German.

Benjaminsen, L. 2016. "Homelessness in a Scandinavian Welfare State: The Risk of Shelter Use in the Danish Adult Population." *Urban Studies* 53:2041–2063.

Bernstein, J. H. 2009. "Nonknowledge: The Bibliographical Organization of Ignorance, Stupidity, Error, and Unreason: Part One." *Knowledge Organization* 36:17–29.

Berscheid, E. 2010. "Love in the Fourth Dimension." *Annual Review of Psychology* 61:1–25.

Betenson, T. 2016. "Anti-theodicy." *Philosophy Compass* 11:56–65.

Bettis, R. A., and S. Hu. 2018. "Bounded Rationality, Heuristics, Computational Complexity, and Artificial Intelligence." In *Behavioral Strategy in Perspective*, Vol. 39, *Advances in Strategic Management*, 139–150. Bingley, UK: Emerald Publishing Limited.

Bick, A., N. Fuchs-Schündeln, and D. Lagakos. 2018. "How Do Hours Worked Vary with Income? Cross-Country Evidence and Implications." *American Economic Review* 108:170–199.

Binet, L. 2017. *The 7th Function of Language*. New York: Farrar, Straus and Giroux.

Bishop, M. 1962. *A History of Cornell*. Ithaca, NY: Cornell University Press.

Blake, P. R., K. McAuliffe, J. Corbit, T. C. Callaghan, O. Barry, A. Bowie, L. Kleutsch, K. L. Kramer, E. Ross, H. Vongsachang, R. Wrangham, and F. Warneken. 2015. "The Ontogeny of Fairness in Seven Societies." *Nature* 528:258–262.

Blanke, O. 2012. "Multisensory Brain Mechanisms of Bodily Self-Consciousness." *Nature Reviews Neuroscience* 13:556–571.

Bloom, P. 2017. "Empathy and Its Discontents." *Trends in Cognitive Sciences* 21:24–31.

Boehm, C., H. B. Barclay, R. K. Dentan, M.-C. Dupre, J. D. Hill, S. Kent, B. M. Knauft, K. F. Otterbein, and S. Rayner. 1993. "Egalitarian Behavior and Reverse Dominance Hierarchy" [and comments and reply]. *Current Anthropology* 34 (3): 227–254.

Bolles, R. C., and M. S. Fanselow. 1980. "A Perceptual-Defensive-Recuperative Model of Fear and Pain." *The Behavioral and Brain Sciences* 3:291–323.

Bonica, A., N. McCarty, K. T. Poole, and H. Rosenthal. 2013. "Why Hasn't Democracy Slowed Rising Inequality?" *Journal of Economic Perspectives* 27:103–124.

Borges, J. L. [1935] 1962a. "The Approach to Al-Mu'tasim." In *Ficciones*, trans. A. Bonner in collaboration with the author. New York: Grove Press.

Borges, J. L. [1941] 1962b. "Tlön, Uqbar, Orbis Tertius." In *Ficciones*, trans. A. Bonner in collaboration with the author. New York: Grove Press.

Borges, J. L. 1964. *Dreamtigers (El Hacedor)*, trans. M. Boyer and H. Morland. Austin: University of Texas Press.

Borges, J. L. 1969. *Elogio de la sombra*. Buenos Aires: Emecé.

Borges, J. L. [1940] 1970a. "The Aleph." In *The Aleph and Other Stories, 1933–1969*, trans. N. T. di Giovanni in collaboration with the author. New York: E. P. Dutton.

Borges, J. L. [1940] 1970b. "The Circular Ruins." In *The Aleph and Other Stories, 1933–1969*, trans. N. T. di Giovanni in collaboration with the author. New York: E. P. Dutton.

Borges, J. L. [1941] 1970c. "The Garden of Forking Paths. In *Labyrinths*, ed. D. A. Yates and J. E. Irby, 44–54. New York: Penguin.

Borges, J. L. [1947] 1970d. "The Immortal." In *The Aleph and Other Stories, 1933–1969*, trans. N. T. di Giovanni in collaboration with the author. New York: E. P. Dutton.

Borges, J. L. 1970e. *Labyrinths*, ed. D. A. Yates and J. E. Irby. New York: Penguin.

Borges, J. L. 1999a. "August 25, 1983." In *Collected Fictions*, trans. Andrew Hurley, 489–493. New York: Penguin.

Borges, J. L. 1999b. "A New Refutation of Time." In *Selected Non-Fictions*, ed. E. Weinberger, 317–332. New York: Viking.

Borges, J. L. [1922] 1999c. "The Nothingness of Personality." In *Selected Non-Fictions*, ed. E. Weinberger, 3–9. New York: Viking.

Borjigin, J., U. Lee, T. Liu, D. Pal, S. Huff, D. Klarr, J. Sloboda, J. Hernandez, M. M. Wang, and G. A. Mashour. 2013. "Surge of Neurophysiological Coherence and Connectivity in the Dying Brain." *Proceedings of the National Academy of Science* 110:14432–14437.

Bossaerts, P., and C. Murawski. 2017. "Computational Complexity and Human Decision-Making." *Trends in Cognitive Sciences* 21:917–929.

Bostrom, N. 2003. "Are You Living in a Computer Simulation?" *Philosophical Quarterly* 53:243–255.

Botvinick, M., and J. Cohen. 1998. "Rubber Hands 'Feel' Touch That Eyes See." *Nature* 391:756.

Bouchat, P., L. Licata, V. Rosoux, C. Allesch, H. Ammerer, M. Babinska, M. Bilewicz et al. 2019. "Greedy Elites and Poor Lambs: How Young Europeans Remember the Great War." *Journal of Social and Political Psychology* 7 (1): 52–75.

Boyd, R., H. Gintis, S. Bowles, and P. J. Richerson. 2003. "The Evolution of Altruistic Punishment." *Proceedings of the National Academy of Science* 100:3531–3535.

Boym, S. 2001. *The Future of Nostalgia*. New York: Basic Books.

Boysen, B. 2008. "I Call That Patriotism: Leopold Bloom and Cosmopolitan *caritas*." *The Comparatist* 32:140–156.

Bradshaw, S., and P. N. Howard. 2018. *Challenging Truth and Trust: A Global Inventory of Organized Social Media Manipulation*. The Computational Propaganda Project. Oxford Internet Institute, University of Oxford. https://comprop.oii.ox.ac.uk/research/cybertroops2018/.

Brady, D., and A. Bostic. 2015. "Paradoxes of Social Policy: Welfare Transfers, Relative Poverty, and Redistribution Preferences." *American Sociological Review* 80:268–298.

Braithwaite, S., and J. Holt-Lunstad. 2017. "Romantic Relationships and Mental Health." *Current Opinion in Psychology* 13:120–125.

Branje, S. 2018. "Development of Parent-Adolescent Relationships: Conflict Interactions as a Mechanism of Change." *Child Development Perspectives* 12:171–176.

Brembs, B. 2011. "Towards a Scientific Concept of Free Will as a Biological Trait: Spontaneous Actions and Decision-Making in Invertebrates." *Proceedings of the Royal Society B* 278:930–939.

Breugelmans, S. M., M. Zeelenberg, T. Gilovich, W.-H. Huang, and Y. Shani. 2014. "Generality and Cultural Variation in the Experience of Regret." *Emotion* 14:1037–1048.

Brewer, W. F., and C. A. Chinn. 1994. "Scientists' Responses to Anomalous Data: Evidence from Psychology, History, and Philosophy of Science." *PSA: Proceedings of the Biennial Meeting of the Philosophy of Science Association, Vol. One: Contributed Papers*, 304–313.

Brielmann, A. A., and D. G. Pelli. 2017. "Beauty Requires Thought." *Current Biology* 27:1–8.

Brinkmann, S. 2014. "Languages of Suffering." *Theory & Psychology* 24:630–648.

Brodsky, J. 1995. "In Praise of Boredom." In *On Grief and Reason—Essays*, 104–113. New York: Penguin.

Bromham, L., R. Dinnage, and X. Hua. 2016. "Interdisciplinary Research Has Consistently Lower Funding Success." *Nature* 534:684–687.

Brosschot, J. F., B. Verkuil, and J. F. Thayer. 2016. "The Default Response to Uncertainty and the Importance of Perceived Safety in Anxiety and Stress: An Evolution-Theoretical Perspective." *Journal of Anxiety Disorders* 41:22–34.

Brouwer, L. E. J. 1952. "Historical Background, Principles and Methods of Intuitionism." *South African Journal of Science October-November*, 139–146.

Brown, E. D., M. D. Seyler, A. M. Knorr, M. L. Garnett, and J.-F. Laurenceau. 2016. "Daily Poverty-Related Stress and Coping: Associations with Child Learned Helplessness." *Family Relations* 65:591–602.

Brown, N., A. Lerer, S. Gross, and T. Sandholm. 2019. "Deep Counterfactual Regret Minimization." In *Proceedings of the 36th International Conference on Machine Learning*, ed. K. Chaudhuri and R. Salakhutdinov. Long Beach, CA.

Buckner, R. L. 2010. "The Role of the Hippocampus in Prediction and Imagination." *Annual Review of Psychology* 61:27–48.

Bulgakov, M. A. 1967. *The Master and Margarita*. Paris: YMCA Press.

Bunge, M. 2017. "The Self-Domesticated Animal and Its Study." In *Neuroscience and Social Science: The Missing Link*, ed. A. Ibáñez, L. Sedeño, and A. M. García, 431–441. New York: Springer.

Bunin, I. A. 1908. "Bird's Shadow" (Тень птицы). *Земля (Earth) Almanac* 1.

Bunin, I. A. 1949. *Dark Avenues and Other Stories*, trans. Richard Hare. London: John Lehmann.

Burns, D. M. 2016. "Providence, Creation, and Gnosticism According to the Gnostics." *Journal of Early Christian Studies* 24:55–79.

Burton, R. 1638. *The Anatomy of Melancholy*. Available online at Project Gutenberg. https://www.gutenberg.org/ebooks/10800.

Burton, R. F. [1855] 1893. *Personal Narrative of a Pilgrimage to El-Medinah and Meccah*. London: Tylston and Edwards. Memorial edition in two volumes. http://www.burtoniana.org/books/.

Burton, R. F. 1885. *The Book of Thousand Nights and a Night*. London: The Burton Club. http://www.burtoniana.org/books/1885-ArabianNights.

Byrne, R. M. J. 2002. "Mental Models and Counterfactual Thoughts About What Might Have Been." *Trends in Cognitive Sciences* 6:426–431.

Callender, C. 2017. *What Makes Time Special?* New York: Oxford University Press.

Campbell, J. 1949. *The Hero with a Thousand Faces*. New York: Pantheon.

Campbell Jr., J. W. 1959. "What Do You Mean . . . Human?" *Astounding Science Fiction*, September, 5–7. Editorial.

Carey, D., and S. Trakulhun. 2007. "Universalism and the Postcolonial Enlightenment." In *The Postcolonial Enlightenment: Eighteenth-Century Colonialism and Postcolonial Theory*, ed. D. Carey and L. Festa, 240–280. New York: Oxford University Press.

Carleton, R. N. 2016. "Fear of the Unknown: One Fear to Rule Them All?" *Journal of Anxiety Disorders* 41:5–21.

Carstensen, L. L. 2006. "The Influence of a Sense of Time on Human Development." *Science* 312:1913–1915.

Carstensen, L. L., and J. A. Michels. 2005. "At the Intersection of Emotion and Cognition: Aging and the Positivity Effect." *Current Directions in Psychological Science* 14:117–121.

Casanova, J. 2005. "The Dark Face of Spanish Anarchism." *International Labor and Working-Class History* 67 (Spring): 79–99.

Chadha, M. 2015. "Time-Series of Ephemeral Impressions: The Abhidharma-Buddhist View of Conscious Experience." *Phenomenology and Cognitive Science* 14:543–560.

Chaitin, G. J. 2018. "Building the World Out of Information and Computation: Is God a Programmer, Not a Mathematician?" In *The Map and the Territory: Exploring the Foundations of Science, Thought and Reality*, ed. S. Wuppuluri and F. A. Doria, 431–438. Cham, Switzerland: Springer.

Chandler, M. A. 2003. "Meno and Mencius: Two Philosophical Dramas." *Philosophy East and West* 53:367–398.

Chater, N., T. Felin, D. C. Funder, G. Gigerenzer, J. J. Koenderink, J. I. Krueger, D. Noble, S. A. Nordli, M. Oaksford, B. Schwartz, K. E. Stanovich, and P. M. Todd. 2018. "Mind, Rationality, and Cognition: An Interdisciplinary Debate." *Psychonomic Bulletin and Review* 25:793–826.

Chatwin, B. 1987. *Songlines*. New York: Penguin.

Cheadle, J. E., and P. R. Amato. 2011. "A Quantitative Assessment of Lareau's Qualitative Conclusions about Class, Race, and Parenting." *Journal of Family Issues* 32:679–706.

Cherniak, C. 1986. *Minimal Rationality*. Cambridge, MA: MIT Press.

Chonody, J. M., and B. Teater. 2016. "Why Do I Dread Looking Old?: A Test of Social Identity Theory, Terror Management Theory, and the Double Standard of Aging." *Journal of Women & Aging* 28:112–126.

Choo, H., and M. Ferree. 2010. "Practicing Intersectionality in Sociological Research: A Critical Analysis of Inclusions, Interactions, and Institutions in the Study of Inequalities." *Sociological Theory* 28:129–149.

Churchland, P. M. 1998. "Towards a Cognitive Neurobiology of the Moral Virtues." *Topoi* 17:83–96.

Cipolla, C. M. 1987. "The Basic Laws of Human Stupidity." *Whole Earth Review*, Spring, 2–7.

Clarke, A. C. 1946. "Rescue Party." *Astounding Science Fiction* 5 (6) (September): 18–30.

Clastres, P. 1987. *Society Against the State: Essays in Political Anthropology*. New York: Zone Books.

Conlon, E. 1986. *The Spanish Civil War: Anarchism in Action*. Workers Solidarity Movement. Pamphlet. http://struggle.ws/spain/pam_intro.html.

Connors, A. L. 2009–2010. "Big Bad Pharma: An Ethical Analysis of Physician-Directed and Consumer-Directed Marketing Tactics." *Albany Law Review* 73:243–282.

Conrad, S. 2012. "Enlightenment in Global History: A Historiographical Critique." *The American Historical Review* 117:999–1027.

Contestabile, B. 2014. "Negative Utilitarianism and Buddhist Intuition." *Contemporary Buddhism* 15:298–311.

Conway, J., and S. Kochen. 2006. "The Free Will Theorem." *Foundations of Physics* 36 (10): 1441–1473.

Couldry, N. 2017. "Surveillance-Democracy." *Journal of Information Technology & Politics* 14 (2): 182–188.

Cozzarelli, C., A. V. Wilkinson, and M. J. Tagler. 2001. "Attitudes toward the Poor and Attributions for Poverty." *Journal of Social Issues* 57:207–227.

Cozzolino, P. J., L. E. R. Blackie, and L. S. Meyers. 2014. "Self-Related Consequences of Death Fear and Death Denial." *Death Studies* 38:418–422.

Craig, A. D. 2002. "How Do You Feel? Interoception: The Sense of the Physiological Condition of the Body." *Nature Reviews Neuroscience* 3:655–666.

Crowder-Meyer, M. 2018. "Baker, Bus Driver, Babysitter, Candidate? Revealing the Gendered Development of Political Ambition among Ordinary Americans." *Political Behavior*.

Cupers, K. 2016. "Human Territoriality and the Downfall of Public Housing." *Public Culture* 29 (1): 165–190.

Curry, O. S. 2016. "Morality as Cooperation: A Problem-Centred Approach." In *The Evolution of Morality*, ed. T. K. Shackelford and R. D. Hansen, 27–51. Cham, Switzerland: Springer.

Curry, O. S., D. A. Mullins, and H. Whitehouse. 2019. "Is It Good to Cooperate? Testing the Theory of Morality-as-Cooperation in 60 Societies." *Current Anthropology* 60:1.

Dąbrowska, E. 2018. "Experience, Aptitude and Individual Differences in Native Language Ultimate Attainment." *Cognition* 178:222–235.

Dąbrowska, E., and J. Street. 2006. "Individual Differences in Language Attainment: Comprehension of Passive Sentences by Native and Non-Native English Speakers." *Language Sciences* 28:604–615.

Dainton, B. 2016. "Some Cosmological Implications of Temporal Experience." In *Cosmological and Psychological Time*, ed. Y. Dolev and M. Roubach, 75–105. New York: Springer.

Daly, M., and M. Wilson. 1988. "Evolutionary Social Psychology and Family Homicide." *Science* 242:512–524.

Danielson, P. 2007. "The Place of Ethics in a Unified Behavioral Science." *Behavioral and Brain Sciences* 30:23–24.

Daqing, W. 2010. "On the Ancient Greek αγον." *Procedia—Social and Behavioral Sciences* 2 (5): 6805–6812.

Davidai, S., and T. Gilovich. 2018. "The Ideal Road Not Taken: The Self-Discrepancies Involved in People's Most Enduring Regrets." *Emotion* 18:439–452.

Davidson, R. 1996. *Desert Places: A Woman's Odyssey with the Wanderers of the Indian Desert.* New York: Penguin.

Decety, J. 2015. "The Neural Pathways, Development and Functions of Empathy." *Current Opinion in Behavioral Sciences* 3:1–6.

Deibert, R. J. 2019. "The Road to Digital Unfreedom: Three Painful Truths about Social Media." *Journal of Democracy* 30 (1): 25–39.

DeLoache, J. S., and V. LoBue. 2009. "The Narrow Fellow in the Grass: Human Infants Associate Snakes and Fear." *Developmental Science* 12:201–207.

Dennett, D. C. 1983. "Intentional Systems in Cognitive Ethology: The 'Panglossian Paradigm' Defended." *Behavioral and Brain Sciences* 6:343–355.

Dennett, D. C. 1984. *Elbow Room: The Varieties of Free Will Worth Wanting.* Cambridge, MA: MIT Press.

Dennett, D. C. 2003. *Freedom Evolves.* New York: Viking.

Dennett, D. C. 2006. *Breaking the Spell: Religion as a Natural Phenomenon.* New York: Viking.

Dennett, D. C. 2008. *Kinds of Minds: Toward an Understanding of Consciousness.* New York: Basic Books.

Deutsch, D. 1997. *The Fabric of Reality.* London: Allen Lane.

Dewey, J. 1903. "Logical Conditions of a Scientific Treatment of Morality." *Decennial Publications of the University of Chicago, First Series* 3:115–139.

Díaz, J. 2012. "The Cheater's Guide to Love." *New Yorker*, July 23, 61–69.

Dick, P. K. 1964. *The Penultimate Truth.* New York: Belmont Books.

Dick, P. K. 1969. *Ubik.* New York: Doubleday.

Dick, P. K. 1974. *Flow My Tears, the Policeman Said.* New York: Doubleday.

Dick, P. K. 1976. *Martian Time-Slip.* New York: Ballantine Books.

Didonna, F., and Y. Rosillo Gonzalez. 2009. "Mindfulness and Feelings of Emptiness." In *Clinical Handbook of Mindfulness*, ed. F. Didonna, 125–152. New York: Springer.

Dipert, R. R. 2003. "Mathematics in Musil." In *Writing the Austrian Traditions: Relations between Philosophy and Literature*, ed. W. Huemer and M.-O. Schuster, 143–159. Edmonton, Alberta: Wirth-Institute for Austrian and Central European Studies.

DiTommaso, L. 1992. "History and Historical Effect in Frank Herbert's 'Dune.'" *Science Fiction Studies* 19 (3): 311–325.

Dobzhansky, T. 1973. "Nothing in Biology Makes Sense Except in the Light of Evolution." *The American Biology Teacher* 35:125–129.

Dolev, Y., and M. Roubach, eds. 2016. *Cosmological and Psychological Time*. New York: Springer.

Dong, X., B. Milholland, and J. Vijg. 2016. "Evidence for a Limit to Human Lifespan." *Nature* 538:257–265.

Doob, A. N., and A. E. Gross. 1968. "Status of Frustrator as an Inhibitor of Horn-Honking Responses." *Journal of Social Psychology* 76:213–218.

Dorey, P. 2010. "A Poverty of Imagination: Blaming the Poor for Inequality." *The Political Quarterly* 81 (3): 333–343.

Doria, F. A. 2018. "El Aleph, or a Monster Lurks in the Belly of Computer Science." In *The Map and the Territory: Exploring the Foundations of Science, Thought and Reality*, ed. S. Wuppuluri and F. A. Doria, 22, 407–417. Cham, Switzerland: Springer.

Draitser, E. A. 1984. "Это непростое дело." In *Пещера неожиданностей (The Cave of Surprises)*, 100–101. New York: Effect. Story available in English: "It's Not a Simple Thing." New York: ELF (Eclectic Literary Forum), 1996.

Droit-Volet, S., and S. Gil. 2009. "The Time-Emotion Paradox." *Philosophical Transactions of the Royal Society B* 364:1943–1953.

Droit-Volet, S., S. Fayolle, M. Lamotte, and S. Gil. 2013. "Time, Emotion and the Embodiment of Timing." *Timing & Time Perception* 1:99–126.

Du Bois, J. W. 2014. "Towards a Dialogic Syntax." *Cognitive Linguistics* 25:359–410.

Dunning, D. 2011. "The Dunning-Kruger Effect: On Being Ignorant of One's Own Ignorance." In *Advances in Experimental Social Psychology*, vol. 44, ed. J. M. Olson and M. P. Zanna, 247–296. Amsterdam: Elsevier.

Dunning, D. 2019. "The Best Option Illusion in Self and Social Assessment." *Self and Identity* 18:349–362.

Durant, W. J. 1917. *Philosophy and the Social Problem*. New York: Macmillan.

Dutkievicz, P., and D. B. Kazarinova. 2017. "Fear as Politics." *Polis. Political Studies* 4:8–21. In Russian.

Dutt, A. J., and H. W. Wah. 2017. "Feeling Sad Makes Us Feel Older: Effects of a Sad-Mood Induction on Subjective Age." *Psychology of Aging* 32:412–418.

Dyde, S. W. 1894. "Hegel's Conception of Freedom." *The Philosophical Review* 3 (6): 655–671.

Easterlin, R. A., R. Morgan, M. Switek, and F. Wang. 2012. "China's Life Satisfaction, 1990–2010." *Proceedings of the National Academy of Science* 109:9775–9780.

Edelman, S. 2008. *Computing the Mind: How the Mind Really Works*. New York: Oxford University Press.

Edelman, S. 2009. "On What It Means to See, and What We Can Do about It." In *Object Categorization: Computer and Human Vision Perspectives*, ed. S. Dickinson, A. Leonardis, B. Schiele, and M. J. Tarr, 69–86. Cambridge: Cambridge University Press.

Edelman, S. 2011. "Regarding Reality: Some Consequences of Two Incapacities." *Frontiers in Theoretical and Philosophical Psychology* 2: article 44.

Edelman, S. 2012. *The Happiness of Pursuit*. New York: Basic Books.

Edelman, S. 2014. *Beginnings*. BookBaby. Available at Amazon, http://www.amazon.com/Beginnings-Shimon-Edelman-ebook/dp/B00IQZBPJG/; and iTunes, https://itunes.apple.com/us/book/beginnings/id828059215?mt=11.

Edelman, S. 2015. "Varieties of Perceptual Truth and Their Possible Evolutionary Roots." *Psychonomic Bulletin and Review* 22:1519–1522.

Edelman, S. 2017. "Language and Other Complex Behaviors: Unifying Characteristics, Computational Models, Neural Mechanisms." *Language Sciences* 62:91–123.

Edelman, S. 2018. "Identity, Immortality, Happiness: Pick Two." *Journal of Evolution and Technology* 28:1–17.

Edelman, S. 2019. "Verbal Behavior without Syntactic Structures: Beyond Skinner and Chomsky. Unpublished ms.

Edelman, S., T. Fekete, and N. Zach, eds. 2012. *Being in Time: Dynamical Models of Phenomenal Experience*. Amsterdam: John Benjamins.

Moyal, R., T. Fekete, and S. Edelman. 2020. "Dynamical Emergence Theory (DET): A Computational Account of Phenomenal Consciousness." *Minds and Machines* 30:1–21.

Egan, G. 1994. *Permutation City*. London: Orion.

Egan, G. 1997. *Diaspora*. New York: HarperCollins.

Egan, G. 1999. "Luminous." In *Luminous*. London: Orion/Millennium.

Ehrsson, H. H. 2007. "The Experimental Induction of Out-of-Body Experiences." *Science* 317:1048.

Eichenbaum, H., C. J. MacDonald, and B. J. Kraus. 2014. "Time and the Hippocampus." In *Space, Time and Memory in the Hippocampal Formation*, ed. Derdikman and J. J. Knierim, 273–301. Vienna: Springer.

Eidelman, S., and C. S. Crandall. 2009. "On the Psychological Advantage of the Status Quo." In *Social and Psychological Bases of Ideology and System Justification*, ed. J. T. Jost, A. C. Kay, and H. Thorisdottir, 85–106. New York: Oxford University Press.

Eidelman, S., C. S. Crandall, and J. Pattershall. 2009. "The Existence Bias." *Journal of Personality and Social Psychology* 97:765–775.

Einstein, A. 1905. "Zur Elektrodynamik bewegter Körper." *Annalen der Physik* 17:891–921. English translation: "On the Electrodynamics of Moving Bodies," in W. Perrett and G. B. Jeffery, *The Principle of Relativity*. London: Methuen, 1923.

Einstein, A. [1949] 2009. "Why Socialism?" *Monthly Review* 61 (1): 55–61.

Einstein, A., and S. Freud. 1939. *Why War? A Correspondence between Albert Einstein and Sigmund Freud.* London: Peace Pledge Union.

Ekert, A., and R. Renner. 2014. "The Ultimate Physical Limits of Privacy." *Nature* 507:443–447.

Eliot, C. 1921. *Hinduism and Buddhism: An Historical Sketch.* London: Routledge & Kegan Paul.

Eliot, T. S. 1943. *Four Quartets.* San Diego: Harcourt.

Ellis, E. C., N. R. Magliocca, C. J. Stevens, and D. Q. Fuller. 2018. "Evolving the Anthropocene: Linking Multi-Level Selection with Long-Term Social-Ecological Change." *Sustainability Science* 13:119–128.

Empson, W. 1960. "The Satan of Milton." *The Hudson Review* 13:33–59.

Engel, P. 2016. "The Epistemology of Stupidity." In *Performance Epistemology: Foundations and Applications*, ed. M. A. Fernandez Vargas, 96–223. New York: Oxford University Press.

Engels, F. 1878. *Anti-Dühring.* Leipzig: Genossenschafts Buchdruckerei. First published in *Vorwärts* in 1877–1878. Translated by Emile Burns from 1894 edition. https://www.marxists.org/archive/marx/works/1877/anti-duhring/.

Ennis, P. H. 1967. "Ecstasy and Everyday Life." *Journal for the Scientific Study of Religion* 6:40–48.

Erasmus, D. [1511] 1876. *In Praise of Folly.* London: Reeves & Turner. English translation.

Erofeev, V. [1969] 1992. *Moscow to the End of the Line.* Chicago: Northwestern University Press. Translated from Russian by H. W. Tjalsma and A. R. Dirik.

Evans, G. W. 2016. "Childhood Poverty and Adult Psychological Well-Being." *Proceedings of the National Academy of Science* 113:14949–14952.

Fajardo-Acosta, F. 1990. "The Character of Anchises and Aeneas' Escape from Troy: Virgil's Criticism of Heroic Values." *Syllecta Classica* 2:39–44.

Falah, G. 1989. "Israeli State Policy toward Bedouin Sedentarization in the Negev. *Journal of Palestine Studies* 18 (2): 71–91.

Falk, R. 1984. "The Kahan Commission Report on the Beirut Massacre." *Dialectical Anthropology* 8:319–324.

Famakinwa, J. O. 2012. "Is the Unexamined Life Worth Living or Not?" *Think* 11 (31): 97–103.

Farine, D. R., P.-O. Montiglio, and O. Spiegel. 2015. "From Individuals to Groups and Back: The Evolutionary Implications of Group Phenotypic Composition." *Trends in Ecology & Evolution* 30:609–621.

Farrell, H., and B. Schneier. 2018. "Common-Knowledge Attacks on Democracy." Research Publication 7, Berkman Klein Center, Harvard Law School.

Fekete, T., and S. Edelman. 2011. "Towards a Computational Theory of Experience." *Consciousness and Cognition* 20:807–827.

Feldman Barrett, L. 2013. "Psychological Construction: The Darwinian Approach to the Science of Emotion." *Emotion Review* 5:379–389.

Feldman Barrett, L., R. Adolphs, S. Marsella, A. M. Martinez, and S. D. Pollak. 2019. "Emotional Expressions Reconsidered: Challenges to Inferring Emotion from Human Facial Movements." *Psychological Science in the Public Interest* 20 (1): 1–68.

Felin, T., J. J. Koenderink, and J. I. Krueger. 2017. "Rationality, Perception, and the All-Seeing Eye." *Psychonomic Bulletin and Review* 24:1040–1059.

Fieder, M., and S. Huber. 2012. "An Evolutionary Account of Status, Power, and Career in Modern Societies." *Human Nature* 23:191–207.

Finlay, B. L., and S. Syal. 2014. "The Pain of Altruism." *Trends in Cognitive Sciences* 18:615–617.

Fischer, C. S., M. Hout, M. Sanchez Jankowski, S. R. Lucas, A. Swidler, and K. Voss. 1996. *Inequality by Design: Cracking the Bell Curve Myth.* Princeton, NJ: Princeton University Press.

Fisher, H. E., X. Xu, A. Aron, and L. L. Brown. 2016. "Intense, Passionate, Romantic Love: A Natural Addiction? How the Fields that Investigate Romance and Substance Abuse Can Inform Each Other." *Frontiers in Psychology* 7: article 687.

Fivush, R., and C. A. Haden. 2003. *Autobiographical Memory and the Construction of a Narrative Self: Developmental and Cultural Perspectives.* Mahwah, NJ: Erlbaum.

Fletcher, G. J. O., J. A. Simpson, L. Campbell, and N. C. Overall. 2015. "Pair-Bonding, Romantic Love, and Evolution: The Curious Case of *Homo sapiens.*" *Perspectives on Psychological Science* 10:20–36.

Fletcher, J. A., and M. Doebeli. 2009. "A Simple and General Explanation for the Evolution of Altruism." *Proceedings of the Royal Society B* 276:13–19.

Flores, R. 2015. "Making Sense of Suffering: Insights from Buddhism and Critical Social Science." In *World Suffering and Quality of Life*, Vol. 56, *Social Indicators Research Series*, ed. R. E. Anderson, 65–73. New York: Springer.

Foa, R. S., and Y. Mounk. 2016. "The Danger of Deconsolidation: The Democratic Disconnect." *Journal of Democracy* 27 (3): 5–17.

Foa, R. S., and Y. Mounk. 2017. "The End of the Consolidation Paradigm: A Response to Our Critics." *Journal of Democracy*, June. Web exchange with P. Norris. http://roberto.foa.name/FoaMounkEndofConsolidationParadigm.pdf.

Fogelin, R. 2003. *Walking the Tightrope of Reason: The Precarious Life of a Rational Animal.* Oxford: Oxford University Press.

Forget, E. L. 2011. "The Town with No Poverty: The Health Effects of a Canadian Guaranteed Annual Income Field Experiment." *Canadian Public Policy / Analyse de politiques* 37 (3): 283–305.

Frank, R. 2016. *Success and Luck: Good Fortune and the Myth of Meritocracy.* Princeton, NJ: Princeton University Press.

Frankfurt, H. G. 2005. *On Bullshit.* Princeton, NJ: Princeton University Press.

Fresco, D. M., D. S. Mennin, R. G. Heimberg, and M. Ritter. 2013. "Emotion Regulation Therapy for Generalized Anxiety Disorder." *Cognitive and Behavioral Practice* 20:282–300.

Friedkin, N. E., and F. Bullo. 2017. "How Truth Wins in Opinion Dynamics along Issue Sequences." *Proceedings of the National Academy of Science* 114:11380–11385.

Frier, D. G. 2005. "José Saramago's 'O Evangelho Segundo Jesus Cristo': Outline of a Newer Testament." *The Modern Language Review* 100:367–382.

Friesen, J. P., K. Laurin, S. Shepherd, D. Gaucher, and A. C. Kay. 2018. "System Justification: Experimental Evidence, Its Contextual Nature, and Implications for Social Change." *British Journal of Social Psychology* (2018): 1–25.

Frith, C. D., and T. Metzinger. 2016. "What's the Use of Consciousness?" In *The Pragmatic Turn: Toward Action-Oriented Views in Cognitive Science*, ed. A. K. Engel, K. J. Friston, and D. Kragic, 193–214. Cambridge, MA: MIT Press.

Fuchs, C., and D. Trottier. 2015. "Towards a Theoretical Model of Social Media Surveillance in Contemporary Society." *Communications: The European Journal of Communication Research* 40 (1): 113–135.

Galloway, T. A., B. Gustafsson, P. J. Pedersen, and T. Österberg. 2015. "Immigrant Child Poverty—The Achilles Heel of the Scandinavian Welfare State." *Research on Economic Inequality* 23:185–219.

Garfield, J. L. 1994. "Dependent Arising and the Emptiness of Emptiness: Why Did Nāgārjuna Start with Causation?" *Philosophy East and West* 44:219–250.

Garfield, J. L. 2010. "Taking Conventional Truth Seriously: Authority Regarding Deceptive Reality." In *Moonshadows: Conventional Truth in Buddhist Philosophy*, ed. T. Cowherds. New York: Oxford University Press.

Garfield, J. L., and G. Priest. 2009. "Mountains Are Just Mountains." In *Pointing at the Moon: Buddhism, Logic, Analysis*, ed. M. D'Amato, J. L. Garfield, and T. Tillemans, 71–82. New York: Oxford University Press.

Garland, E. L., and M. O. Howard. 2013. "A Transdiagnostic Perspective on Cognitive, Affective, and Neurobiological Processes Underlying Human Suffering." *Research on Social Work Practice* 24:142–151.

Gel'man, V. 2015. "The Politics of Fear." *Russian Politics & Law* 53 (5–6): 6–26.

Gier, N., and P. K. Kjellberg. 2004. "Buddhism and the Freedom of the Will." In *Freedom and Determinism: Topics in Contemporary Philosophy*, ed. J. K. Campbell, D. Shier, and M. O'Rourke, 277–304. Cambridge, MA: MIT Press.

Gigerenzer, G., and R. Garcia-Retamero. 2017. "Cassandra's Regret: The Psychology of Not Wanting to Know." *Psychological Review* 124:179–196.

Gil, S., and S. Droit-Volet. 2009. "Time Perception, Depression and Sadness." *Behavioral Processes* 80:169–176.

Gilbert, D. T., and T. D. Wilson. 2007. "Prospection: Experiencing the Future." *Science* 317:1351–1354.

Gilbert, P. 2019. "Explorations into the Nature and Function of Compassion." *Current Opinion in Psychology* 28:108–114.

Gino, F., and D. Ariely. 2012. "The Dark Side of Creativity: Original Thinkers Can Be More Dishonest." *Journal of Personality and Social Psychology* 102:445–459.

Gintis, H. 2003. "The Hitchhiker's Guide to Altruism: Gene-Culture Coevolution, and the Internalization of Norms." *Journal of Theoretical Biology* 220:407–418.

Gintis, H. 2007. "A Framework for the Unification of the Behavioral Sciences." *Behavioral and Brain Sciences* 30:1–16.

Glenberg, A. M. 1997. "What Memory Is For." *Behavioral and Brain Sciences* 20:1–55.

Gödel, K. 1931. "Über formal unentscheidbare Sätze der Principia Mathematica und verwandter Systeme, I." *Monatshefte für Mathematik und Physik* 38:173–198.

Godfrey-Smith, P. 2016a. "Individuality, Subjectivity, and Minimal Cognition." *Biology and Philosophy* 31:775–796.

Godfrey-Smith, P. 2016b. "Mind, Matter, and Metabolism." *Journal of Philosophy* 113:481–506.

Godfrey-Smith, W. 1979. "The Value of Wilderness." *Environmental Ethics* 1:309–319.

Goodarzi, J. M. 2009. *Syria and Iran: Diplomatic Alliance and Power Politics in the Middle East*. New York: I. B. Tauris.

Goranson, A., R. S. Ritter, A. Waytz, M. I. Norton, and K. Gray. 2017. "Dying Is Unexpectedly Positive." *Psychological Science* 28:988–999.

Gordon, A. 2017. "Bar Kochba's Homelands: Prague Zionists on National Soil and Rootedness." *International Journal of Political Culture and Society* 30:157–169.

Gowdy, J., and L. Krall. 2016. "The Economic Origins of Ultrasociality." *Behavioral and Brain Sciences* 39: e92.

Graham, J., P. Meindl, S. Koleva, R. Iyer, and K. M. Johnson. 2015. "When Values and Behavior Conflict: Moral Pluralism and Intrapersonal Moral Hypocrisy." *Social and Personality Psychology Compass* 9:158–170.

Griffin, D. R. 1978. "Prospects for a Cognitive Ethology." *Behavioral and Brain Sciences* 1:527–538.

Gruber, J., I. B. Mauss, and M. Tamir. 2011. "A Dark Side of Happiness? How, When, and Why Happiness Is Not Always Good." *Perspectives on Psychological Science* 6:222–233.

Gu, J., C. Strauss, R. Bond, and K. Cavanagh. 2015. "How Do Mindfulness-Based Cognitive Therapy and Mindfulness-Based Stress Reduction Improve Mental Health and Wellbeing? A Systematic Review and Meta-Analysis of Mediation Studies." *Clinical Psychology Review* 37:1–12.

Hagemann, S. 2015. "Feeling at Home in the Occupied Territories: Emotion Work of the Religious Settler Movement." *Emotion, Space and Society* 15:11–18.

Hájek, A. 2003. "Waging War on Pascal's Wager. *The Philosophical Review* 112:27–56.

Hamilton, C. 2015. "The Theodicy of the 'Good Anthropocene.'" *Environmental Humanities* 7:233–238.

Hamlin, C. 2017. "Towards a Theory of Universes: Structure Theory and the Mathematical Universe Hypothesis." *Synthese* 194:571–591.

Hansen, H., P. Bourgois, and E. Drucker. 2014. "Pathologizing Poverty: New Forms of Diagnosis, Disability, and Structural Stigma under Welfare Reform." *Social Science & Medicine* 103:76–83.

Hardy, B. W., M. Tallapragada, J. C. Besley, and S. Yuan. 2019. "The Effects of the 'War on Science' Frame on Scientists' Credibility." *Science Communication* 41 (1): 90–112.

Harman, E. 2009. "Critical Study: David Benatar. *Better Never To Have Been: The Harm of Coming into Existence* (Oxford: Oxford University Press, 2006)." *Noûs* 43 (4): 776–785.

Harris, R. 1981. *The Language Myth*. London: Duckworth.

Harrison, M. John. 2002. *Light*. London: Gollancz.

Hart, B., and T. R. Risley. 1995. *Meaningful Differences in the Everyday Experience of Young American Children*. Baltimore, MD: Brooks.

Haushofer, J., and E. Fehr. 2014. "On the Psychology of Poverty." *Science* 344: 862–867.

Heisig, J. P. 2011. "Who Does More Housework: Rich or Poor? A Comparison of 33 Countries." *American Sociological Review* 76:74–99.

Held, B. S. 2004. "The Negative Side of Positive Psychology." *Journal of Humanistic Psychology* 44:9–46.

Herbert, F. 1965. *Dune*. New York: Chilton.

Hesse, H. 1949. *The Glass Bead Game*. New York: Holt, Rinehart and Winston.

Hesse, H. 1972. "Chagrin d'Amour." In *Stories of Five Decades*, trans. Ralph Manheim, 146–151. London: Macmillan.

Heydrich, L., T. J. Dodds, J. E. Aspell, B. Herbelin, H. H. Bülthoff, B. J. Mohler, and O. Blanke. 2013. "Visual Capture and the Experience of Having Two Bodies—Evidence from Two Different Virtual Reality Techniques." *Frontiers in Psychology* 4: article 946.

Heyes, C. 2018. "Empathy Is Not in Our Genes." *Neuroscience & Biobehavioral Reviews* 95:499–507.

Heyes, C. M. 1998. "Theory of Mind in Nonhuman Primates." *Behavioral and Brain Sciences* 21:101–134.

Hirschberger, G., T. Pyszczynski, T. Ein-Dor, T. Shani Sherman, E. Kadah, P. Kesebir, and Y. C. Park. 2016. "Fear of Death Amplifies Retributive Justice Motivations and Encourages Political Violence." *Peace and Conflict: Journal of Peace Psychology* 22:67–74.

Hoerl, C., and T. McCormack. 2016. "Making Decisions about the Future: Regret and the Cognitive Function of Episodic Memory." In *Seeing the Future: Theoretical Perspectives on Future-Oriented Mental Time Travel*, ed. K. Michaelian, S. B. Klein, and K. Szpunar, 241–266. Oxford: Oxford University Press.

Hoffman, D. D., M. Singh, and C. Prakash. 2015. "The Interface Theory of Perception." *Psychonomic Bulletin and Review* 22:1480–1506.

Hofstadter, D. R. 1979. *Gödel, Escher, Bach: An Eternal Golden Braid*. New York: Basic Books.

Hofstadter, D. R. 1985. "Variations on a Theme as the Crux of Creativity." In *Metamagical Themas*, 232–259. Harmondsworth, UK: Viking.

Hofstadter, D. R. 1995. "On Seeing A's and Seeing As." *Stanford Humanities Review* 4:109–121.

Holm, N. 1982. "Ecstasy Research in the 20th Century—An Introduction." *Scripta Instituti Donneriani Aboensis* 11:7–26.

Horkheimer, M., and T. W. Adorno. [1944] 2002. *Dialectic of Enlightenment*, ed. Gunzelin Schmid Noerr, trans. Edmund Jephcott. Stanford, CA: Stanford University Press.

Howard, S. R., A. Avarguès-Weber, J. E. Garcia, A. D. Greentree, and A. G. Dyer. 2019. "Numerical Cognition in Honeybees Enables Addition and Subtraction." *Science Advances* 5 (2): eaav0961.

Hoyle, F., and N. C. Wickramasinghe. 1999. "The Universe and Life: Deductions from the Weak Anthropic Principle." *Astrophysics and Space Science* 268:89–102.

Hume, D. 1740. *A Treatise of Human Nature*. http://www.gutenberg.org/etext/4705.

Hupfeld, S. 2009. "Rich and Healthy—Better Than Poor and Sick? An Empirical Analysis of Income, Health, and the Duration of the Pension Benefit Spell." *Journal of Health Economics* 28:427–443.

Hurley, A. 1999. "What I Lost When I Translated Jorge Luis Borges." *Cadernos de Tradução* 1:289–303.

Immordino Yang, M. H., A. McColl, H. Damasio, and A. Damasio. 2009. "Neural Correlates of Admiration and Compassion." *Proceedings of the National Academy of Science* 106:8021–8026.

Inbar, E. 1990. "Attitudes toward War in the Israeli Political Elite." *Middle East Journal* 44 (3): 431–445.

Ioannidis, J. P. A. 2012. "Why Science Is Not Necessarily Self-Correcting." *Perspectives on Psychological Science* 7:645–654.

Irons, B., and C. Hepburn. 2007. "Regret Theory and the Tyranny of Choice." *The Economic Record* 83 (261): 191–203.

Iverach, L., R. G. Menzies, and R. E. Menzies. 2014. "Death Anxiety and Its Role in Psychopathology: Reviewing the Status of a Transdiagnostic Construct." *Clinical Psychology Review* 34:580–593.

Iyengar, S., and D. S. Massey. 2019. "Scientific Communication in a Post-Truth Society." *Proceedings of the National Academy of Science* 116:7656–7661.

Jablonka, E., and M. Lamb. 2006. *Evolution in Four Dimensions.* Cambridge, MA: MIT Press.

Jackson, T. 2009. *Prosperity without Growth: Economics for a Finite Planet.* London: Earthscan.

Jakobson, R. 1960. "Linguistics and Poetics." In *Style in Language*, ed. T. Sebeok, 350–359. Cambridge, MA: MIT Press.

James, D. 2012. "Subjective Freedom and Necessity in Hegel's 'Philosophy of Right.'" *Theoria* 59 (131): 41–63.

James, W. 1890. *The Principles of Psychology.* New York: Holt. http://psychclassics.yorku.ca/James/Principles/.

Johnson, K. 2008. "26 Monkeys, Also the Abyss." *Asimov's* 32 (July): 81–89.

Johnson, K. 2016. *The Dream Quest of Vellitt Boe.* New York: Tor.

Joshanloo, M., and D. Weijers 2014. "Aversion to Happiness across Cultures: A Review of Where and Why People Are Averse to Happiness." *Journal of Happiness Studies* 15:717–735.

Joyce, J. 1922. *Ulysses.* Paris: Sylvia Beech.

Kadir, D. 2017. "Agnotology and the Know-Nothing Party: Then and Now." *Review of International American Studies* 10 (1): 117–131.

Kahn, D. 2009. "How I Discovered World War II's Greatest Spy." *Cryptologia* 34 (1): 12–21.

Karageorgou-Bastea, C. 2017. "El lugar del olvido en la poesía de Borges." *Hispanófila* 180:173–188.

Karpinski, R. I., A. M. Kinase Kolb, N. A. Tetreault, and T. B. Borowski. 2018. "High Intelligence: A Risk Factor for Psychological and Physiological Overexcitabilities." *Intelligence* 66:8–23.

Katz, A. Z. 2017. *When Democracies Choose War: Politics, Public Opinion, and the Marketplace of Ideas.* Boulder, CO: Lynne Rienner.

Kavanagh, J., and M. D. Rich. 2018. *Truth Decay: An Initial Exploration of the Diminishing Role of Facts and Analysis in American Public Life*. Santa Monica, CA: RAND Corporation.

Kay, A. C., D. Gaucher, J. M. Peach, K. Laurin, K. Friesen, J. Friesen, M. P. Zanna, and S. J. Spencer. 2009. "Inequality, Discrimination, and the Power of the Status Quo: Direct Evidence for a Motivation to See the Way Things Are as the Way They Should Be." *Journal of Personality and Social Psychology* 97:421–434.

Keller, H. 2018. "Universality Claim of Attachment Theory: Children's Socioemotional Development across Cultures." *Proceedings of the National Academy of Science* 115:11414–11419.

Kelsay, J. 2015. "Political Practice: The Nexus between Realisms and Just War Thinking." *Soundings* 98:38–58.

Keyes, K. M., J. Platt, A. S. Kaufman, and K. A. McLaughlin. 2017. "Association of Fluid Intelligence and Psychiatric Disorders in a Population-Representative Sample of US Adolescents." *JAMA Psychiatry* 74 (2): 179–188.

Kihlstrom, J. F. 1995. "The Rediscovery of the Unconscious." In *The Mind, the Brain, and Complex Adaptive Systems*, Vol. 22, *Santa Fe Institute Studies in the Sciences of Complexity*, ed. H. Morowitz and J. Singer, 123–143. Reading, MA: Addison-Wesley.

Killingsworth, M. A., and D. T. Gilbert. 2010. "A Wandering Mind Is an Unhappy Mind." *Science* 330:932.

King, S. B. 2016. "Through the Eyes of Auschwitz and the Killing Fields: Mutual Learning between Engaged Buddhism and Liberation Theology." *Buddhist-Christian Studies* 36:55–67.

Kintsch, W. 2012. "Musings about Beauty." *Cognitive Science* 36:1–20.

Kissel, M., and N. C. Kim. 2019. "The Emergence of Human Warfare: Current Perspectives." *American Journal of Physical Anthropology* 168 (S67): 141–163.

Kleene, S. C. 1952. *Introduction to Meta-Mathematics*. Amsterdam: North-Holland.

Kolodny, O., and S. Edelman. 2018. "The Evolution of the Capacity for Language: The Ecological Context and Adaptive Value of a Process of Cognitive Hijacking." *Philosophical Transactions of the Royal Society B* 373:20170052.

Kornbrot, D. E., R. M. Msetfi, and M. J. Grimwood. 2013. "Time Perception and Depressive Realism: Judgment Type, Psychophysical Functions and Bias." *PLoS ONE* 8 (8): e71585.

Kriner, D. L., and F. X. Shen. 2016. "Invisible Inequality: The Two Americas of Military Sacrifice." *University of Memphis Law Review* 46:545–635.

Krylov, A. 2016. "The Role of the Religious Factor in Political Processes in Israel." *Annual Report of the Institute for International Relations, Moscow* 1(15): 98–108. In Russian.

LaBar, K. S., and R. Cabeza. 2006. "Cognitive Neuroscience of Emotional Memory." *Nature Reviews Neuroscience* 7:54–64.

LaBerge, S. 1990. "Lucid Dreaming: Psychophysiological Studies of Consciousness during REM Sleep." In *Sleep and Cognition*, ed. R. R. Bootzen, J. F. Kihlstrom, and D. L. Schacter, 109–126. Washington, DC: American Psychological Association.

Lachmann, M., S. Számadó, and C. T. Bergstrom. 2001. "Cost and Conflict in Animal Signals and Human Language." *Proceedings of the National Academy of Science* 98:13189–13194.

Ladyman, J., and K. Wiesner. 2018. *What Is a Complex System*. Princeton, NJ: Princeton University Press.

Laland, K. N. 2017. "The Origins of Language in Teaching." *Psychonomic Bulletin and Review* 24:225–231.

Laland, K. N., T. Uller, M. W. Feldman, K. Sterelny, G. B. Müller, A. Moczek, E. Jablonka, and J. Odling-Smee. 2015. "The Extended Evolutionary Synthesis: Its Structure, Assumptions and Predictions." *Proceedings of the Royal Society B* 282:20151019.

Lancy, D. 2015. *The Anthropology of Childhood: Cherubs, Chattel, and Changelings*. Cambridge: Cambridge University Press.

Lange, M. 2003. "Voices from the Kalahari." *Current Writing: Text and Reception in Southern Africa* 15 (3): 57–71.

Lao Tze [Laozi]. 1904. *The Book of the Simple Way*, trans. W. G. Old. London: Philip Wellby.

Laurent, V., and B. W. Balleine. 2015. "Factual and Counterfactual Action-Outcome Mappings Control Choice between Goal-Directed Actions in Rats." *Current Biology* 25:1074–1079.

Laureys, S. 2005. "Death, Unconsciousness and the Brain." *Nature Reviews Neuroscience* 6:899–909.

Lazarus, R. S. 2003a. "Does the Positive Psychology Movement Have Legs?" *Psychological Inquiry* 14:93–109.

Lazarus, R. S. 2003b. "The Lazarus Manifesto for Positive Psychology and Psychology in General." *Psychological Inquiry* 14:173–189.

Le Guin, U. K. 1967. *City of Illusions*. New York: Ace Books.

Le Guin, U. K. 1968. *A Wizard of Earthsea*. Berkeley, CA: Parnassus Press.

Le Guin, U. K. 1969. *The Left Hand of Darkness*. New York: Ace Books.

Le Guin, U. K. 1971. *The Lathe of Heaven*. New York: Avon Books.

Le Guin, U. K. 1972. *The Farthest Shore*. New York: Atheneum Books.

Le Guin, U. K. 1973. "The Ones Who Walk Away from Omelas." In *New Dimensions 3*, ed. R. Silverberg, 1–8. New York: Nelson Doubleday.

Le Guin, U. K. 1974a. "The Day before the Revolution." *Galaxy Science Fiction Magazine* 35 (8): 17–30.

Le Guin, U. K. 1974b. *The Dispossessed*. New York: Harper & Row.

Le Guin, U. K. 1985. *Always Coming Home*. New York: Harper & Row.

Le Guin, U. K. 1988. "Buffalo Gals, Won't You Come Out Tonight." In *Buffalo Gals and Other Animal Presences*. New York: Plume Books.

Le Guin, U. K. 2001. *The Telling*. New York: Ace.

Le Guin, U. K. 2002. "Solitude." In *The Birthday of the World*, 119–152. New York: HarperCollins.

Le Guin, U. K. 2016. *Out Here: Poems and Images from Steens Mountain Country*. Astoria, OR: Raven Studios.

Leary, M. R. 2004. *The Curse of the Self*. New York: Oxford University Press.

Ledford, H. 2015. "CRISPR, the Disruptor." *Nature* 522 (7554): 20–24.

Lem, S. [1971] 1999. *A Perfect Vacuum*, trans. M. Kandel. Chicago: Northwestern University Press.

Lem, S. 1974a. *The Cyberiad*, trans. Michael Kandel. San Francisco: Seabury Press.

Lem, S. [1971] 1974b. *The Futurological Congress*, trans. Michael Kandel. San Francisco: Seabury Press.

Lem, S. [1981] 1984. "Golem XIV." In *Imaginary Magnitude*, trans. M. E. Heine. New York: Harcourt Brace Jovanovich.

Lem, S. 1986. *One Human Minute*, trans. C. S. Leach. New York: Harcourt Brace Jovanovich.

Lem, S. [1986] 1987. *Fiasco*, trans. Michael Kandel. London: Andre Deutsch.

Lenggenhager, B., T. Tadi, T. Metzinger, and O. Blanke. 2007. "Video Ergo Sum: Manipulating Bodily Self-Consciousness." *Science* 317:1096–1099.

Leon, N. 2018. "Aftershocks of the 1977 '*Mahapach*' (Upheaval) and Their Effect on Religious Politics in Israel." *Israel Affairs* 24:944–957.

Levine, D. H. 1988. "Assessing the Impacts of Liberation Theology in Latin America." *The Review of Politics* 50:241–263.

Levine, T. R. 2014. "Truth-Default Theory (TDT): A Theory of Human Deception and Deception Detection." *Journal of Language and Social Psychology* 33:378–392.

Levy, Y. 1998. "Militarizing Inequality: A Conceptual Framework." *Theory and Society* 27:873–904.

Liang, F., V. Das, N. Kostyuk, and M. M. Hussain. 2018. "Constructing a Data-Driven Society: China's Social Credit System as a State Surveillance Infrastructure." *Policy and Internet* 10:415–452.

Liang, R. 2011. "Digitality, Granularity and Ineffability." *Language Sciences* 33:30–39.

Lieblich, A. 2010. "A Century of Childhood, Parenting, and Family Life in the Kibbutz." *The Journal of Israeli History* 29:1–24.

Lightman, A. 1993. *Einstein's Dreams*. New York: Pantheon.

Ligotti, T. 2010. *The Conspiracy against the Human Race: A Contrivance of Horror*. New York: Hippocampus Press.

Linell, P. 2013. "Distributed Language Theory, with or without Dialogue." *Language Sciences* 40:168–173.

Livni, J. 2017. "Cultural Evolution of an Institution: The Sabbath." *Cliodynamics: The Journal of Quantitative History and Cultural Evolution* 8:59–74.

Livraghi, G. 2009. *The Power of Stupidity*. Pescara, Italy: Monti & Ambrosini.

Lloyd, S. 2012. "A Turing Test for Free Will." *Philosophical Transactions of the Royal Society A* 370:3597–3610.

Longxi, Z. 2002. "The Utopian Vision, East and West." *Utopian Studies* 13:1–20.

Love, N. 2004. "Cognition and the Language Myth." *Language Sciences* 26:525–544.

Lucas, J. R., K. E. Gentry, K. E. Sieving, and T. M. Freeberg. 2018. "Communication as a Fundamental Part of Machiavellian Intelligence." *Journal of Comparative Psychology* 132:442–454.

Mace, R. 2016. "The Evolutionary Ecology of the Family." In *Handbook of Evolutionary Psychology*, ed. D. M. Buss, 561–577. New York: Wiley.

MacIver, M. A. 2009. "Neuroethology: From Morphological Computation to Planning." In *The Cambridge Handbook of Situated Cognition*, ed. P. Robbins and M. Aydede, 480–504. New York: Cambridge University Press.

Madison, G. 2016. "'Home' Is an Interaction, Not a Place." *Existential Analysis* 27 (1): 28–38.

Malaclypse the Younger. 1965. *Principia Discordia, or How the West Was Lost*. http://www.principiadiscordia.com/downloads/Principia%20Discordia%20(Wholly%201st%20Edition).pdf.

Malcolm, G. L., I. I. A. Groen, and C. I. Baker. 2016. "Making Sense of Real-World Scenes." *Trends in Cognitive Sciences* 20:843–856.

Mameli, M., and P. Bateson. 2006. "Innateness and the Sciences." *Biology and Philosophy* 21:155–188.

Mani, A., S. Mullainathan, E. Shafir, and J. Zhao. 2013. "Poverty Impedes Cognitive Function." *Science* 341:976–980.

Margrett, J., P. Martin, J. L. Woodard, L. S. Miller, M. MacDonald, J. Baenziger, I. C. Siegler, A. Davey, and L. Poon. 2010. "Depression among Centenarians and the Oldest Old: Contributions of Cognition and Personality." *Gerontology* 56:93–99.

Marquis, J.-P. 2018. "A View from Space: The Foundations of Mathematics." In *The Map and the Territory: Exploring the Foundations of Science, Thought and Reality*, ed. S. Wuppuluri and F. A. Doria, 357–375. Cham, Switzerland: Springer.

Martin, L. T., L. D. Kubzansky, K. Z. LeWinn, L. P. Lipsitt, P. Satz, and S. L. Buka. 2007. "Childhood Cognitive Performance and Risk of Generalized Anxiety Disorder." *International Journal of Epidemiology* 36:769–775.

Marx, K. [1843] 1970. *Critique of Hegel's Philosophy of Right*, trans. Joseph O'Malley. New York: Oxford University Press.

Marx, K. [1859] 1977. *A Contribution to the Critique of Political Economy*. Moscow: Progress Publishers.

Marx, K. [1867] 1887. *Capital: A Critique of Political Economy*, trans. Samuel Moore and Edward Aveling, ed. Frederick Engels. Moscow: Progress Publishers.

Marzec, R. P. 2018. "Reflections on the Anthropocene Dossier." *MFS Modern Fiction Studies* 64 (4): 585–616.

Mascaro, S., K. B. Korb, A. E. Nicholson, and O. Woodberry. 2010. *Evolving Ethics: The New Science of Good and Evil*. Charlottesville, VA: Imprint Academic.

Mavelli, L. 2016. "Governing Uncertainty in a Secular Age: Rationalities of Violence, Theodicy and Torture." *Security Dialogue* 47:117–132.

McCulloch, W. 1956. "Toward Some Circuitry of Ethical Robots or an Observational Science of the Genesis of Social Evolution in the Mind-like Behavior of Artifacts." *Acta Biotheoretica* 11:147–156. Reprinted in McCulloch, *The Embodiments of Mind* (1965).

McLaren, P., and P. Jandrić. 2018. "Karl Marx and Liberation Theology: Dialectical Materialism and Christian Spirituality in, against, and beyond Contemporary Capitalism." *tripleC* 16:598–607.

Merchant, C. 2006. "The Scientific Revolution and the Death of Nature." *Isis* 97 (3): 513–533.

Mercier, H., and D. Sperber. 2011. "Why Do Humans Reason? Arguments for an Argumentative Theory." *Behavioral and Brain Sciences* 34:57–111.

Merker, B. 1993. "Vehicles of Hope: Hidden Structures in Man's Great Religions and Ideologies." Unpublished manuscript. http://www.pathsplitter.net/toc.php?visa =1.3.2.

Merker, B. 2004. "Cortex, Countercurrent Context, and Dimensional Integration of Lifetime Memory." *Cortex* 40:559–576.

Merker, B. 2013. "The Efference Cascade, Consciousness, and Its Self: Naturalizing the First-Person Pivot of Action Control." *Frontiers in Psychology* 4 (501): 1–20.

Mesoudi, A., A. Whiten, and K. N. Laland. 2006. "Towards a Unified Science of Cultural Evolution." *Behavioral and Brain Sciences* 29:329–383.

Metzinger, T. 2003. *Being No One: The Self-Model Theory of Subjectivity*. Cambridge, MA: MIT Press.

Metzinger, T. 2004. "The Subjectivity of Subjective Experience: A Representationalist Analysis of the First-Person Perspective." *Networks* 3–4:33–64.

Metzinger, T. 2017. "Suffering, the Cognitive Scotoma." In *The Return of Consciousness*, ed. K. Almqvist and A. Haag, 237–262. Stockholm: Axel and Margaret Ax:son Johnson Foundation.

Metzinger, T. 2018. "Splendor and Misery of Self-Models: Conceptual and Empirical Issues Regarding Consciousness and Self-Consciousness." *ALIUS Bulletin* 1 (2): 53–73. Interviewed by J. Limanowski and R. Millière.

Mieder, W. 2004. *Proverbs: A Handbook*. Westport, CT: Greenwood Press.

Mijs, J. J. B. 2016. "The Unfulfillable Promise of Meritocracy: Three Lessons and Their Implications for Justice in Education." *Social Justice Research* 29:14–34.

Mills, C., and D. Zavaleta. 2015. "Shame, Humiliation and Social Isolation: Missing Dimensions of Poverty and Suffering Analysis." In *World Suffering and Quality of Life*, Vol. 56, *Social Indicators Research Series*, ed. R. E. Anderson, 251–266. New York: Springer.

Mirsu-Paun, A., and J. A. Oliver. 2017. "How Much Does Love Really Hurt? A Meta-Analysis of the Association between Romantic Relationship Quality, Breakups and Mental Health Outcomes in Adolescents and Young Adults." *Journal of Relationships Research* 8 (e5): 1–12.

Miyamoto, Y., R. E. Nisbett, and T. Masuda. 2006. "Culture and Physical Environment: Holistic versus Analytic Perceptual Affordances." *Psychological Science* 17:113–119.

Moberg, D. O. 1987. "Holy Masquerade: Hypocrisy in Religion." *Review of Religious Research* 29:3–24.

Moerk, E. L. 1996. "Input and Learning Processes in First Language Acquisition." *Advances in Child Development and Behavior* 26:181–228.

Moody-Adams, M. M. 2017. "Moral Progress and Human Agency." *Ethical Theory and Moral Practice* 20:153–168.

Moore, G. E. 1903. *Principia Ethica.* Cambridge, UK: Cambridge University Press.

Mor, N., and J. Winquist. 2002. Self-Focused Attention and Negative Affect: A Meta-Analysis." *Psychological Bulletin* 128:638–662.

Morris, W. 1890. *News from Nowhere; Or, An Epoch of Rest.* London: Kelmscott Press.

Morris, W. 1896. *The Well at the World's End.* London: The Kelmscott Press.

Morton, W. S. 1971. "The Confucian Concept of Man: The Original Formulation." *Philosophy East and West* 21:69–77.

Mougin, G., and E. Sober. 1994. "Betting against Pascal's Wager." *Noûs* 28:382–395.

Musil, R. [1937] 1979. "On Stupidity." *PN Review* 5 (3 & 4), 5–10; 39–41. Translation of a lecture delivered in Vienna in March 1937.

Musil, R. [1978] 1995. *The Man without Qualities*, trans. Sophie Wilkins and Burton Pike. New York: Alfred A. Knopf.

Myers West, S. 2019. "Data Capitalism: Redefining the Logics of Surveillance and Privacy." *Business & Society* 58 (1): 20–41.

Nagel, T. 1970. "Death." *Noûs* 4:73–80.

Nagel, T. 1971. "The Absurd." *Journal of Philosophy* 68:716–727.

Neal, J. W., and Z. P. Neal. 2011. "Power as a Structural Phenomenon." *American Journal of Community Psychology* 48:157–167.

Neisser, U. 1967. *Cognitive Psychology.* New York: Appleton-Century-Crofts.

Neitzke, A. B. 2016. "An Illness of Power: Gender and the Social Causes of Depression." *Cultural and Medical Psychiatry* 40:59–73.

Nesse, R. M. 2004. "Natural Selection and the Elusiveness of Happiness." *Philosophical Transactions of the Royal Society B* 359:1333–1348.

Nichols, S., N. Strohminger, A. Rai, and J. Garfield. 2018. "Death and the Self." *Cognitive Science* 42:314–332. Suppl. 1.

Nicholson, J. M., and J. P. A. Ioannidis. 2012. "Conform and Be Funded." *Nature* 492:34–36.

Nisbett, R. E., and T. Masuda. 2003. "Culture and Point of View." *Proceedings of the National Academy of Science* 100:11163–11170.

Nisbett, R. E., and Y. Miyamoto. 2005. "The Influence of Culture: Holistic versus Analytic Perception." *Trends in Cognitive Sciences* 9:467–473.

Norenzayan, A. 2016. "Theodiversity." *Annual Review of Psychology* 67:465–488.

Norenzayan, A., I. G. Hansen, and J. Cady. 2008. "An Angry Volcano? Reminders of Death and Anthropomorphizing Nature." *Social Cognition* 26:190–197.

Norris, P. 2017. "Is Western Democracy Backsliding? Diagnosing the Risks." *Journal of Democracy* 28 (2). Web exchange with R. S. Foa and Y. Mounk. https://www .journalofdemocracy.org/online-exchange-democratic-deconsolidation/.

Norton, H. 2017. "Government Speech and the War on Terror." *Fordham Law Review* 86:543–563.

Öhman, C., and L. Floridi. 2017. "The Political Economy of Death in the Age of Information: A Critical Approach to the Digital Afterlife Industry." *Minds & Machines* 27:639–662.

Oishi, S., S. Kesebir, and E. Diener. 2011. "Income Inequality and Happiness." *Psychological Science* 22:1095–1100.

Ostrom, E., J. Walker, and R. Gardner. 1992. "With and without a Sword: Self-Governance Is Possible." *The American Political Science Review* 86:404–417.

Otto, K., R. Roe, S. Sobiraj, M. Mabundo Baluku, and M. E. Garrido Vásquez. 2017. "The Impact of Career Ambition on Psychologists' Extrinsic and Intrinsic Career Success: The Less They Want, the More They Get." *Career Development International* 22 (1): 23–36.

Panksepp, J. 2001. "The Neuro-Evolutionary Cusp between Emotions and Cognitions: Implications for Understanding Consciousness and the Emergence of a Unified Mind Science." *Evolution and Cognition* 7:141–163.

Panksepp, J. 2005. "Affective Consciousness: Core Emotional Feelings in Animals and Humans." *Consciousness and Cognition* 14:30–80.

Parfit, D. 1984. *Reasons and Persons*. Oxford: Clarendon Press.

Parfit, D. 2011. *On What Matters*. Oxford: Oxford University Press.

Payne, C. 2000. "Unbearable Witness." *JAMC* 163:1176–1178.

Pearlman, W. 2016. "Narratives of Fear in Syria." *Perspectives on Politics* 14 (1): 21–37.

Pearsall, Z. 2016. "Adam Smith's Circle of Ambition." Master's thesis, Georgia State University.

Pecastaing, C. 2013. "The Politics of Apology: Hollande and Algeria." *World Affairs* 175 (6): 51–56.

Peled, N. 2017. "Kibbutz Mothering in Transition: Bringing the Children Home." *Journal of the Motherhood Initiative* 8:57–73.

Pelevin, V. [1996] 2001. *Buddha's Little Finger*, trans. A. Bromfield. New York: Penguin. Russian original, titled Чапаев и Пустота, published by Vagrius.

Pelevin, V. 1997. *The Blue Lantern and Other Stories*, trans. A. Bromfield. New York: New Directions.

Pelevin, V. 1998. "Tai Shou Chuan USSR." In *A Werewolf Problem in Central Russia and Other Stories*, trans. A. Bromfield, 80–94. New York: New Directions Publishing Corporation.

Pennycook, G., J. A. Cheyne, N. Barr, D. J. Koehler, and J. A. Fugelsang. 2015. "On the Reception and Detection of Pseudo-Profound Bullshit." *Judgment and Decision Making* 10:549–563.

Pereboom, D. 1995. "Determinism Al Dente." *Noûs* 29 (1): 21–45.

Peters, M. A. 2017a. "Ecopolitical Philosophy, Education and Grassroots Democracy: The 'Return' of Murray Bookchin (and John Dewey?)." *Geopolitics, History, and International Relations* 9 (2): 7–14.

Peters, M. A. 2017b. "Education in a Post-Truth World." *Educational Philosophy and Theory* 49:563–566.

Peters, M. A., and P. Jandri. 2017. "Dewey's Democracy and Education in the Age of Digital Reason: The Global, Ecological and Digital Turns." *Open Review of Educational Research* 4:205–218.

Piff, P. K., D. M. Stancato, S. Côtéb, R. Mendoza-Denton, and D. Keltner. 2012. "Higher Social Class Predicts Increased Unethical Behavior." *Proceedings of the National Academy of Science* 109:4086–4091.

Polanyi, M. 1936. "The Struggle between Truth and Propaganda." *The Manchester School* 7:105–118.

Popper, K. R. 1992. *In Search of a Better World*. London: Routledge.

Powell, L., and E. Neiva. 2006. "The Pharisee Effect: When Religious Appeals in Politics Go Too Far." *Journal of Communication & Religion* 29:70–102.

Prelec, D. 2004. "A Bayesian Truth Serum for Subjective Data." *Science* 306:462–466.

Priest, G. 2009. "The Structure of Emptiness." *Philosophy East & West* 59:467–480.

Proffitt, D. R. 2006. "Embodied Perception and the Economy of Action." *Perspectives on Psychological Science* 1:110–122.

Putnam, H. 2004. *Ethics without Ontology*. Cambridge, MA: Harvard University Press.

Putnam, H. 2012. *Philosophy in an Age of Science: Physics, Mathematics, and Skepticism*, ed. M. De Caro and D. Macarthur. Cambridge, MA: Harvard University Press.

Quine, W. V. O. 1960. *Word and Object*. Cambridge, MA: MIT Press.

Raleigh, J. H. 1977. "Bloom as a Modern Epic Hero." *Critical Inquiry* 3:583–598.

Ramírez, E., A. R. Ortega, A. Chamorro, and J. M. Colmenero. 2014. "A Program of Positive Intervention in the Elderly: Memories, Gratitude and Forgiveness." *Aging & Mental Health* 18:463–470.

Ramscar, M., and H. Baayen. 2013. "Production, Comprehension, and Synthesis: A Communicative Perspective on Language." *Frontiers in Psychology* 4: article 233.

Ramscar, M., P. Hendrix, C. Shaoul, P. Milin, and H. Baayen. 2014. "The Myth of Cognitive Decline: Non-linear Dynamics of Lifelong Learning." *Topics in Cognitive Science* 6:5–42.

Rawls, J. 1971. *A Theory of Justice*. Cambridge, MA: Harvard University Press.

Redford, J., J. A. Johnson, and J. Honnold. 2009. "Parenting Practices, Cultural Capital and Educational Outcomes: The Effects of Concerted Cultivation on Academic Achievement." *Race, Gender & Class* 16:25–44.

Rees, W. E. 2019. "End Game: The Economy as Eco-Catastrophe and What Needs to Change." *Real-World Economics Review* 87:132–148.

Renna, M. E., J. M. Quintero, A. Soffer, M. Pino, L. Ader, D. M. Fresco, and D. S. Mennin. 2018. "A Pilot Study of Emotion Regulation Therapy for Generalized Anxiety and Depression: Findings from a Diverse Sample of Young Adults." *Behavior Therapy* 49:403–418.

Reyna, S. P. (2016). *Deadly Contradictions: The New American Empire and Global Warring*. Oxford: Berghahn Books.

Richards, B. A., and P. W. Frankland. 2017. "The Persistence and Transience of Memory." *Neuron* 94:1071–1084.

Richter, D., and U. Kunzmann. 2011. "Age Differences in Three Facets of Empathy: Performance-Based Evidence." *Psychology and Aging* 26:60–70.

Robinson, P. 2017. "Learning from the Chilcot Report: Propaganda, Deception and the 'War on Terror.'" *International Journal of Contemporary Iraqi Studies* 11(1 & 2): 47–73.

Robinson, W. I., and M. Barrera. 2012. "Global Capitalism and Twenty-First Century Fascism: A US Case Study." *Race & Class* 53 (3): 4–29.

Rochat, F., and A. Modigliani. 1995. "The Ordinary Quality of Resistance: From Milgram's Laboratory to the Village of Le Chambon." *Journal of Social Issues* 51:195–210.

Rogers, M. L., and T. E. Joiner. 2017. "Rumination, Suicidal Ideation, and Suicide Attempts: A Meta-Analytic Review." *Review of General Psychology* 21:132–142.

Rogerson, K. S. 2003. "Addressing the Negative Consequences of the Information Age: Lessons from Karl Polanyi and the Industrial Revolution." *Information, Communication & Society* 6 (1): 105–124.

Rolland, R. 1920. "Shakespeare the Truthteller." *The Dial* 69 (2): 109–121. Trans. Helena Van Brugh de Kay.

Romeo, R. R., J. A. Leonard, S. T. Robinson, M. R. West, A. P. Mackey, M. L. Rowe, and J. D. E. Gabrieli. 2018. "Beyond the 30-Million-Word Gap: Children's Conversational Exposure Is Associated with Language-Related Brain Function." *Psychological Science* 29:700–710.

Roscigno, V. J. 2011. "Power, Revisited." *Social Forces* 90:349–374.

Roy, D. J. 2015. "We All Die Unfinished: A Meditation on Existential Suffering." *Journal of Palliative Care* 31:3–4.

Royce, E. C. 2009. "Poverty as a Social Problem." In *Poverty and Power: A Structural Perspective on American Inequality*, 1–26. Lanham, MD: Rowman & Littlefield Publishers, Inc.

Rucker, D. D., and A. D. Galinsky. 2017. "Social Power and Social Class: Conceptualization, Consequences, and Current Challenges." *Current Opinion in Psychology* 18:26–30.

Rucker, R. 2016. *The Lifebox, the Seashell, and the Soul*, 2nd ed. San Francisco: Transreal Books.

Rusho, W. L. 1983. *Everett Ruess: A Vagabond for Beauty*. Salt Lake City, UT: Peregrine Smith Books.

Sa'di. [1258] 1966. *The Gulistan*, trans. E. Rehatsek. New York: Capricorn Books. Originally published by the Kama Shastra Society, London, 1888.

Said, E. W. [1984] 2000. "Reflections on Exile." In *Reflections on Exile and Other Essays*, 173–186. Cambridge, MA: Harvard University Press.

Sallach, D. L. 2000. "Classical Social Processes: Attractor and Computational Models." *Journal of Mathematical Sociology* 24 (4): 245–272.

Sánchez-Romero, M., and A. Prskawetz 2017. "Redistributive Effects of the US Pension System among Individuals with Different Life Expectancy." *The Journal of the Economics of Ageing* 10:51–74.

Sandberg, A., and N. Bostrom. 2008. *Whole Brain Emulation: A Roadmap*. Future of Humanity Institute 3, Oxford University. http://www.fhi.ox.ac.uk/reports/2008-3.pdf.

Sandeford, D. S. 2019. "An Energetic Analysis of the Human Subsistence System and Its Intensification." University of Arizona preprint, August.

Sandos, J. A. 1997. "Between Crucifix and Lance: Indian-White Relations in California, 1769–1848." *California History* 76:196–229.

Sartre, J.-P. [1943] 1956. *Being and Nothingness (L'être et le néant)*. London: Philosophical Library. Originally published in French.

Sartre, J.-P. 1963a. *The Age of Reason*. London: Penguin.

Sartre, J.-P. 1963b. *Iron in the Soul*. London: Penguin.

Sartre, J.-P. 1963c. *The Reprieve*. London: Penguin.

Saslow, L. R., R. Willer, M. Feinberg, P. K. Piff, K. Clark, D. Keltner, and S. R. Saturn. 2013. "My Brother's Keeper? Compassion Predicts Generosity More among Less Religious Individuals." *Social Psychological and Personality Science* 4:31–38.

Saunders, E. N. 2015. "War and the Inner Circle: Democratic Elites and the Politics of Using Force." *Security Studies* 24 (3): 466–501.

Schacter, D. L., and D. R. Addis. 2007. "The Cognitive Neuroscience of Constructive Memory: Remembering the Past and Imagining the Future." *Philosophical Transactions of the Royal Society B* 362:773–786.

Scharfstein, B. 1993. *Ineffability: The Failure of Words in Philosophy and Religion*. Albany: SUNY Press.

Scheffer, M., B. van Bavel, I. A. van de Leemput, and E. H. van Nes. 2017. "Inequality in Nature and Society." *Proceedings of the National Academy of Science* 114: 13154–13157.

Schmidhuber, J. 2009. "Simple Algorithmic Theory of Subjective Beauty, Novelty, Surprise, Interestingness, Attention, Curiosity, Creativity, Art, Science, Music, Jokes." *Journal of SICE* 48:21–32.

Scholes, R. 1977. "The Reality of Borges." *The Iowa Review* 8 (3): 12–25.

Schooler, J. W., D. Ariely, and G. Loewenstein. 2003. "The Pursuit and Monitoring of Happiness Can Be Self-Defeating." In *Psychology and Economics*, ed. J. Carrillo and I. Brocas, 41–70. Oxford: Oxford University Press.

Schultz, P. W., L. Zelezny, and N. J. Dalrymple. 2000. "A Multinational Perspective on the Relation between Judeo-Christian Religious Beliefs and Attitudes of Environmental Concern." *Environment and Behavior* 32 (4): 576–591.

Schwarcz, V. 1991. "No Solace from Lethe: History, Memory, and Cultural Identity in Twentieth-Century China." Special issue: The Living Tree: The Changing Meaning of Being Chinese Today. *Daedalus* 120:85–112.

Scott, J. C. 2012. *Two Cheers for Anarchism: Six Easy Pieces on Autonomy, Dignity, and Meaningful Work and Play*. Princeton, NJ: Princeton University Press.

Seidman, M. 1982. "Work and Revolution: Workers' Control in Barcelona in the Spanish Civil War, 1936–38." *Journal of Contemporary History* 17:409–433.

Seli, P., R. E. Beaty, J. A. Cheyne, D. Smilek, J. Oakman, and D. L. Schacter. 2018. "How Pervasive Is Mind Wandering, Really?" *Consciousness and Cognition* 66: 74–78.

Selye, H. 1973. "The Evolution of the Stress Concept: The Originator of the Concept Traces Its Development from the Discovery in 1936 of the Alarm Reaction to Modern Therapeutic Applications of Syntoxic and Catatoxic Hormones." *American Scientist* 61:692–699.

Shafer-Landau, R., ed. 2013. *Ethical Theory: An Anthology*, 2nd ed. Malden, MA: Wiley.

Shaver, J. H., C. G. Sibley, R. Sosis, D. Galbraith, and J. Bulbulia. 2019. "Alloparenting and Religious Fertility: A Test of the Religious Alloparenting Hypothesis." In *Evolution and Human Behavior* 40:315–324.

Sheckley, R. 1957. "The Language of Love." *Galaxy Science Fiction* 14 (1) (May): 39–50.

Sheldon, A. B. 1973. "The Women Men Don't See." *Fantasy and Science Fiction* 45 (6): 4–29. Published under the pseudonym James Tiptree Jr.

Sherman, S. M., and R. W. Guillery. 2006. *Exploring the Thalamus and Its Role in Cortical Function*. Cambridge, MA: MIT Press.

Shklar, J. N. 1979. "Let Us Not Be Hypocritical." *Daedalus* 108 (Summer): 1–25.

Shklar, J. N. 1982. "Putting Cruelty First." *Daedalus* 111:17–27.

Shneidman, E. S. 2005. "Anodyne Psychotherapy for Suicide: A Psychological View of Suicide." *Clinical Neuropsychiatry* 2:7–12.

Sidanius, J., S. Cotterill, J. Sheehy-Skeffington, N. Kteily, and H. Carvacho. 2016. "Social Dominance Theory: Explorations in the Psychology of Oppression." In *The Cambridge Handbook of the Psychology of Prejudice*, ed. C. G. Sibley and F. K. Barlow, 149–187. Cambridge: Cambridge University Press.

Siderits, M. 2003. "On the Soteriological Significance of Emptiness." *Contemporary Buddhism* 4 (1): 9–23.

Siderits, M. 2007. *Buddhism as Philosophy*. Indianapolis, IN: Hackett.

Siegal, M., and R. Varley. 2002. "Neural Systems Involved in 'Theory of Mind.'" *Nature Reviews Neuroscience* 3:411–486.

Sill, C. R. 2013. "A Survey of Androids and Audiences: 285 BCE to the Present Day." Master's thesis, Simon Fraser University.

Silverberg, R. 1973. "Breckenridge and the Continuum." In *Showcase*, ed. F. Elwood. New York: Harper & Row.

Simon, H. A. 1956. "Rational Choice and the Structure of the Environment." *Psychological Review* 63 (2): 129–138.

Sinclair, P. R. 1976. "Fascism and Crisis in Capitalist Society." *New German Critique* 9 (Autumn): 87–112.

Sinha, N. C. 1968. "The Refuge: India, Tibet and Mongolia." *Bulletin of Tibetology* 5 (1): 23–39.

Skinner, B. F. 1971. *Beyond Freedom and Dignity*. New York: Knopf.

Skoll, G. R. 2016. *Globalization of American Fear Culture*. London: Palgrave Macmillan.

Slezkine, Y. 2004. *The Jewish Century*. Princeton, NJ: Princeton University Press.

Smeeding, T., and C. Thévenot. 2016. "Addressing Child Poverty: How Does the United States Compare with Other Nations?" *Academic Pediatrics* 16:S67–S75.

Smith, J. 2017. "Climate Change: Scientific Evidence and the Industry of Denial." *The Missouri Review* 40 (3): 187–201. Review.

Smith, J. D., W. E. Shields, and D. A. Washburn. 2003. "The Comparative Psychology of Uncertainty Monitoring and Metacognition." *Behavioral and Brain Sciences* 26:317–373.

Smith, P. K., and W. Hofmann. 2016. "Power in Everyday Life." *Proceedings of the National Academy of Science* 113:10043–10048.

Smith, R. 2010. "Beyond Growth or Beyond Capitalism?" *Real-World Economics Review* 53:28–42.

Smyth, J. 2017. *The Toxic University: Zombie Leadership, Academic Rock Stars, and Neoliberal Ideology*. London: Palgrave Macmillan.

Snow, N., and P. M. Taylor. 2006. "The Revival of the Propaganda State: US Propaganda at Home and Abroad Since 9/11." *The International Communication Gazette* 68 (5–6): 389–407.

Snyder, T. 2019. "What Turing Told Us about the Digital Threat to a Human Future." *The New York Review of Books Daily*, May 6.

Squire, L. R. 2004. "Memory Systems of the Brain: A Brief History and Current Perspective." *Neurobiology of Learning and Memory* 82:171–177.

Ssorin-Chaikov, N. 2018. "Hybrid Peace: Ethnographies of War." *Annual Review of Anthropology* 47:251–262.

Stark, F. [1948] 2013. *Perseus in the Wind*. London: Tauris Parke.

Stavans, I. 2017. "Against Representation: A Note on Jorge Luis Borges' Aleph." *Studies in 20th & 21st Century Literature* 42 (1): 8.

Steinberg, L. 2005. "Cognitive and Affective Development in Adolescence." *Trends in Cognitive Sciences* 9:69–74.

Stephan, Y., A. R. Sutin, A. Kornadt, J. Caudroit, and A. Terracciano. 2018. "Higher IQ in Adolescence Is Related to a Younger Subjective Age in Later Life: Findings from the Wisconsin Longitudinal Study." *Intelligence* 69:195–199.

Stephenson, S. 2000. "The Russian Homeless: Old Problem—New Agenda." In *Poverty in Transition Economies*, ed. S. Hutton and G. Redmond, 14–34. London: Routledge.

Sterelny, K. 2010. "Moral Nativism: A Sceptical Response." *Mind & Language* 25: 279–297.

Stetson, C., M. P. Fiesta, and D. M. Eagleman. 2007. "Does Time Really Slow Down During a Frightening Event?" *PLoS ONE* 2: (12): e1295.

Still, S., D. A. Sivak, A. J. Bell, and G. E. Crooks. 2012. "Thermodynamics of Prediction." *Physical Review Letters* 109:120604.

Stout, D. 2018. "Archaeology and the Evolutionary Neuroscience of Language: The Technological Pedagogy Hypothesis." *Interaction Studies* 19:256–271.

Strugatsky, A., and B. Strugatsky. 1978. *Definitely Maybe: A Manuscript Discovered Under Unusual Circumstances*. London: Macmillan. Original title: *A Billion Years before the End of the World*.

Summerfield, D. 2004. "Cross-Cultural Perspectives on the Medicalization of Human Suffering." In *Posttraumatic Stress Disorder: Issues and Controversies*, ed. G. M. Rosen, 233–246. Chichester, UK: John Wiley & Sons.

Swanwick, M. 1991. *Stations of the Tide*. New York: William Morrow and Company.

Swanwick, M. 1993. *The Iron Dragon's Daughter*. London: Millennium.

Syal, S., and B. L. Finlay. 2010. "Thinking Outside the Cortex: Social Motivation in the Evolution and Development of Language." *Developmental Science* 14:417–430.

Szathmáry, E., and J. Maynard Smith. 1995. "The Major Evolutionary Transitions." *Nature* 374:227–232.

't Hooft, G. 2016. *The Cellular Automaton Interpretation of Quantum Mechanics*. Cham, Switzerland: Springer Nature.

't Hooft, G. 2019. "Free Will in the Theory of Everything." In *Determinism and Free Will: New Insights from Physics, Philosophy, and Theology*, ed. F. Scardigli, G. 't Hooft, E. Severino, and P. Coda, 21–48. Cham, Switzerland: Springer Nature.

Tappan, M. B., and L. M. Brown. 1989. "Stories Told and Lessons Learned: Toward a Narrative Approach to Moral Development and Moral Education." *Harvard Educational Review* 59:182–205.

Thacker, E. 2018. *Infinite Resignation*. New York: Penguin Random House.

The BIG Bell Test Collaboration. 2018. "Challenging Local Realism with Human Choices." *Nature* 557:212–222.

Theofanopoulou, C., S. Gastaldon, T. O'Rourke, B. D. Samuels, A. Messner, P. T. Martins, F. Delogu, S. Alamri, and C. Boeckx. 2017. "Self-Domestication in Homo sapiens: Insights from Comparative Genomics." *PLoS ONE* 12 (10): e0185306.

Thomsen, D. K. 2006. "The Association between Rumination and Negative Affect: A Review." *Cognition and Emotion* 20:1216–1235.

Tillyris, D. 2015. "The Virtue of Vice: A Defence of Hypocrisy in Democratic Politics." *Contemporary Politics* 22 (1): 1–19.

Tolkien, J. R. R. 1954. *The Lord of the Rings*, 3 vols. London: George Allen & Unwin.

Tolkien, J. R. R. 1977. *The Silmarillion*. London: George Allen & Unwin.

Torres-Sánchez, R., P. Brandon, and M. 't Hart. 2018. "War and Economy. Rediscovering the Eighteenth-Century Military Entrepreneur." *Business History* 60 (1): 4–22.

Treisman, A. 1986. "Properties, Parts, and Objects." In *Handbook of Perception and Human Performance*, Vol. 2, ed. K. R. Boff, L. Kaufman, and J. P. Thomas, 1–70. New York: Wiley.

Trivers, R. 1972. "Parental Investment and Sexual Selection." In *Sexual Selection and the Descent of Man*, ed. B. Campbell, 137–179. London: Aldine.

Trivers, R. L. 1971. "The Evolution of Reciprocal Altruism." *The Quarterly Review of Biology* 46:35–57.

Tsai, J. 2018. "Lifetime and 1-Year Prevalence of Homelessness in the US Population: Results from the National Epidemiologic Survey on Alcohol and Related Conditions-III." *Journal of Public Health* 40:65–74.

Tsai, J. L. 2017. "Ideal Affect in Daily Life: Implications for Affective Experience, Health, and Social Behavior." *Current Opinion in Psychology* 17:118–128.

Tulving, E. 2002. "Episodic Memory: From Mind to Brain." *Annual Review of Psychology* 53:1–25.

Turing, A. M. 1950. "Computing Machinery and Intelligence." *Mind* 59:433–460.

Unamuno, M. de. 1972. *The Tragic Sense of Life in Men and Nations*, trans. A. Kerrigan. Princeton, NJ: Princeton University Press. Introduction by S. de Madariaga and afterword by W. Barrett.

Usher, M. 2018. "Agency, Teleological Control and Robust Causation." *Philosophy and Phenomenological Research* (2018): 1–23.

Van Den Broek, R. 1983. "The Present State of Gnostic Studies." *Vigiliae Christianae* 37:41–71.

van Rooij, I., M. Blokpoel, R. de Haan, and T. Wareham. 2019a. "Tractable Embodied Computation Needs Embeddedness." Forthcoming in *Reti, saperi, linguaggi: Italian Journal of Cognitive Sciences*.

van Rooij, I., M. Blokpoel, J. Kwisthout, and T. Wareham. 2019b. *Cognition and Intractability: A Guide to Classical and Parameterized Complexity Analysis*. Cambridge: Cambridge University Press.

Verbunt, P., and A.-C. Guio. 2019. "Explaining Differences within and between Countries in the Risk of Income Poverty and Severe Material Deprivation: Comparing Single and Multilevel Analyses." *Social Indicators Research* 144:827–868.

Vila Matas, E. 2000. *Bartleby &Co.*, trans. J. Dunne. New York: New Directions.

Vilanova, M. 1992. "Political Participation, and Illiteracy in Barcelona between 1934 and 1936." *The American Historical Review* 97:96–120.

Vinge, V. 1993. "The Coming Technological Singularity: How to Survive in the Post-Human Era." *Whole Earth Review Winter*. http://www-rohan.sdsu.edu/faculty/vinge/misc/singularity.html.

von Uexküll, J. [1934] 2010. *A Foray into the World of Animals and Humans: With a Theory of Meaning*, trans. J. D. O'Neill. Minneapolis: University of Minnesota Press.

Voynich, E. L. 1897. *The Gadfly*. New York: Henry Holt & Company.

Vučković, S., D. Srebro, K. Savić Vujović, Č. Vučetić, and M. Prostran. 2018. "Cannabinoids and Pain: New Insights from Old Molecules." *Frontiers in Pharmacology* 9: article 1259.

Warren, W. H. 2006. "The Dynamics of Perception and Action." *Psychological Review* 113:358–389.

Waterfall, H. R., B. Sandbank, L. Onnis, and S. Edelman. 2010. "An Empirical Generative Framework for Computational Modeling of Language Acquisition." *Journal of Child Language* 37 (Special issue 03): 671–703.

Watts, M. J. 2018. "It's All Over Now, Baby Blue." *American Historical Review* 123 (5): 1583–1595.

Wearden, J. H. 2015. "Passage of Time Judgements." *Consciousness and Cognition* 38:165–171.

Wegemer, C., and K. Hinze. 2013. "Compromised Stability and Security in the 'Race to the Bottom.'" *Journal of Critical Thought and Praxis* 2 (1): 1–15.

Wegner, D. M. 2004. "Precis of *The Illusion of Conscious Will*." *Behavioral and Brain Sciences* 27:649–692.

Weinrich, H. [1997] 2004. *Lethe. The Art and Critique of Forgetting*. Ithaca, NY: Cornell University Press. Translated from German by S. Rendall.

Welizarowicz, G. 2016. "California Mission Gulags: Putting Junípero Serra's Canonization in Perspective." *Polish Journal for American Studies* 10:195–216.

Whyte, K. P. 2018. "Indigenous Science (Fiction) for the Anthropocene: Ancestral Dystopias and Fantasies of Climate Change Crises." *Environment and Planning E: Nature and Space* 1 (1–2): 224–242.

Wieck, C., and U. Kunzmann. 2015. "Age Differences in Empathy: Multidirectional and Context-Dependent." *Psychology and Aging* 30:407–419.

Wigner, E. P. 1960. "The Unreasonable Effectiveness of Mathematics in the Natural Sciences." *Communications on Pure and Applied Mathematics* 13:1–14.

Wilkins, J. F., and P. Godfrey-Smith. 2009. "Adaptationism and the Adaptive Landscape." *Biology and Philosophy* 24:199–214.

Williams, B. 1973. "The Makropulos Case: Reflections on the Tedium of Immortality." In *Problems of the Self*, ed. B. Williams, 82–100. Cambridge: Cambridge University Press.

Williams, D. C. 1962. "Dispensing with Existence." *The Journal of Philosophy* 59 (23): 748–763.

Williams, L. 2007. "Anarchism Revived." *New Political Science* 29:297–312.

Wills, T. A. 1981. "Downward Comparison Principles in Social Psychology." *Psychological Bulletin* 90:245–271.

Wilson, D. S. 2015. *What's Wrong (& Right) about Evolutionary Psychology*. Technical report, Binghamton, NY: The Evolution Institute.

Wilson, D. S., and E. O. Wilson. 2007. "Rethinking the Theoretical Foundation of Sociobiology." *Quarterly Review of Biology* 82:327–348.

Wilson, D. S., S. C. Hayes, A. Biglan, and D. Embry. 2014. "Evolving the Future: Toward a Science of Intentional Change." *Behavioral and Brain Sciences* 37:395–460.

Wilson, T. D., and D. T. Gilbert. 2005. "Affective Forecasting: Knowing What to Want." *Current Directions in Psychological Science* 14:131–134.

Wimber, M., A. Alink, I. Charest, N. Kriegeskorte, and M. C. Anderson. 2015. "Retrieval Induces Adaptive Forgetting of Competing Memories via Cortical Pattern Suppression." *Nature Neuroscience* 18:582–589.

Wittgenstein, L. 1958. *Philosophical Investigations*, 3rd ed., trans. G. E. M. Anscombe. Englewood Cliffs, NJ: Prentice Hall.

Wittgenstein, L. 1961. *Tractatus Logico-philosophicus*, trans. D. F. Pears and B. F. McGuinness. London: Routledge.

Woergoetter, W., and B. Porr. 2007. "Reinforcement Learning." *Scholarpedia* 3 (3): 1448.

Wolbert, L. S., D. J. de Ruyter, and A. Schinkel. 2018. "What Attitude Should Parents Have towards Their Children's Future Flourishing?" *Theory and Research in Education* 16:82–97.

Wolff, R. P. 1970. *In Defense of Anarchism*. New York: Harper and Row.

Wright, E. O. 2013. "Transforming Capitalism through Real Utopias." *American Sociological Review* 78:1–25.

Yahel, H., and R. Kark. 2016. "Reasoning from History: Israel's 'Peace Law' and Resettlement of the Tel Malhata Bedouin." *Israel Studies* 21 (2): 102–132.

Yang, L. 1993. "Water in Traditional Chinese Culture." *Journal of Popular Culture* 27 (2): 51–56.

Yuchtman-Yaar, E., Y. Alkalay, and T. Aival. 2018. "Effects of Religious Identity and Ethnicity on the Israeli-Jewish Electorate." *Israel Studies Review* 33 (3): 1–20.

Zagzebski, L. 2010. "Exemplarist Virtue Theory." *Metaphilosophy* 41:41–57.

Zahavi, A., and A. Zahavi 1997. *The Handicap Principle: A Missing Piece of Darwin's Puzzle*. New York: Oxford University Press.

Zapffe, P. W. [1933] 2004. "The Last Messiah." *Janus* 9. In *Philosophy Now* 45 (2004). Translated from Norwegian by G. R. Tangenes.

Zeelenberg, M., K. van den Bos, E. van Dijk, and R. Pieters. 2002. "The Inaction Effect in the Psychology of Regret." *Journal of Personality and Social Psychology* 82:314–327.

Zeki, S., J. P. Romaya, D. M. T. Benincasa, and M. F. Atiyah. 2014. "The Experience of Mathematical Beauty and Its Neural Correlates." *Frontiers in Human Neuroscience* 8: article 68.

Index